The Nature of the Child

Other Books by Jerome Kagan

Birth to Maturity
WITH HOWARD A. MOSS

Change and Continuity in Infancy

Infancy: Its Place in Human Development
WITH RICHARD KEARSLEY AND PHILIP ZELAZO

The Second Year

THE NATURE
OF
THE CHILD

Jerome Kagan

Basic Books, Inc., Publishers

NEW YORK

Library of Congress Cataloging in Publication Data

Kagan, Jerome.
 The nature of the child.

 Bibliography: p. 281
 Includes index.
 1. Child psychology. I. Title.
BF721.K158 1984 155.4 83-45263
ISBN 0-465-04850-1

Copyright © 1984 by Basic Books, Inc.
Printed in the United States of America
Designed by Vincent Torre
10 9 8 7 6 5

For Cele, Janet, and Steve,

who waited so patiently

while each day I wove on the loom

and every night unwove it.

Every age has its myths and calls them higher truths.

ANONYMOUS

We must use plain words and display such goodness or purity as we have at the bottom of the pot.

MONTAIGNE

Contents

Contents

Preface

IT HAS ALWAYS STRUCK ME as odd that we come to understand an exotic phenomenon, like the eclipse of the sun, before so many commonplace events, like the beginning of a baby's birth. Although children have been scurrying under the watchful eyes of interested and intelligent adults for a very long time, we have a less satisfying explanation of human psychological development than of the life cycle of the fruit fly, which has been an object of study for less than one hundred years.

There are four reasons for this embarrassing imbalance in scientific progress. The first is ascribable to the complexity of our interests. Thought, emotion, and intention are simply more difficult to study than eating, reproduction, and locomotion. Second, the experiment is the most powerful way to gain deep understanding, but moral imperatives do not permit us to perform with children the kinds of experiment that are commonplace in scientific investigations of animals. Third, most observers of children begin their work with a deeply held personal philosophy about what human nature is or should be, and how it attains its adult form. These philosophies are influenced by the politics, the economy, and the social structure of the society in which the observer lives. Of course, biologists also come to their work with biases, but most citizens have stronger opinions about the reasons for aggression in children than they do about fighting among ants or territorial defense by male robins. Finally, the combination of invisible events, limitations on experiments, and preferred interpretations have prevented agreement on concepts and methods and slowed the progress in human development that was hoped for a century ago when European scholars turned their attention to the young child.

I do not wish to minimize what we have learned. Hence, along with personal reflections on the issues and underlying suppositions that guide current study of the child, this book contains synopses of some of these victories. Some chapters—especially the first four—include historical and philosophical arguments which, strictly speaking, may not seem relevant to a book on human psychological development. I believe, however, that current scholarship is comprehended more completely if one appreciates the historical context of present research and the philosophical assumptions that guide the selection of concepts. Hence, I regard these sections as relevant to my mission and our joint adventure.

Major scientific advance is often marked by a fresh theoretical perspective that challenges a popular idealistic conception. Kepler questioned the idealistic assumptions of planetary orbits that were circular and of constant velocity. Darwin rejected the idealism contained in the Biblical explanation of the creation. The theory of relativity challenged the idealism in Newton's view of a universe in which space and time were absolute. Behaviorism criticized the ideal of a person with a will free to choose how to behave, and Freud's suggestion of unconscious sexual motives questioned the idealistic innocence of the child.

Contemporary views of human development contain equally idealistic assumptions. One is that a mother's love for her infant is necessary for the child's future mental health. A second is that the events of infancy seriously influence the future mood and behavior of the adolescent. A third is that a person should be psychologically described as possessing a set of abstract psychological qualities that are displayed across a wide variety of situations, with local circumstances being of minimal relevance. The chapters of this book offer a critique of these favored premises.

The major impetus for these essays, which were written over the past seven years, is to repair an imbalance in our current attitudes toward the central ideas in human development. It is almost a general truth that the understanding of every complex phenomenon requires a simultaneous appreciation of complementary concepts. The chemist Niels Bohr persuaded his colleagues that if one assumes that on some occasions matter is composed of particles, while at other times it is a wave, one gains a deeper appreciation of nature than if only one perspective is used. Bohr's insight is relevant for contemporary writing on the development of the child. Each of the six substantive chapters, following the introductory one, is an attempt to bring into relief a theme that, despite an earlier popularity, has been neglected during most of this century.

The selection of topics was guided by a complicated weighting of theoretical significance and my expertise. The nature of the infant, the influence of the family, and the development of morality, emotion, and thought must be included in any serious discussion of the child. But many readers may object to the absence of extensive consideration of the deviations of childhood and the important role of schools and of peer friendships. These ideas are touched on only indirectly, in part because of my limited knowledge; in part, because of the belief that the evidence does not permit many robust conclusions. And now for a preview of what is to come.

The initial chapter examines five complementary themes every scientist studying the growth of living forms must confront. The first four, which apply to all organisms, are the balance between the inherent characteristics of a developing form and surrounding environmental forces; connectedness, in contrast to discontinuity, between phases of growth; qualitative versus quantitative differences between organisms and their characteristics; and fourth, the utility of broad versus specific concepts to describe the entities that change with growth. The fifth theme, which is especially relevant to those who study human development, places the subjective frame of the person being studied in opposition to the frame of the scientist who tries to choose terms that are minimally ambiguous. Each of the six succeeding chapters highlights one or more of these themes.

The second chapter, which is a summary of the growth of both intellectual functions and social attachments during infancy, reminds the reader that the maturation of new cognitive abilities is the hub around which emotions and actions play out their stories. The child's first ideas are constrained by the way the brain works, and the infant's fears, sense of self, and inferences must wait until the requisite cognitive talents are in place. Even the attachment bonds to parents, so necessary for socialization, rest upon natural inclinations to embrace, to vocalize, and to laugh with those who care for the baby. This discussion of the infant contrasts the emphasis on family experience, which has dominated writings about the child since the second decade of this century, with the forces inherent in the child's biology.

In the third chapter, I examine the fugue created from the pattern of stable and changing strands in development. Something must be preserved out of the dramatic transformations that turn an infant into an adolescent, for the child cannot leap from one stage to another, leaving all victories and scars on the platform just vacated, and arrive at his new location as innocent as he was at the beginning of life. Having granted that some qualities are carried along, the task is to discover which ones enjoy that privilege. Western scholars, long before any sound evidence had been accumulated, assumed that there had to be a material connection between the infant and the adult, and likened development to a journey in which the mind absorbs each new experience, never discarding any of its acquired treasures. Despite the vulnerability of the evidence, the facts are not in accord with that traditional belief, and I will suggest the usefulness of a skeptical attitude toward a strong form of connectedness between the distant past and the present.

The fourth chapter probes the idea of a moral standard, which parents know as *conscience* and psychologists call *superego*. All young children appreciate the ideas of good and bad by their third birthday, and many human motives are moral missions. Children and adults seek ways to satisfy a desire to feel virtuous and are not always trying to slake a parched palate. This position, which has not been strong in this century, was held by a small number of Enlighenment philosophers who rejected an early version of the physiological materialism that is overwhelmingly popular today. Construction of a persuasive rational basis for behaving morally has been the problem on which most moral philosophers have stubbed their toes. I believe they will continue to do so until they recognize what Chinese philosophers have appreciated for a long time: namely, feeling, not logic, sustains the superego. This suggestion has the important consequence of explaining the paradox of extraordinary variety of surface virtues that characterize societies and historical eras, despite apparent agreement on the deeper meanings of everyday ethical imperatives.

The chapter on emotion criticizes the currently popular view that emotions are Platonic ideals, and suggests that we must first discover the relations among provocative events, changes in internal feeling states, and interpretations, and only then invent names for the qualitatively distinct trios that cluster together. When that mission is accomplished, words like *joy, sadness,* and *anger* will probably be replaced with more useful terms that specify the event that gave rise to the emotion in the first place, and will correct the belief held by some that all of the emotions are simply quantitative variations on a generalized state of internal arousal.

The chapter on the development of thought should be the richest discussion, yet I find it not wholly satisfying. Despite the availability of more scientific facts on human cognitive function than on emotions, standards, and the family, they are tiny ones. Small facts restrain irresponsible theorizing, but they also prevent a synthesis that, although premature, can be temporarily pleasing. It has proven useful during the formative phase of every discipline to invent two kinds of hypothetical terms: one for units, and one for the processes that act on the units to produce the observable consequences that scientists count. I will posit four different kinds of units of thought, although the basic division is between those that stay faithful to reality—my image of a friend's face—and those that ignore their source and live in a heady world of abstraction, as does my idea of justice. There are also two kinds of process. One set selects events, detects similarities, places information in memory, and retrieves knowledge. But we cannot understand the niceties of perception and inference unless we assume first that the cognitive competences are very specific to classes of problems and are not broadly generalized talents. Additionally, we have to posit a set of managers that monitors the working functions and redirects their efforts when the mission is not going well. The relation between the units in the cytoplasm that continually construct proteins and the watchful eye of the nuclear DNA is a reasonably good analogy.

Sentimental views of the role of parents on a child's development are rampant, and in the last chapter I try to analyze why. Most modern American parents hold two strong beliefs. The first is that they have only a few years to set the course of their child's life. If they fail to implement the proper actions, the child is doomed. The second, potentially faulty, premise is that physical affection and firmness are the two vital ingredients. The first promotes self-confidence; the second prevents self-indulgence. Although there is insufficient scientific support for either of these views, they are so strongly held by most parents that it is hard to persuade them that they are folk beliefs. One reason they remain strong is that the subjective experiences of parents and commentators support them; and it may be helpful to recognize that an objective description can be intellectually powerful and yet not accommodate to the subjective frame.

In this last chapter, as in the ones before, I emphasize the meanings children impose on experience. It is not what parents do to children or siblings do to each other that matters, but rather the intention the child imputes to those who act on and with him or her. If it were otherwise, we could not explain why the children of Puritan parents were not less well adapted than today's youth, or why the young adolescent boys of an isolated New Guinea tribe who perform ritual fellatio on older boys regard themselves neither as sexually deviant nor as an oppressed minority.

A second theme, also threaded through all the chapters, is that our current descriptions of development use terms that are much too broad, and our explanations do not acknowledge either the power of maturation or the possibility of serious change and discontinuity, especially during the opening decade of life.

Most scientists rely on sister disciplines for metaphors to shape initial, unformed ideas. Biologists often steal from chemistry, and chemists borrow from physics. I, like many social scientists, use biology—in particular, embryology—as a model for psychological growth. There are three reasons for this preference. First, the growth of the organs from the fertilized egg to the fully formed newborn reveals extraordinary specificity. The principles that account for the growth and final structure of the brain are different from those that explain the establishment of the lungs or the muscles of the hand. Second, there is an orderly sequence of growth—controlled, in part, by the genetics of the cell—that guarantees that the first signs of the spinal cord will appear before the heart and the heart before the fingers. Finally, there are major discontinuities in the growth of the fetus. The smooth, spherical egg is suddenly transformed into a hollow tube, and sets of cells that had a major function in the young embryo disappear when they are no longer needed. Specificity, orderly growth, and discontinuity are as much a part of psychological development as are their complements—broad forces, variability of script, and continuity. Consideration of both sets of ideas is helpful in interpreting the child's development. I have tried to use these themes to aid understanding of the child, rather than as a whining critique of contemporary scholarship.

Although I shall try to persuade the reader that many statements about development may be true, it is important that the reader appreciate the bases for these claims and the reasons they deserve reflection. Ideally, the main burden of persuasion should rest on firm empirical evidence and as little as possible on the statements of authority. I will use evidence wherever it is relevant, and resist retreating to the testimony of expert witnesses. But the youth and complexity of psychology require some reliance on deductions from reasonable premises honed from many days of watching children and many nights of reading history and anthropology. Reflective intuition is always a dangerous basis for argument; and so the reader will be warned whenever the facts fail and this strategy is called into service. But reliance on intuition forced me to choose continually between limiting a conclusion in order to be more accurate and surrendering to what I thought most readers would regard as pleasing. I once said impulsively to a friend that, when he had a choice between writing what was true and what seemed beautiful, he was likely to select the latter. Although novelists must side with pleasingness, I have tried to favor precision and to resist yielding either to the poetic impulse or to what I suspected most readers would like to hear. I hope that decision makes this book informative rather than turgid. Every age has favorite myths about the child and family which it regards as obviously true. By examining, and perhaps discarding, some of these myths we make ourselves vulnerable to a temporary period of uncertainty, but eventually gain an appreciation of many new possibilities.

I am grateful to the Foundation for Child Development, the John D. and Catherine T. MacArthur Foundation, and the National Institute of Child Health and Human Development for their support of some of the research that is described in this book. I also wish to thank Cambridge University Press for allowing me, in chapter 5, to draw on material in *Emotion, Cognition and Behavior* (1984) by Carroll E. Izard, Jerome Kagan, and Robert B. Zajonc. I am especially appreciative of the extraordinary editorial skill of Phoebe Hoss who ferreted out obfuscation in what I regarded as the simplest of sentences. I also wish to thank Judith Greissman for her wise advice on matters of organization and her friendship. Many of the ideas have profited from frequent discussions over the last decade with Orville G. Brim, Jr., Joseph Campos, Marshall Haith, Robert McCall, and Steven Reznick. I have gained much from their candor and good will. Finally I thank Whitney Walton and Micaela Elchediak for their care and patience in preparing this manuscript.

The Nature of the Child

I

Guiding Themes
in Human Development

A great truth is a truth whose opposite is
also a great truth.

THOMAS MANN,
Essay on Freud

THREE PAIRS OF QUESTIONS motivate contemporary scholarship
on development. The first seeks facts. What characteristics are
common to all children during the sequential phases of development, and which qualities are unique to particular times and
places? It is so natural to suppose that there is a special purpose
hidden in the facts of growth that most scholars who posit a universal scenario add, as a statement of faith, that children are moving toward a higher plane where they will be more free, more
logical, more loving, more moral, or more detached, depending
upon the favored metaphysical theme.

All sciences first select phenomena to study and then gather evidence in order to explain why certain events occur together—
whether the joined events be the presence of bacteria and a high
fever, or the association between an extra chromosome and mental
retardation. But the scientists who study human nature, especially
psychologists and sociologists, often add an additional question.

3

They ask, To what end, or, For what purpose, are the events related? and usually have a favored purpose in mind before they begin their work. A great many child psychologists, for example, believe that maternal love toward a child should produce a less anxious and more self-confident adolescent. They expend a great deal of energy trying to prove that this idea is correct, and far less effort in trying to determine *how* maternal love might create any set of consequences. I shall try to keep these two questions separate and will stress the *how* of development over the *why*. Thus, a second pair of questions seeks the reasons for the phenomena of development. Why do the abilities and moods of children exhibit similar changes, and why are children of the same age so different? It is understood that we will need different explanations for these two kinds of variation.

The final pair of questions springs naturally from a desire to predict the future. Which of the many qualities observed in infants and children are preserved for years, and what conditions maximize the stability of a belief, a talent, a desire, or style of behavior?

The attempts to solve this trio of conundrums are guided, as is all scholarship, by deep premises that the physicist Gerald Holton (1973) calls *themata*. Each theme is defined by a pair of complementary assumptions that can be neither proven nor refuted. Each scientist is loyal to one or the other of the assumptions, and his or her research gains coherence through that point of view. Five themata currently guide developmental inquiry, and the chapters of this book engage one or more of them.

Biology and Experience

The first theme involves the balance between biology and experience. There have been two contrasting views of the child. One emphasizes the strong hand of maturation, which releases new talents as it gradually relaxes its hold over the first dozen years. The complementary view places the formative power in the richness of encounters and comes very close to claiming that almost anything is possible if adults are clever enough in the way they handle children. Theorists who side with Aristotle and modern behavioral geneticists award considerable potency to the qualities that are inherent in the biological nature of the child. These potentials guarantee the appearance of speech and reason in all youngsters and vulnerability to fear or psychosis in some. The most important biological influences on psychological development are contained in the maturation of central nervous system structures that permit motor and cognitive abilities—such as walking, speech, symbolism, and self-awareness—to appear at regular times. The brain is still completing its growth during the early years, and the cortex of the young infant resembles that of the adult rat. Nerve fibers must still finish their growth, important connections must be made, and all of the neurotransmitters that are essential to adult functioning may not be operative in the infant.

Contrary to popular intuition, brain growth during childhood is characterized by the elimination of synapses that were laid down during the months before and immediately after birth. This pruning of connections permits the surviving cells to expand their contacts with neighbors, much as an animal species comes to dominate an ecological niche as its competitors are eliminated. The victor in the neuronal competition is determined, in part, by asymmetry of stimulation and use. If the right hand is used more than the left, the neural connections that serve the right hand expand their sphere of dominance; those serving the left lose some power. There may be a material basis for the folk belief that those who are unusually skilled at languages are a little less proficient with their hands. Although loss, as well as gain, is inherent in the growth of the brain, the loss of synapses is accompanied by greater specificity of response, decreased malleability, and a capacity to inhibit an automatic reaction. As I shall illustrate in chapters 2, 4, and 6, the qualities that are direct consequences of maturation are inevitable, as long as children are growing in any reasonably varied environment where minimal nutritional needs are met and children can exercise emerging abilities.

These two caveats are necessary, for the competences that are dependent upon growth of the nervous system can be affected, often seriously, if animals or children are deprived of stimulation or an opportunity to act. Although rhesus monkeys raised in isolation, with no visual access to humans or monkeys, eventually display to a human face the same signs of fear that are shown by normal monkeys, the fear occurs about a month later than it does in animals who are exposed to other monkeys and humans (Kenney, Mason, and Hill 1979). But almost all children, save for an unfortunate few who are locked in empty rooms or housed in barren institutions, experience sufficient variety to permit the biological changes natural to our species to occur. As brain structures reach certain levels of organization, new cognitive abilities emerge which make new motives possible. For example, it is not until after the second birthday that the child appreciates that her behavior is evaluated by others with respect to standards of excellence.* When the child becomes aware of these evaluations, a motive for task mastery emerges. By age seven, when the child can compare some properties of self with those of others, he generates either a motive of hostility toward, or a motive for acceptance by, those peers who possess desired characteristics he does not have. Finally, cognitive abilities that appear at puberty generate a motive for logical consistency between beliefs and between beliefs and behavior. Thus, the emergence of cognitive talents during the first dozen years is accompanied by motives that, although they may appear to be the same as, or derivative of, earlier ones, are often novel desires.

Scholars who regard the environment as more formative treat evolution through natural selection as a generative model for growth, because that perspective emphasizes the child's malleability in response to challenge and the potential for change that follows an individual's attempt to cope with real or imagined threat. But the environmentalists also see history as limiting change. Each person lives simultaneously in nested social spheres—extending from the home to the neighborhood to the fuzzy boundaried culture—that constrain what the child values, believes, and dreams. Karl Marx (1867) saw this principle operating on the large stage of class membership. B. F. Skinner's (1938) script is written for a pair of players in a smaller theater. But both theorists have insisted that because each person is partly imprisoned by his or her past, the potential for change is not limitless.

*Throughout this book I have followed an informal pattern of alternating the gender pronouns for the child; however, when speaking of the child and the caregiver, who is usually female, I have used the masculine pronoun for the child for the sake of convenience and clarity.

The main catalyst for environmentally mediated change is information. One source of information is contained in those events that have become associated with strong feelings. A child looking outside a window at a large red bus is startled by an unexpected clap of thunder, feels frightened, and cries. The next time she sees a large red bus, or perhaps any bus, she may re-experience the feeling of fright. Sometimes the child's own behavior becomes predictive of a desired goal. A one-year-old cries when his mother tucks him into bed, turns out the light, and leaves the room. The cry provokes the mother to return, turn on the light, and go to the infant's side. The return of the mother, regarded as a rewarding event, increases the likelihood that in the future the child will cry when the mother puts him to bed.

However, it is not possible to specify the characteristics of the rewarding events most likely to change the probability of actions that precede them. In the past, most scholars stated, without argument, that the important component of the rewarding event was its ability to provide pleasure to an actor. But because one does not feel pleasure every time one performs an action that attains a goal, many psychologists argue that if a response is simply followed by any change in experience—especially one that is alerting—the probability that the behavior will occur again is enhanced. But that conclusion is not quite accurate either, for new actions always produce changes. I move my pencil to produce a change in experience, but that sequence of events does not necessarily increase the probability of my repeating that action. The depth of the enigma is apparent when we watch a baby who has just acted in a way that seems to provide pleasure. The baby strikes a balloon full of beads, causing it to move and make a noise. The baby laughs and repeats the action. The movement and noise occur again and again, and the baby smiles. If this sequence were an example of the principle of instrumental conditioning, the baby should repeat the act until exhausted. But after only a few minutes, the baby stops smiling, as if she were bored. The common phenomenon of boredom following attainment of a goal suggests that we must know something about the motivational state and knowledge of the child. If the child does not desire the goal, the response that ordinarily gains it will not occur.

A third source of information is contained in the unfamiliar and the unexpected, for such events provoke the child to attempt to relate them to his knowledge in a process that changes what he originally knew. Consider a five-month-old whose only representation of a human is the mother's form and face—a structure we call a *schema.* The infant scans the face and form of the first unfamiliar adult he has seen, detects a relation between the stranger and the schema of the mother's face, and, in relating the former to the latter, becomes sensitized to the possibility of unfamiliar faces. This single experience with the novel face probably alters the child's ability to assimilate the next stranger more rapidly.

A two-year-old notes her first animal with horns and tries, at first unsuccessfully, to relate it to a schema of the dogs and cats she has often encountered in the past. As a result, she changes her schema for animals to include the possibility of one with horns. Encounters with new information change beliefs, too; an eight-year-old who learns that her friend's father locked her in a room may brood for the first time on the possibility of cruel fathers and deeply angry children.

New ideas are also created through reflective thought. The child is continually making inferences from information that is not immediately comprehensible. An incompletely understood event provokes a child to generate hypotheses that facilitate understanding. If one of the guesses is followed by a sense of resolution, whether or not it is valid, the child treats it as correct, until it is disconfirmed by experience. A twenty-month-old child is shown a toy cup, a car, and a cat and correctly gives the examiner the toy requested on three successive occasions. The examiner then replaces these three toys with two new, but equally familiar, objects and one odd-shaped piece of wood that is totally unfamiliar. The examiner waits a few seconds to permit the child to scan the toys and then, in a matter-of-fact tone, asks, "Give me the zoob." The child pauses for a moment and then gives the odd-shaped piece of wood to the adult. The confidence of the child's reply implies that she regards the question as reasonable and assumes that the unfamiliar object must be the correct referent for the unfamiliar word (Kagan 1981).

Reflective thought is often provoked by communications from others. The child tries to maintain consistency among his beliefs and actions. Discovery of an inconsistency leads the child to change one or the other. The child who believes reading is an important skill but fails reading tests for three years in a row is troubled by the implication that he might be incompetent at a task he values. Since this conclusion is inconsistent with his view of self as capable, he may reclassify the task as unimportant. Failure does not generate disparagement of reading skill in all children; some continue to treat it as sacred and live with the anxiety that comes from acknowledging their incompetence.

The structure of beliefs about self and world that are most resistant to change is called a *frame.* The frame determines the events that will be selected for accommodation and imposes biases on the conclusions drawn from experience. Most children hold a frame that assumes their parents are wise, competent, just, and affectionate. For a much smaller group, the premises of the frame are reversed. Hence, a particular event will not be interpreted similarly by these two classes of children. A chastisement, for example, is viewed by a majority as motivated by the parent's desire to raise a socialized child, and is treated as serving the child's welfare. A smaller group of children interpret the punishment as a sign of parental hostility.

Although the maturation of cognitive functions can initiate a change in frame—for example, adolescents examine their beliefs on a topic as a related set and, when they detect inconsistencies, change some of these beliefs—most of the time, new experiences produce a change in frame. One of the most significant experiences for an only child is the arrival of a new baby, especially if the older child is between two and five years of age. Many mothers report changes in the behavior of their three-year-old that do not occur as often in three-year-olds who remain only children. The former child first shows a brief period of anxiety; he may lose bowel and bladder control and want to be with the mother continually. But soon a spurt of more mature behavior appears, characterized by more initiative and a loss of fearfulness. One basis for the new boldness is the realization that, for the first time, there is a person less potent than the child, not unlike the lightening of mood that follows discovery of someone who carries a more serious burden. The basis for change is not based primarily on special interactions with the sibling or on new patterns of behavior with the parents. The new qualities are a product of the mental comparison of self with sibling and a realization of the differences in size, strength, and competence. Thus, it is necessary to assume, with John Locke (1690) and Leon Festinger (1957), that the mind is prepared to be altered simply by detecting novelty in the world or inconsistency among one's ideas. It is reassuring to note that recent essays on conditioning also acknowledge that a discrepancy between what the animal wants and what happens is fundamental for a conditional association (Mackintosh 1983).

But we must never treat the biological and the experiential as separate, independent forces. The complementarity of the two is best illustrated by the early growth of the brain. Although the number of neurons a particular species will possess seems to be determined strictly by its genetic constitution, the locations of those nerve cells and the pattern of final synaptic connections in the central nervous system are influenced by both local physical and chemical conditions and experience and, therefore, are much more variable. Indeed, whether a particular cell appearing in the earliest phases of neural development becomes part of the spinal column or part of the eye depends in large measure on the cells it meets as it travels from the neural crest to its final destination.

Some social scientists have accepted the unprofitable and misleading dichotomy between biology and experience, in part, because they inherited statistical models that assume that influences due to endogenous forces can be separated from those due to exogenous ones. Biologists and physicists have more successfully avoided the fallacy of treating complementary forces as having independent causal status. An embryo capable of cell division is formed when the sperm and egg unite; neither is the more important cause of the first division of the fertilized egg. Or, consider a pond in the process of freezing. Water has one set of inherent properties over 32 degrees Fahrenheit and another set when the outside temperature falls below that point. Physicists do not explain the pond's freezing by assuming that the formation of ice can be apportioned into one set of factors attributable to the inherent properties of water and into another ascribable to external change in temperature. Freezing is a unitary event resulting from a particular quality of the outside air acting upon a closed body of water. In a similar vein, the cognitive development of a premature infant who grows up in an economically disadvantaged home will follow a different developmental course than will that of a premature infant who grows up in a middle-class home (Werner and Smith 1982). It is not possible to determine the differential importance of being born premature and subsequent family experience on a child's profile of intellectual abilities.

Connectedness and Discontinuity in Development

A second theme, probed deeply in chapter 2, contrasts the belief in continuous, connected growth from infancy to adulthood with the possibility of serious discontinuity, where some earlier characteristics vanish completely and new ones emerge with relatively short histories. Put plainly, what qualities of infants and children are preserved, and for how long?

No era in the history of Western society is without its share of scholars, ministers and statesmen who declare that part of the adult character is formed during the opening years of life. Plato believed that the baby who is rocked frequently becomes a better athlete; German Reformation leaders declared that the hand that rocks the cradle shapes the destiny of a society; nineteenth-century New England ministers in Sunday sermons told parents that the way they handled their infants would determine the child's future character. Rousseau's diagnosis of society's problems is modern in tone:

When mothers deign to nurse their own children then will be a reform in morals; natural feeling will revive in every heart; there will be no lack of citizens for the state; this first step by itself will restore mutual affection. . . . As women become good mothers men will be good husbands and fathers. (Rousseau 1911 [1762], pp. 13–14)

Concern with the initial period of development, which is part of a general curiosity about the origins of natural phenomena, rests on the premise that each life is an unbroken trail on which one can trace a psychological quality from any point back to its beginning. Each child provides the discerning mind with clues that are subtle previews of adolescence and adulthood. Hence, parents fear that their quiet, timid three-year-old will become an adolescent loner, or anticipate that their effusive energetic six-year-old will be elected president of her high school class.

The possibility of serious change in psychological profile complements the theme of stability. Classic Chinese premises form a compelling contrast to those of the West, for an emphasis on change, rather than on permanence, has dominated philosophical writings during most of Chinese history. An important third-century essay—the "Chuang-tzû Commentary"—captures this theme: "Of the forces which are imperceptible forces, none is greater than that of change. . . . All things are ever in a state of change . . . therefore the I of the past is no longer the I of today" (cited in Fung 1973, p. 213).

Despite the Western preference for stability, Americans invest so much of public and private resources in purchasing the services of psychologists, psychiatrists, and counselors, and in supporting government intervention programs, they must believe that a child's behavior can be changed through benevolent intervention. Americans, from colonial times, have trusted the power of education to remove incompetence and to civilize the vagrant and the criminal. A threatening consequence of the scientific evaluations of benevolent efforts like Head Start and increased expenditures for schools is the general pessimism regarding their permanent benefit to the child. On the other hand, some delinquents do stop stealing and apply to college, and some successful executives leave their jobs and families to write poetry in isolated mountain cabins. Even though these cases are not the rule, their existence forces us to acknowledge the possibility of some change at any point in the life span (Brim and Kagan 1980).

Qualities and Quantities

A third theme deals with our descriptions of human characteristics. There are two ways to think about natural events. A tree, the taste of salt, the sound of a crashing wave, and a suicide seem to be qualitatively distinctive events, not parts of a graded series. By contrast, the depth of blue in a morning sky, the temperature of a cup of tea, the perceived speed of our heartbeat, and the feeling of fatigue in a particular moment seem to be points on a continuum of similar events that differ from each other only in degree.

Most of the properties of matter that are of concern to physicists are continuous, like weight, length, temperature, and, for an object in motion, velocity. But the biological qualities of living creatures—irritability, reproduction, disease—are generally not continuous. A nerve cell is or is not in an irritable state; a female is or is not reproducing an offspring. There is no state of "partial pregnancy."

This dichotomy between qualitatively discrete properties and continuous quantities has been a persistent source of debate in essays on the essence of natural phenomena. On the one hand, there was Aristotle's insistence on qualitative differences among events; and, on the other, Plato's view that the unique qualities that seem to compose phenomenal experience are derived from invisible continuities in their basic elements. The status and intellectual power of mathematics, which were enhanced in the subsequent two millenniums, persuaded most Enlightenment scholars to side with Plato and to declare, with Galileo, that God used mathematics as the language of nature, even though the power of mathematics in the natural sciences remains mysterious and defies rational explanation. Therefore, the best scientific explanation should eventually rest on continuous mathematical functions. Explanations that rely on qualities are preliminary, less powerful, and always less pleasing.

Despite the fact that many psychological phenomena seem to be best described as discrete qualities, psychologists prefer, whenever possible, to flatten the bumpy qualities into tiny points on a graded series. Consider the perception of color. Qualitatively different cells in the retina and the thalamus respond selectively to light of different wavelengths, even though the physicist describes the light in a continuous metric of nanometers. And infants, like adults, treat the differences between the hues as discrete categories rather than as visual experiences on a continuum. After becoming bored with a circle that is crimson in color, infants show far less excitement when a pink circle replaces the crimson one than when the change is from pink to green, even though the physical changes are of equivalent wavelengths, as measured in nanometers.

Similarly, psychological phenomena like schizophrenia and Down's syndrome are not instances on a continuum of psychic disturbance or intelligence, but coherent sets of distinctive qualities. A biologist who correlated the speed of completing a mating episode with the size of reproductive organs in a variety of species of animals, and invented the continuous concept of "mating efficiency," would probably invite a sarcastic critique from colleagues. Yet most social scientists do not deride a scientist who computes ratios of brain to body weight in different species in order to infer a continuum of intelligence, because psychologists are attracted to characteristics like intelligence that fall on a continuum, and are less friendly than biologists or linguists to the idea of distinctive classes. One of the sharpest controversies in modern linguistics concerns whether human language is a distinctive characteristic of our species, or a talent that lies on a continuum with the communicative competence of apes.

One of the unfortunate consequences of regarding discrete qualities as points on a continuum is the practice of comparing children of vastly different ages on the same characteristic (for example, the number of ideas that can be recalled or the magnitude of increase in heart rate to a threat), with the assumption that the conditions that produced the behavior are identical for all age groups and differ only in intensity. But infants are qualitatively different from older children and should not be conceptualized as having less of some quality than ten-year-olds possess.

One reason psychologists prefer continua is that the statistical techniques available to them—correlations, analysis of variance, and path analysis—assume an underlying continuum of causation, with both extreme and less extreme values produced by the same forces. I shall argue in chapters 2 and 5 that the temperamental characteristics of infants and the basic classes of emotions are better conceptualized as discrete qualities than as continua.

General and Specific Constructs

The selection of the most appropriate level of analysis, which lies at the heart of the fourth theme, contrasts broad with narrow concepts. Until recently, psychologists have preferred very broad ideas. Freud, for example, felt he needed only three basic forces—id, ego, and superego—to explain most behavior. Both Piagetians and behaviorists also base their explanations of behavior on a very small number of concepts. Their strategy is to use a limited empirical fact to invent a broad explanatory idea—a leap away from specificity. I suspect that one reason for this ambition is traceable to the sociology of science. Disciplines, like individuals, imitate those with higher status. Mathematics, acknowledged to be the queen of sciences, enjoys the greatest respect in the academy, and most mathematicians, especially those who call themselves formalists, regard complex deductive arguments from a small set of axioms as the ideal of scholarship. But biology provides a productive counterexample. There are only a few broad ideas in biology, but many powerful specific ones. The concepts of cell, nucleus, and DNA were all inductively derived, and each has a specific set of functions that cannot be deduced from a small set of assumptions. I believe psychology should follow biology, not mathematics, at this point in its short history.

There is, therefore, a tension in psychology over how general or specific psychological concepts should be. Most contemporary psychologists prefer constructs that are minimally constrained by local conditions like setting, incentive, and target. Descriptive terms such as "need for achievement," "anxiety," "hostility," "working memory," and "intelligence" are popular examples. But people do not possess these abstract qualities in all situations. No one desires to achieve in all settings or is hostile to all people. A psychologist friendly to the view that names for human competences or dispositions should be constrained by context, would use constructs that include a clear reference to the locus of action, and replace "need for achievement" and "hostility" with "need for intellectual achievement" and "hostility toward male authority."

Every psychological procedure is a specific context in which a person reacts. Therefore, the meaning of a quality inferred from a person's reactions often must be limited to that scientific procedure, as we shall see in chapter 6. But psychologists habitually use seriously different procedures to measure what they think is the same quality. One scientist asks the child if she is afraid of her father; another watches the child's behavior with the parent at home; a third puts electrodes on the child to see if her heart rate changes when she sees a picture of man punishing a small child. It is not surprising that each procedure yields a different answer. But rather than conclude that there is no single meaning to "a child's fear of the father," investigators throw stones at the procedures they distrust.

The relation of procedure to conclusion is nicely illustrated in the work of particle physicists who wish to determine the elementary constituents of the atom. When scientists build a more powerful accelerator that increases the velocity of the stream of protons striking a target, they typically discover new particles that were not present when they used the less powerful machine. The new particles are to be viewed as the joint product of the structure of the atom and the energy of the bombarding protons, and not as parts of the atomic target that had always been there just waiting to be released.

Each method elicits from its target of study a special profile of characteristics. Many of these characteristics are not stable components of the target—as wetness is a continuous characteristic of the ocean—but rather potential qualities that are actualized under very specific experimental conditions. An adult who is told by a white-coated experimenter to administer shock to a stranger in an adjoining laboratory room will do so, even though the stranger protests vigorously (Milgram 1964). The compliance does not mean that most American adults have a stable disposition to conform to the inhumane requests of authority; rather, it means that the combination of this special procedure and the person's characteristics create the conformity and apparent indifference to the distress of another human being. A different procedure would not have produced the conformity. Hence, the unquestioning obedience is not a continuous property of the adult, but a characteristic that is provoked only under specific conditions. That is why the physicist Freeman Dyson has written, "It is hopeless to look for a description independent of the mode of observation" (1979, p. 249).

When a nineteenth-century observer made a statement about a child's lability or fear, his colleagues knew that the source of the statement was the child's overt behavior, for this was the method of choice. Today psychologists use questionnaires, interviews, projective tests, memory problems, and polygraphic display of neural discharge. Even if we ignore the fact that these methods may not be accurate evaluations of either lability or fear, scientists who use any of them make statements about the degree to which a child possesses these properties, and are often indifferent to the real possibility that the measurement methods are not equivalent. The proposition "the newborn is labile" has one meaning if it is based on watching the baby in a crib for two hours, quite another if one is looking at the infant's heart rate, and still another if the evidence comes from the amplitude of the baby's brain waves in response to one hundred brief flashes of light.

The intimate relation between a procedure and a description of a child's qualities becomes increasingly relevant as social scientists begin to study physiological correlates of psychological states. The construct that best fits the biological data often has no obvious synonym in terms used to describe what seem to be related psychological characteristics.

I recently studied a large group of three-year-old children and their mothers. One of the most striking differences between the children was based on their heart-rate profiles when they were being administered a series of tests. One group had high and stable heart rates across all the test procedures. The contrasting group had low and variable heart rates. Experimental work with older children and adults has shown that, when a person is doing mental work (for example, listening carefully to a list of numbers in order to remember them), heart rate rises and stabilizes; but this pattern does not occur when the person is simply listening to words or looking at pictures. It is believed that the profile of an increasing and more stable heart rate is due to an increase in physiological arousal.

How shall we describe the children who show these two different patterns? Terms like "motivated," "anxious," and "hopeful of success"—which historically have been used to summarize similar data—do not seem to be appropriate for the states associated with the heart-rate profiles. The facial expressions or bodily movements of the children with the higher and more stable heart rates, for example, do not reflect more intense motivation or greater anxiety. Because the mothers of the children with the higher and more stable heart rates told an interviewer that they held high standards for their children's intellectual competence, we might suggest terms like "aroused," "uncertain about quality of performance," or "involved in the tasks." But no aspect of a child's behavior warranted those labels; hence, these descriptions originate in and take their meaning from the heart-rate evidence. This situation is not unlike that of the electroencephalographer who says of a subject with closed eyes that his brain-wave pattern indicates a state of alertness. Indeed, the phrase "paradoxical sleep" was invented to account for the odd phenomenon of a sleeping subject whose brain waves resemble those of an alert person at high noon.

Consider the following hypothetical situation. One person is allowed only to see an apple at a distance; two others are blindfolded, and one is permitted to taste the apple but not feel it, while the other can only feel it. After all process their source of information, each declares, "This object is an apple." These statements do not have the same meaning because the sources of the experience are different. If this example does not seem persuasive, change the apple to a gold harp to which three persons have access through only one sensory modality: sight, sound, or touch. Should all three declare, "This object is beautiful," it should be more obvious that the three statements have different meanings.

The psychologist more often uses terms to name hypothetical qualities like beauty than to label concrete objects like apples. The idealist who believes there is a unitary essence of "apple" or "beauty" behind the different sensory experiences should be reminded that phlogiston and witches do not exist, despite initial signs that were persuasive of their reality.

The scientist's task is to detect the relations among events and, subsequently, to apply names to the events and the newly discovered relations. But the best scientific procedures reveal only a portion of the total phenomena to be understood; and the names, therefore, denote what has been revealed by the procedures and not the events as they occur in nature. The position of empiricists is much like that of two blind persons, one with scissors and the other with a jackknife, who, after being told the characteristics of a rose petal, are instructed to find one and to separate it from its surroundings so that the product is perfectly faithful to the original petal. Even if our blind adventurers should be fortunate enough to find a rose bush, it is unlikely that they would cut away one complete petal and nothing more. Each would probably detach part of a petal, part of a stem, and perhaps a bit of the bush and return with these non-identical products, convinced that each of them had found the perfect rose petal.

This argument may appear to be a restatement of Percy Bridgman's (1958) philosophy of operationalism, which had a brief period of high popularity after the First World War and is now in disrepute. Bridgman and the philosophers of the Vienna circle urged that the meaning of all theoretical terms, including the qualities of organisms, rested only on their measurement operations. Application of that view to modern psychology would mean, for example, that intelligence is only a particular set of answers on the Wechsler Intelligence Scale. There are good reasons to reject this conclusion as too restrictive and obstructive of theoretical progress. I favor a more permissive mood. The investigator has license to ascribe qualities to organisms for settings that were not observed, but he or she is obligated to specify the nature of those unrealized settings.

Subjective and Objective Frames

Description and explanation of psychological phenomena can be constructed from the frame of the subject or the frame of another who is trying to understand the subject. Although there can be as many "other" frames as there are observers, the special perspective of the scholar who is trying to improve theoretical understanding by using evidence to eliminate incorrect hypotheses is usually called the *objective frame*. The objective frame is not always more correct, but it does try to be more consistent in its application of rules of inference. The subjective and the objective frames have different functions and different criteria for validity, and the two need not be consonant. Here lies the essence of the fifth theme, which is most relevant to chapter 5 on emotion and chapter 7 on the family.

Although statements cast in an objective frame, usually based on empirical data gathered by an observer or a machine, are only one source of understanding (intuition is an equally valuable source), such statements need not have a relation to the subjective experience or explanation of the agent being described. The truth of this statement is obvious when animals are the targets of description. Karl Von Frisch's (1974) elegant reports on the dance of returning honey bees describe a lawful relation between the distance of the pollen source from the hive and the movement patterns of the returning bees. Von Frisch need not tell us what the bees' experience might be. From the perspective of the person—what Wendell Garner (1981) calls the primary epistemology of the subject—perception is holistic, immediate, and unanalyzed. But the psychologist, loyal to an objective epistemology, self-consciously analyzes into separate mechanisms what was unanalyzed by the subject.

Students of perception regard the distinction between the two frames as a contrast between appearance and reality. When a bullseye of alternating black and white segments is rotated rapidly, people have the subjective impression that the thin segment of black bordering the white is darker than the rest of the black segment. However, objective measurements reveal that the entire black segment is at the same level of brightness. In this case, the two frames are irreconcilable.

The philosophical distinction between a person's belief and knowledge also acknowledges the two frames, but philosophers would like to see more consonance between the two perspectives in order to avoid legitimizing individual beliefs that are not shared by the community. After infancy, each person has a subjective awareness and interpretation of his or her behavior, wishes, and feelings. From the perspective of an objective description, this private interpretation is to be regarded as an event to be understood, and not as a competing account or one to which the statement in the objective frame must accommodate. If not, there would be no need for the diagnostic categories of the psychiatrist, which, most of the time, bear little relation either to the patient's description or explanation of his symptoms (Kleinman 1980).

The problem is not only that a person's private experience does not contain events unavailable to conscious awareness; but, more important, the person's description of his private experience to another has a unique structure (objects followed by predicates, rules of sentence construction which respect temporal order and causality, and no terms that refer to fragments of experience) that is unlikely to be faithful to the structure of the processes being summarized. Sentences are not finely tooled to the events they are supposed to describe. When a person exploring the interior of a deep hole with a stick is asked to describe what she is experiencing, she will talk about the shape of the hole. But the original perceptual information on which the description is based, which is not in awareness, is composed of a mosaic of pressures between the stick and the hand (Polanyi 1966). Each linguistic description of one's conscious experience can be likened to a pair of mechanical hands attempting to retrieve a set of small fragile forms of clumped sand whose shapes are so imperfectly matched to the mechanical hands that they cannot be grasped easily. Hence, what is retrieved represents an odd fragment of what is present. Although one's report of one's experiences or thoughts has validity in the subjective frame, it may not have much validity in the objective frame (see Marcel 1983 for a recent essay on this issue).* Some contemporary concepts—"a feeling of anonymity," for example—have their clearest meaning in the subjective frame; while others—like "relative dominance of left over right hemisphere"—only have meaning in the objective frame. One form of resolution of the conflict between the determinism of natural science and the humanistic belief in an individual's free will is to view the former premise as belonging to the objective and the latter to the subjective frame. Because the two frames need not be consistent, there is no conflict between the two views.

The complementary relation between the two frames is illustrated in the area of human motivation. Most persons do not think about their motives in the terms chosen by the psychologist. An adolescent girl, for example, wants to become the friend of a specific person; the psychologist says she has an affiliative motive. Another adolescent wants an A in English or an athletic letter in tennis; the scientist says he has an achievement motive. Whereas the individual's motive is typically for a specific event, the scientist's term embraces a broad class of events, because the investigator assumes that the motive to spend an hour drinking with a specific person is only one instance of a more inclusive desire that includes the potential to seek a different person and a different activity if the first is not available. But the more abstract category is in the

---

* The recent revival of interest in hermeneutics represents a theoretical attempt to interpret a person's statements from an objective perspective.

objective frame of the investigator, not the subjective frame of the individual.

Consider the robust phenomenon called *interference* in human memory. When you ask a subject why he cannot remember a set of animal words after he has listened to, and successfully recalled, two prior sets, he simply says, "I can't remember." He does not feel as though anything is interfering with his ability to remember the words. A psychologist might say of the same phenomenon, that there was elimination, replacement, dampening, or simply forgetting. The point is that use of interference in the objective description is not regarded by the subject as the reason for his forgetting the words.

Objectively framed explanations of the relation between social class and early school achievement in children rely on heritability of intelligence, lack of preparation for school tasks, motivation, and expectancy of success. But a ten-year-old boy who is asked why he is failing is likely to reply that the work is too hard or that the teacher is unfair or incompetent. The boy is not likely to say that he has inherited inferior intelligence, or did not learn the alphabet at home, or does not want to succeed. Although psychologists may regard the child's interpretation as a defense—a way of externalizing the failure—many ten-year-olds do believe that an unjust teacher is the reason for their poor achievement. The child's subjective report that the teacher is unjust is a fact that might be used in an objective explanation of the relation between social class and past experience; but it is not necessarily inconsistent with the objective interpretation, or less true.

The difference between the two frames is revealed in a comparison of the stability of personality traits based on objective observations of adolescents, on the one hand, and on self-reports, on the other. Most longitudinal research in an objective frame, using observations and tests, finds that qualities like intellectual achievement, sociability, and dominance are moderately stable over the period of ten to fourteen years of age. But when adolescents were asked on three occasions (grades nine, ten, and eleven) to rate themselves, in a subjective frame, on twenty-one adjectives dealing with such qualities as degree of anxiety, feelings of intellectual ability, kindness, sociability, and dominance over others, there was no relation between the self-reports given in grade nine and those given in grade eleven. The youngsters felt subjectively that they had undergone a great deal of change in these qualities (Dusek and Flaherty 1981). However, empirical data on similar groups of adolescents, summarized in an objective frame, suggest far less change in these qualities (Kagan and Moss 1962).

Another illustration of the two frames is revealed in a comparison of office workers' subjective reports of how often they talked with fellow workers during a particular week, and the objective accounts of observers who walked through the office area every thirty minutes of the working day. There was a serious discrepancy between each person's impression of how often he or she communicated with others and the objective information (Bernard, Killworth, and Sailer 1982).

The different meanings of descriptions that emanate from the two frames are clearly illustrated in studies that ask children or adults to talk about their personal characteristics. Of a large group of nine-year-old boys who were regarded uniformly by their classmates and teachers as extremely unpopular, over one third insisted that they were well liked and popular with all of their classmates at school. This discrepancy between the opinions of others and that of the self is not troubling, for it is always possible for a person to hold a positive, subjective opinion of self despite less flattering perceptions by friends. The special quality of the subjective evaluation, however, was revealed when the psychologist attempted to evaluate the child's conception of self in the objective frame. Each child was given the names of three children in his classroom and asked to select the two that were most similar in personality. In some of these trios, the child under study was a member of the trio being evaluated. Because many of the children who said they were popular placed themselves consistently with the less, rather than with the more, popular children, it is reasonable to infer that they did not regard themselves as popular. But that conclusion is in the objective frame (Kagan et al. 1982). It is not necessary to determine whether the subjective or the objective conclusion is more correct, for the two conclusions are not logically inconsistent. The meaning of the statement "John believes he is popular" depends on the frame adopted—a special case of the earlier conclusion that the meaning of a conclusion always depends upon the method used.

Thus, psychologists must be careful about attributing special significance to verbal replies to their questions. A person's verbal report of private feelings is one datum in a puzzle, and few scientists would wish to make judgments on a single fact. A zoologist who wanted to assign a newly discovered animal to its proper species would never rely on only one characteristic, be it the shape of the beak, the length of the forelimb, or reproductive behavior, but would use a combination of characteristics. So, too, with the classification of a child's beliefs, hopes, or feeling states. No single piece of evidence is likely to be sufficient.

Subjective reports have a special quality, for they pass through consciousness and are transformed in that passage. Psychologists use varied probes to detect the presence of beliefs, intentions, feelings, and competences; each imposes a unique distortion on the information desired. A drawing of the self is not an accurate representation of what the person believes he or she looks like, because the child may have poor artistic skills. A story told to a picture is influenced by the objects in the picture. But because a verbal reply travels through consciousness, it is subject to two serious influences: it must be rational and logical and should not reveal too much that is undesirable about the self. The original information used to construct the answer is altered to fit these requirements. Because so much information is viewed by the person as evaluative of self, a verbal report is often an extremely distorted sign of the essential quality the scientist wishes to know in its less disguised form.

The hard-nosed natural scientist usually wants to dismiss subjective evidence as being unreliable, while some social scientists wish to make it the central explanation. But the latter ignore the fact that each person's frame is unique and limited in scope and illuminates only a small part of the event to be understood in the objective frame—three criticisms that were also leveled eighty years ago at those who believed that the primary problem in psychology was the contents of consciousness, and that introspection was the method of choice.

The reader is not to interpret this discussion as an attack on the utility of the subjective frame. Quite the contrary. Most of each day's decisions flow from that frame, and the coherence that each of us feels compelled to impose on a day, a week, or a life originates in the subjective frame. But the goal of science is to generate statements in the objective frame; hence, subjective information is to be regarded as having the same degree of disguise as rapid eye movements during sleep or a rise in heart rate to an insult. However, treating a person's subjective report of her mood or explanation of her behavior as a datum whose significance is to be discovered is different from regarding it on the same level as the explanation in the objective frame. Thus, I shall try to be careful in my discussion to distinguish these two sources of information and the complementary explanations they generate.

These five themes are the counterpoint for the detailed summaries contained in the chapters that follow. Although an awareness of each of them will enrich one's reading, I regard the fourth theme as the most important. There may come a time when the terms psychologists use to describe human qualities will be broad—as is the concept of energy in modern physics—but this is not that time. Hence, every conclusion about children and families is to be viewed as limited to its source of evidence. Such austerity is necessary during this temporary period of relatively weak theory and an insufficient number of trustworthy facts.

2

The Infant

Natural science does not describe and
explain nature; it is part of the interplay
between nature and ourselves; it describes
nature as exposed to our method of
questioning.

WERNER HEISENBERG,
Physics and Philosophy

WHEN MOST EUROPEANS LIVED their entire lives in the same villages in which they were born, and 40 percent of all children died
by their fifth birthday, a deep understanding of the infant was of
neither interest nor value, for the adult profile of any child who
survived the first few years was determined in large measure by the
parents' economic security and class position. But by the middle of
the seventeenth century, both ascent and descent in social status
had become a real possibility for a significant proportion of youth
whose families had acquired some measure of freedom and the
expectation that their children's lives might be different from their
own. Historical events had made each child's future less knowable
and, therefore, a source of parental apprehension. Now, the community needed an explanation of the variations in life histories that
implied some simple practices that parents could implement in order to reduce the uncertainty that invaded consciousness when
they wondered about the position their child might occupy two
decades later.

The Infant

Of all the causes thoughtful observers might have invented to explain the dramatic differences in adult talent, wealth, happiness, status, and morality, most Western theorists assumed that the experiences of infancy (either quality of physical care or specific encounters with objects and people) were the most relevant. The moods, values, skills, and habits created during the first few years were supposed to persist indefinitely and to form the adult's character, competence, and capacity for joy. Contemporary American parents are ready to believe that the adult's happiness, which has become the most popular criterion for a successful life, is influenced by the events of infancy.

There is also a political motivation that ensures a preoccupation with the first period of childhood, at least among American families. The disturbing differences in economic resources and technical competence between adolescents from disadvantaged ethnic minorities and youngsters from middle-class families are inconsistent with the American ideal of an egalitarian society. Most Americans believe that if the conditions of early rearing were improved and the proper environments engineered, our social problems would be eased. Hence, discovery of the principles of growth would reveal the correct pattern of encounters for all children. This chapter considers some of the important information we have gained about the infant, even though the most profound insights continue to evade us.

The properties of the infant are so distinct from those of the older child that it is not surprising that all societies regard the first two years of life as a special period of development. Infants are often defined not by what they can do but by absence of the qualities adults possess, especially language, intention, appreciation of right and wrong, symbolism, planfulness, guilt, empathy, and self-consciousness. William James's description of the baby's world as a "blooming, buzzing confusion" was rendered credible by the popular notion of the infant as an inherently helpless creature with little power to resist environmental intrusion.

The behavior of the infant is so ambiguous it is easy for the culture's beliefs about human nature to influence observers' interpretations of what they think they see. These influences are nicely illustrated in the different descriptions of the infant by Sigmund Freud, Erik Erikson, and Jean Piaget. Each of these influential theorists highlighted a special aspect of the child's first year because of suppositions originating in the larger cultural context in which each scholar lived.

At the turn of the century, when Freud was forming his theoretical ideas, Darwinian evolutionary theory was a source of metaphors for human behavior. Darwinian theory held that the human infant was the link between animals and human adults. Ernst Haeckel's famous declaration that ontogeny recapitulates phylogeny suggested one form that link might take: the human infant should be governed by the same forces that control primitive animal forms for whom a single orifice served both ingestion of food and sexuality. This imaginative idea—combined with the new doctrine that nerves have specific energies that are linked to different qualities of experience, and the older principle of the conservation of physical energy—probably led Freud to suggest that each child was born with a fixed amount of libidinal energy, with the mouth, tongue, lips, and their usual functions serving as the initial reservoir for this force. Although the bold hypothesis of the oral stage sounds strange today, it was more credible during the early decades of the century—in part, because it bore a close resemblance to major principles in the respected disciplines of zoology, physiology, and physics and satisfied the desire held by many scholars to bring humans and animals conceptually closer.

But half a century later, when Erik Erikson was developing the eight stages of man, politically liberal scholars wanted to increase the psychological distance between animals and humans and to make social experience, rather than inherited instincts, the source of the obvious variation in human talent and character. One reason for this theoretical preference was a desire to quiet a small but vocal group of eminent biologists and psychologists who claimed that the economic and social failure of European immigrant groups was partially biological in origin. Because a growing audience of intellectuals was receptive to the view that social experience, not biology, was formative, it was reasonable for a theorist, during the years between the two world wars, to see the actively nursing infant as a passively fed child and to transform a solitary, instinctive behavior into a social event. Two important qualities in this dyadic relation are the caregiver's affective involvement and her reliability. If she does not feed the crying baby within a reasonable period of time, the infant becomes extremely distressed. Erikson's labeling the first era of development as a time of trust had the same ring of truth in the 1950s that Freud's oral stage had had half a century earlier.

Piaget's conception of infancy, like Freud's, was influenced by debates on the mechanisms of evolutionary change. Piaget sided with those who wanted to award most of the power for change to the organism's commerce with the environment rather than to genetic mutation. Piaget likened the development of cognitive functions to the evolution of organs and bodily processes because, in his conception, the infant's cognitive abilities derive from active interaction with objects in the world and from successive accommodations to new challenges. When Piaget looked at the infant, he saw a baby playing with the mother's face and fingers. Nursing, being nurtured, and exploring the caregiver's fingers are all characteristic of infancy. It is not obvious that one of these functions is most central; theory awards one of them greater status than the others.

The ease with which scholars attribute special meaning to an aspect of infancy reflects a general tendency to ascribe to the young child properties that are opposite to or undeveloped beginnings of the characteristics adults prize. Americans, who value independence and individuality, see the baby as dependent, undiffferentiated, and not yet aware of being separate from others—undesirable contrasts to the qualities the Western adult is supposed to attain.

But dependence on others and an undifferentiated self are not ascribed universally to young children. The Japanese, who prize close interdependence between child and adult, regard the infant as having a small component of autonomy that is part of the baby's unique nature. Japanese mothers, who believe they must tempt the infant into a dependent role, rush to soothe a crying infant, respond quietly to the baby's excited babbling, and sleep with the young child at night in order to encourage the mutual bonding necessary for adult life.

Historical shifts in the traits theorists ascribe to infants can reveal secular changes in the qualities that are admired. During the 1930s, when control of childhood aggression was regarded as both highly desirable and attainable, the British psychoanalyst Melanie Klein awarded to the infant unrestrained aggressive impulses and explained the nursing infant's biting of the mother's nipple as an expression of that primitive instinct. Since the Second World War, childhood aggression has become more acceptable and, accordingly, Klein's description has become obsolete.

When strict conformity to parents and benevolent authority was the ideal, nineteenth-century American children were described as willful. The goal of socialization was to teach them the mature posture of obedience to elders. As historical events began to taint the moral imperatives laid down by authority, theorists felt it necessary to promote a private conscience. Hence, children who regularly conformed to the commands of adults out of fear of punishment were reclassified as immature, because anxiety over the disapproval of others is not as desirable a foundation for morality as is an inhibition that rests on an internal commitment to be good.

Attitudes toward the restraint of strong desire have also changed profoundly during the last two centuries. The inhibition of behavior motivated by anger, the promise of sensory delight, or enhanced power—called *self-control*—was the central criterion for morality in the early nineteenth century. But by the first decade of this century, adjustment to social demands began to replace self-control as the ideal each child was supposed to attain. Successful adjustment required yielding to desires for pleasure, friends, status, and wealth; hence, excessive self-control was undesirable, and the profile valued in 1800 had been reclassified as potentially detrimental to happiness.

Contemporary psychologists have chosen to celebrate two other characteristics of the infant. One group, partly derivative of the Eriksonian view, regards affectionate and playful interaction between mother and infant as critical for the attachment of baby to caregiver—a distinguishing feature of this era. A second group has selected for study qualities that comprise the central interests of modern cognitive science: perception, memory, and categorical functioning. If the renewed concern with morality continues to grow, it is possible that, by the end of this century, many observers, like those who wrote at the end of the last century, will award centrality to the behavioral previews of will, intention, and choice because they are the essential elements of conscience.

This chapter attempts to summarize a conception of infancy that is informed by three ideas. The first awards primacy to maturing cognitive talents: in part, because these qualities were ignored in past descriptions; and, in part, because I believe developmental changes in emotions and social behavior are best understood by relating them to the growth of cognitive processes.* I shall argue that the most essential catalyst for change is the relation between the events that enter the child's perceptual field and his knowledge at that moment, and that the child's corpus of knowledge is monitored by inherent biases in the way experience is segmented and by a growing ability to remember the past and to compare it with the present.

The infant's attachment to those who provide care is a second initial process in the first year. The actualization of this process also involves a relation between the child and the world outside, but the attachment relation unites the infant's inborn repertoire of actions with the responsiveness of those persons who care for and play with the infant.

Acquiring knowledge and forming attachments are universal, but there is extraordinary variation among children in the rate and form of these acquisitions. Although differences in rearing environments make a substantial contribution to this variation, an infant begins life with a particular temperamental style, which profoundly influences the way others treat the child and how he or she reacts to the unexpected.

The Growth of Initial Knowledge

The infant's first knowledge is dependent on actions and perceptual experience. The newborn is ready to experience most, if not all, of the basic sensations given our species from the moment of birth. The baby can see, hear, and smell and is sensitive to pain, touch, and changes in bodily position. Although the sensitivity of these modalities is not yet at its maximum—the newborn's retina, for example, is not fully functional at birth (Abramov et al. 1982)—the infant is responsive to information from all of the senses. The infant can detect the difference between a pattern com-

---

*Some modern essays on conditioning are also cognitive in perspective, regarding conditioning as a process by which representations of events become related (MacKintosh 1983).

posed of stripes only one eighth of an inch wide and a completely gray patch, between vertical and oblique gratings, between linear and curved lines, and between richly contoured, in contrast to minimally contoured, designs. In the auditory mode, the young infant can discriminate between the musical notes C and C sharp and between the spoken syllables "pa" and "ba," and is acutely sensitive to rate of change in sound energy during the first half-second of an auditory event. If change is slow, the baby opens her eyes in interest; if it is rapid, the baby closes them in defensive avoidance.

Psychologists use a simple strategy in determining whether an infant can detect the difference between two events. When infants become bored with a particular event, they usually show increased attention to a different one if they recognize it as different from the original. If infants are shown two identical red spheres until they look away out of boredom, and are subsequently shown one of the red spheres next to a red cube, they will show more interest

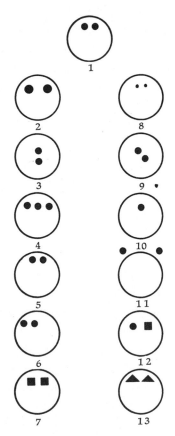

in the cube, implying that they detect a difference between old and new events. For example, ten-month-old infants were shown two identical plain circles (representing faces) with dots for the eyes (frame 1 in figure 2.1). After the infants became bored with this simple stimulus, some of them saw a new pair of circles—one just like the original and one with the "eyes" lying outside the frame (frame 11). Although the infants did not look longer at the figure with the circles outside the frame, they are capable of detecting the difference between the two stimuli (Linn et al. 1982).

These findings reflect a common problem in inferring both knowledge and mental states in another. Suppose one is tracking a man walking in the forest and notes that, on the average, he glances at a tree, a bush, or an animal for about two seconds. If he looks at a particular plant for ten seconds, one would be relatively certain that he sees something special there. But if the man passes a distinctive elm tree and does not glance at it for more than a second, one cannot infer that he does not distinguish it from the other trees in the area, only that the particular elm tree does not interest him. This rule also holds for the baby. Once the child acquires representations of the world—and she does so from the first days— she relates a new experience to what she knows, not to the immediately preceding event. When I hear the sound of a truck on a street that has been quiet for an hour, I may not pause to assimilate it if I perceive it at once for what it is, even though the sound is different from the quiet of the immediately preceding moments. Most of the time humans compare an event to their knowledge about that event, and not to the fading sensory trace of prior moments. Thus, a baby who does not react in an obvious way to a new event may have detected it as different from her last experience but was able to categorize it either quickly or not at all.

The temptation to view the absence of a reactive behavior as due to the absence of the same forces that are responsible for its appearance is a serious problem in psychological theorizing. When the subjects are older children, investigators will acknowledge that minimal motivation or the wrong cognitive set can be responsible for failure to solve a problem a child has the competence to resolve. But because the infant is regarded as cognitively simpler, scientists find it easier to assume that response failure is due to a fundamental incompetence, rather than being a temporary state. One reason for this error in reasoning, as I noted in the first chapter, is that each procedural probe is only one of many that could be used to assess a child's psychological state; another method might have elicited the expected response. Black seven-year-old children from inner-city Baltimore who did not give a correct answer to an examiner who asked, "What should you do to make water boil?" had no problem providing a correct answer when the question was changed to, "What do you do to make water boil?" Changing the simplest aspect of a psychological procedure often leads to a totally unexpected response (Weiskrantz 1977; Donaldson 1978). A psychological quality can be likened to the inside of a house with many tiny portholes, each constructed with a glass of different and unknown convexity. Each view from the outside, like each psychological procedure, produces a different view of what lies within.

CONDITIONS FOR ATTENTION: CHANGE AND PATTERN

New knowledge is most often acquired when the infant's attention is focused on an event, and change is one of the central qualities governing the alerting and maintenance of the infant's attention. Movements of objects, dark-light borders, sudden touches, and pulsing sounds universally attract and maintain attention (Haith 1980). But amount of contour or movement is not the only determinant of attention in the visual mode. Particular changes in the pattern or arrangement of elements also have the ability to hold the infant's attention, at least during the first year of life. Because it is difficult to explain these results as a function of the child's experience, we are forced to conclude that certain patterns have psychological significance. Let us return to the frames in figure 2.1.

Ten-month-old infants were first shown a pair of identical frames (frame 1) in figure 2.1. Thirteen different groups of infants were then shown a new pair of stimuli. One member of the pair was the circle with dots for eyes they had just seen (frame 1); the other was one of the other twelve frames. The thirteenth group of infants continued to see the same pair of circles. Only two of the changed patterns produced a large increase in attention: two vertically arranged circles (frame 3) and two slightly larger circles (frame 2).

It is not easy to invent commanding explanations of this unexpected finding. It might be adaptive for infants to be alerted by the larger circles, which, in the real world, can be a clue to an approaching object. But it is less obvious why the change from horizontal to vertical had such potency. This is not an eccentric phenomenon; in all modalities, a few events usually have great power to capture a child's interest.

These observations are relevant to one of the most persistent questions Western scholars have asked about the source of knowledge. Following John Locke, many philosophers, joined by psychologists during the late nineteenth century, wanted to trace all knowledge and ability to experience originating in the outside world. But the special sensitivity to a change from horizontal to vertical circles seems to be an inborn bias, as are the migrating bird's receptivity to polarized light, the duck's attraction to the call of its mother, and the honeybee's sensitivity to the speed and direction of the dance of returning foragers who have discovered flowers three hundred yards from the hive. Rhesus monkeys isolated from birth from visual access to other animals or humans show signs of excited emotion to a mirror reflection of themselves (lip smacking reflects such a state) and signs of fear to a human face (as evidenced by a grimace) (Kenney, Mason, and Hill 1979). Because the different reactions cannot be due to prior experience with other monkeys or humans, it is necessary to posit an inborn mechanism that leads the monkey to treat these two events differently. The mind that Locke thought of as empty of habit at birth is full of ways to process experience that demand certain uniformities in the acquisition of knowledge, regardless of the culture in which an infant begins life.

THE FORM OF KNOWLEDGE: THE SCHEMA

The *schema,* which is the first form of the infant's knowledge, resembles John Locke's conception of the contents of the human mind. The schema is a representation of experience that bears a relation to an original event. The knowledge that represents a street in which you lived as a child is contained in schemata. Infants create schematic representations that originate in what they see, hear, smell, taste, and touch. Schemata permit recognition of the past, an ability that exists in fragile form during the first days of life. Newborns who were shown, first, a checkerboard composed of sixteen black and white squares and, then, one with only nine squares—that is, one with less black and white contour—showed renewed interest, indicating they recognized that the number of black and white squares had been altered. The unit that permits the recognition is the schema.

The schema cannot be an exact copy of reality, for the mind cannot register every feature of an event, even one as meaningful as the mother's face. Further, succeeding exposures to an event are never identical; and because the mind relates the second experience to the first, and the third to the second, while recognizing the subtle variations, it probably creates a composite of all the experiences. The composite, called a *schematic prototype,* is not identical with any single prior experience and, therefore, is the mind's construction. Original support for that statement came from experiments in which children were shown a series of similar events— say, a schematic face—that had various distances between the eyes, between eyes and nose, or between nose and mouth. After studying these similar faces, the children were shown a face they had never seen but one that represented the average of all the prior faces, a new face that was not the average, and one of the faces they had seen earlier. Children looked longer at the latter two faces than at the average one, suggesting that they regarded the average as the most familiar face, even though they had never seen it before (Strauss 1979). Plato would have been pleased with this result, for he claimed that each event in the world has a basic essence that the mind, through the motion of its elements, represents.

If infants extract a schematic prototype from experience, they must be attending to separate dimensions of an event. This possibility implies that they might represent abstract qualities, independent of any concrete experience, and recognize the abstraction in a modality other than the one that has given rise to the original schema. There is some evidence that infants are able to do this.

Babies who first hear either a pulsing or a continuous tone, and then are shown both a broken and a continuous line, look longer at the broken line after they had heard the pulsing tone, but look longer at the continuous line after they have heard the continuous tone (Wagner et al. 1981). If infants without language can create schemata representing qualities like continuity and discontinuity extracted from auditory and visual experience, then philosophers who have argued for the existence of universals are partially vindicated.

The Infant

Young children may be sensitive to other perceptual contrasts beside continuity versus discontinuity. Some reasonable candidates are the presence versus the absence of an object, single versus multiple representations of an event, spatial locations above and below the child's head, agents acting or being acted upon, and the contrast between an event immediately preceded by a prior event and one that appears to be spontaneous. Each of these pairs shares a significant dimension but contains many unshared dimensions. The child's first language provides some support for these conclusions. When an object disappears, two- and three-year-olds will frequently say, "All gone" or, "Bye-bye," implying a readiness to notice the contrast between presence and absence. Children will say, "More" when they note the presence of a second toy similar to a first and "Down" and "Up" to name appropriate changes in the spatial location of a person or an object. The early appearance of these words implies an appreciation of these contrasting categories of experience.

As the child acquires schemata, the relation between them and immediate experience competes with the original power of contour, movement, color, and curvature to attract and to hold the child's attention. Specifically, events that are a partial transformation of existing schemata begin to dominate the infant's attention. These events are called *discrepant*. This principle is common in development; one mechanisms dominates the functioning of an organism until its mission is completed and it is replaced by or subordinated to another.

The discrepant events likely to generate the longest bouts of attention and excited thrashing and babbling share a sufficient number of dimensions with the child's schemata to be recognized as related to them, but each is a partial transformation—a rearrangement, an addition, or a deletion of an element or dimension that is central to the stored schema. A doll without a head and a doll whose head is placed between the legs represent two such transformations for six-month-olds. A doll without ears does not, because ears are not a salient dimension in the schema for a human, at least not for six-month-old babies. A four-month-old infant with a schema for her parents' faces will look a long time at a picture or sculpture of a face in which the placement of eyes is rearranged, but will not look very long at a face that does not contain eyes or a mouth.

The principle hidden behind these facts—the discrepancy principle—states that the relation between the duration of sustained attention awarded to an event and its relation to the child's schema is often curvilinear (McCall, Kennedy, and Appelbaum 1977). Events that transform noncentral elements and events that transform all central elements elicit far less attention and excitement than do those that transform some, but not all, of the central dimensions. Thus, eight-month-olds with a firm schema for an adult human become excited when they see pictures of infants, but not when they see pictures of butterflies. Two-year-olds, for whom women and infants are very familiar, become excited to pictures of butterflies (Reznick 1982).

The infant's emotional state is affected by his ability or inability to assimilate discrepant events. An event that can be assimilated after some effort produces excitement, but one that cannot be assimilated produces *uncertainty,* a state that will bear a heavy explanatory burden in this and succeeding chapters.

Uncertainty is not synonymous with the states of fear or anxiety, although it may precede them. If the infant continues to attempt assimilation of an event, remains unsuccessful, and, additionally, has no way to deal with the comprehension failure, a different state is generated. Some psychologists call this subsequent state *fear* or *anxiety.* This process is operative as early as three months of age (Mast et al. 1980). Three groups of infants were trained to kick mobiles constructed of two, six, or ten wooden blocks. After learning to produce the kick in order to make the mobile move, all infants were exposed subsequently to a mobile containing only two units. The children who had been originally exposed to the two-unit mobile showed no change in their behavior; those who experienced the change from a ten- or a six-block mobile to one of two blocks fretted and cried, suggesting that they were upset by the change. Their distress can be viewed as a response to a comparison of the amount of movement produced by the two-unit mobile in front of them with their schema of the previous day's more exciting experience with the larger mobile. The fact that each kick produced less variety than it had formerly occasioned their dysphoric state.

The ability to predict the appearance of a discrepant event or to make a response to the unexpected reduces the uncertainty. If one-year-olds watch a mechanical toy that is regularly activated and inactivated every four seconds, they show much less fear than if the same toy moves at irregular, unpredictable times (Gunnar et al. 1983).

Interest, emotion, and action typically follow a partial alteration of the usual. Thus, the mind grows at the edge where the expected does not occur or is moderately transformed. The child's base of knowledge makes a substantial contribution to the mind's growth; hence, there probably is no absolutely best regimen for rearing all infants. The nursery with a ten-unit mobile is not better than one with a six-unit mobile, but alternating from one to the other every five days might produce a more alert infant. Although change forces the mind to work, the events that are best able to provoke mental work will change with the child's cognitive structures. At any one time, the infant is maximally sensitive to a narrow band of events. As one set of experiences is understood, and as a new structure is created or an old one modified, the child becomes maximally receptive to a new set of events.

The discrepancy principle, which implies that humans are prepared to remain attentive to events that are somewhat similar to past experience, may be adaptive. The most informative signs adults give to children are contained in variations in facial expression and vocal emphasis; each is an important basis for socialization.

The discrepancy principle has an analogue in conceptual functioning. Receptivity to and acceptance of new ideas seem to follow a version of the discrepancy principle. The ideas that generate the most heated discussions are those that engage our current beliefs but are slight transformations upon them. Opinions that are too different from those that are held are either ignored or actively rejected. Plays and novels about homosexuality stimulate a degree of thought and debate in 1984 that would have been impossible one hundred years earlier. Although gross discrepancies are alerting, they are unlikely to lead to sustained attempts at comprehension. If a respondent replies to the question, "How are you feeling today?" with the reply, "I feel too angry to go with you," that answer is discrepant from the interrogator's expectation, and he or she works at understanding. If, however, the respondent says, "World's end is that time," the interrogator probably will invest less effort at assimilation. The tendency for a structure to be activated by an event with which it shares some properties is a conserving principle, protecting systems from reacting to all new events while remaining sensitive to the narrow band of experience that permits change.

THE GROWTH OF MEMORY

The ability to relate an experience in the present to relevant schemata is one of the central maturing functions of the first year of life. In plainer language, the child becomes able to remember the past. But that phrase hides at least three different functions—recognition of the past, retrieval of the past, and the ability to compare past and present on the stage of active memory. The three-month-old infant can recognize a familiar event in her perceptual field because it shares properties with her schemata. But during the first half-year, new schemata, created from a brief encounter with an event, fade quickly if they are not renewed or if there is too long a delay between the original experience and the next encounter.

Infants often announce their recognition of a familiar event by looking back and forth between a new and an old object. For example, an infant was shown three identical toys mounted on a card in a triangular pattern. This card was then replaced with a second one also containing three toys after either a one- or a seven-second delay. Sometimes the second card replaced one of the toys, sometimes it replaced two toys, and sometimes all three toys were replaced. Occasionally, the second card contained the same three toys as the first. If the second card appeared after only a one-second delay, eight-month-olds looked back and forth many times between the new and the old toy, indicating that they recognized that one of the toys had been replaced. However, these same infants showed much less shifting between the toys when the second card appeared after a longer, seven-second delay, suggesting they had forgotten the colors and shapes of the toys that were present initially (Kagan and Hamburg 1981).

A second component of memory, emerging after the middle of the first year, is the ability to retrieve a schema when there are minimal clues—or hints—in the immediate field. Four-month-olds can recognize whether a face in front of them is similar to one they have seen before, but are less able to retrieve the schema for a familiar face while lying alone in their cribs.

A convenient and intuitively reasonable procedure for evaluating the ability to retrieve a schema requires the infant to wait awhile after an attractive object has been hidden, before she is allowed to reach for it. A group of infants was tested on such a problem once a month from eight to twelve months of age. Each child had to find a toy that was hidden under one of two identical cloths in front of him or her. But each infant had to wait one, three, or seven seconds before being permitted to reach for the toy. In addition, a transparent screen, an opaque screen, or no screen separated the child from the toy during the delay. The infants improved steadily in their ability to remember the location of the toy across the four months of observation. No eight-month-old was able to remember the toy's location with a one-second delay when the opaque screen was lowered during the brief interval. But by one year, all infants could find the toy when the opaque screen was lowered for three seconds, and a majority could solve the problem when the opaque screen was lowered for as long as seven seconds (Kagan, Kearsley, and Zelazo 1978).

Jean Piaget believed that before nine months the child does not know that an object that has disappeared continues to exist. This supposition is based on the fact that, prior to eight months, the infant will not reach for a toy she has seen someone hide under a cloth. After eight months, she easily retrieves the hidden toy.

Additionally, the eight- to nine-month-old child who can reliably reach for a toy that he has watched being covered under one cloth, remains vulnerable for a month or two to another class of error. The child is now shown two cloths, A and B. The examiner hides a toy under cloth A (on the left or the right) and permits the baby to retrieve it two or three times. The examiner then hides the toy under the other cloth—cloth B. The puzzle is that most nine-month-old babies go to cloth A. The conditions that reduce the probability of this error provide a clue to its origin. If the delay between the hiding under cloth B and the opportunity to reach is short (less than a second or two) the error is much less likely to occur. Further, if the nine-month-old child does not make the error with a two-second delay, the error will occur if the delay is increased to six seconds. Indeed, throughout the second half of the first year, one can increase the likelihood of the error simply by increasing the delay between the hiding under location B and the time when the child is permitted to reach. At eight months, a delay of five seconds is sufficient; by twelve months, a delay of ten or twelve seconds is necessary to produce the error (Diamond 1983).

A third memorial competence accompanies the ability to retrieve the past over longer delays. When older children and adults read a sentence or listen to a conversation, they are able to integrate the incoming information with their knowledge over a period of time that can last as long as thirty seconds. Most adults who read or hear the sentence, "The Senegalese woman whose father had fought against the French decided before the end of colonialism to live in Nigeria," will understand and mentally rephrase this sentence, despite its length, because they are able to hold all the information in awareness while retrieving the knowledge of Senegal, French rule, and the location of Nigeria. The hypothetical process that permits this integration to occur is called *active memory*. It is likely that this process is also enhanced around eight months of age, permitting the infant to compare and relate incoming information with past knowledge over a period of time. The infant now automatically relates the present to the immediate past, which means she is comparing information from two sources.

A nice demonstration of this ability is found in an experiment with eight-, nine-, and eleven-month-old infants which, through the use of a special mirror, allowed the children to feel an object that was different from the one they were seeing or had just seen. On other trials, they felt and saw the same object. If the infants were actively comparing the tactile and the visual information, one would expect them to be more exploratory on the trick trials when the two objects were different than on the ordinary trials when the two objects were the same. The eight-month-olds did not behave differently on the two kinds of trial, while the older children were more likely to behave as if they were puzzled when they saw and felt different objects. In order to be puzzled, the infant would have to be relating the information from the two senses (Bushnell 1982).

Many puzzling phenomena that appear during the last third of the first year become more understandable if we assume that the child's ability to retrieve the past and to hold it in active memory are being enhanced. For example, if masks of human faces are shown to children four to twenty-four months of age, attention is prolonged at four months of age, is markedly lower for the next four months, but increases at the end of the first and through the second year. The increased attention after eight months is due to the fact that the infant spontaneously relates her perception of the mask to existing schemata of faces she has encountered, keeps both schemata in active memory, and tries to figure out the relation between what she sees and what she knows. It is probably not a coincidence that it is precisely at this age that deaf children learning sign language first use signs to refer to objects in the environment, an act that requires them to relate what is present in their experience to schemata they acquired earlier (Petitto 1983).

In less than one year, the growth of the central nervous system has allowed the infant to move from simple recognition of an event experienced a moment earlier to the ability to remember and integrate separate ideas experienced in the more remote past. These changes seem to occur in all healthy children at roughly similar ages. The vacillation between old and new objects occurs between four and seven months; retrieval of a hidden toy and the relating of two schemata between eight and twelve months. The remarkable uniformity in the appearance of these milestones across different rearing environments suggests that these talents follow orderly changes in the central nervous system, especially maturation of the prefrontal cortex, because this part of the brain is activated when a monkey is presented with a problem in which it must remember under which of two covers a piece of food has been hidden.

THE COGNITIVE BASES OF FEAR

The ability to retrieve and hold schemata in active memory, while relating discrepant events to their possible origins, helps to demystify the universal appearance of certain "fears" characteristic of the second half of the first year, especially fear of unfamiliar adults and fear following temporary separation from a primary caregiver. Infants do not display the facial expression suggestive of fear—mouth retracted, eyes widened, brows raised—until six or seven months of age, even though the ability to make these muscle movements is present at birth. The appearance of this distinctive facial expression implies that the quality of internal experience to discrepant events has changed.

Of course, local conditions in a culture can create unique fears.

No dolls are present in the homes of families living on many of the small atolls in the Fiji chain. Hence, when a Western visitor shows one-year-olds a doll, most children cry, run to their mother, and become inhibited (Katz 1981).

The two most common fears of the first year have been called, in this century, *stranger anxiety* and *separation anxiety*. If a stranger approaches an eight-month-old in a quiet manner and does not smile or talk, the infant wrinkles her face, looks back and forth between the stranger and the mother, and, after a few seconds, begins to cry. If the mother of a one-year-old who is playing happily in an unfamiliar room leaves, the child will gaze at the door where the mother was last seen and begin to cry. Blind one-year-olds will cry when they hear their mother leave the room. They do not have to see the mother to be protected against distress; they only have to know that she is in the room to remain content.

The enhanced cognitive competences I have just considered may permit the appearance of these two reactions. As an unfamiliar woman approaches, the eight-month-old studies her face, automatically retrieves schemata for the familiar faces he knows, compares the two ideas in active memory, and tries to relate them in order to resolve the inconsistency. If the child cannot assimilate the new person, despite an attempt to do so, and has no behavior to deal with the subsequent state of uncertainty, he may cry. At the least, he will turn away from the stranger, stop playing, and perhaps seek the parent.

A similar analysis can be applied to separation anxiety. Following departure of the mother, the twelve-month-old retrieves from memory the schema of the mother's former presence and compares that knowledge with the present situation in active memory. If the child cannot resolve the inconsistency inherent in the comparison, he becomes uncertain and may cry. Macaque monkeys removed from their mothers become depressed only when they remain in the same cage where they had been with their mothers and, therefore, have reminders of her earlier presence. If the infants are removed to a new cage they do not show the depression.*

However, since some children begin to cry as their mother moves toward the door, other factors must be operative. One possi-

*I. C. Kaufmann, personal communication, 1981.

bility is that the enhanced retrieval and comparison capacities are accompanied by the ability to anticipate the future and to make inferences about possible causes (for example, what will happen now? will my mother return? what can I do?) The child who cannot generate a prediction, or do something that might resolve the uncertainty, becomes vulnerable to distress and may cry as a way to bring the mother back or to prevent her from leaving. The child who can generate a prediction, however, may laugh; laughter in anticipation of a novel event increases dramatically after eight months of age.

This interpretation of separation distress differs from an earlier one that assumed that the child cries after maternal departure because he anticipates pain or danger as a consequence of maternal absence—what most psychologists call a *conditioned fear reaction*. Another popular interpretation holds that separation distress reflects the quality of the child's emotional relationship to the mother or primary caregiver. But neither of these explanations can account for the fact that the timing and the form of appearance of separation distress across the first two-and-a half years of life are very similar for children blind from birth, and for children raised in American nuclear families, in kibbutzim in Israel, in barrios in Guatemala, in Indian villages in Central America, in orphanages, or in American day-care centers. Why should all these infants, growing up under such different conditions, learn a conditioned fear reaction to caregiver departure at the same age? It also strains credibility to assume that despite the extraordinary variation in the amount of time infants spend with their mother across these different settings, the developmental function for the emotional relationship to the caregiver is similar.

Even though the intensity of distress displayed by the child during the period from eight to twenty-four months may be related, in part, to the infant's relationship with the caregiver, I favor the view that the appearance of separation anxiety between eight and twelve months of age is due, in part, to the emergence of the ability to retrieve the past, to compare past and present in active memory, and to generate events that might occur in the immediate future.

We are left with one final puzzle. Why does the presence of a familiar person, like the father, or of a familiar setting, like the home, decrease the likelihood of crying and distress in response to maternal departure or the approach of unfamiliar adults? The presence of a familiar person or setting may provide the child with an opportunity to make some response when she is in a state of uncertainty. Action often dispels anxiety in infants as well as in adults. Indeed, one-year-olds who can control the movements of a toy by hitting a panel show less fear of the unpredictable toy than do infants who have no control over the toy's sudden motion (Gunnar 1980). Similarly, to know one can do something when in a state of anxiety tends to mute that state. When the mother leaves but the father remains in the room with the child, the father's presence provides the child with a potential target for particular behavior; the child can approach if she wishes, vocalize, or simply turn to the other parent. That knowledge keeps uncertainty under some control.

Separation distress recedes after two years of age because an older child is able to understand the event, predict the return of the mother, and issue a useful reaction. The child knows where the mother is, or knows that she will return. The child's experiences during the second year create knowledge that permits solution of the puzzle that has engendered the anxiety.

The behavior of monkeys in an unfamiliar environment also reveals that the onset of fear of the unusual depends upon maturation of the central nervous system. Six rhesus monkeys were raised individually with an inanimate toy (a hobbyhorse) in a restricted environment that permitted visual access to the outside world but no interaction with any living creature. Six other monkeys were raised individually with a dog in an environment that permitted considerably more freedom and playful interaction. Each monkey was placed alone in an unfamiliar environment on a regular schedule, and the investigator measured how fearful each monkey became: the animal's heart rate and distress calls were the indexes of fear. Although the monkeys raised with the dogs showed more fear than did those raised with the inanimate toy, both groups of animals showed a major increase in fear between two and four months of age; distress calls were most frequent at four months (Mason 1978). Four months is also the age when monkeys reared in total isolation become distressed when they see photographs of monkeys posturing threat displays (Sackett 1972), and the age when monkeys reared with no visual exposure to humans or animals first show fear in response to a human face (Kenney, Mason, and Hill 1979). These findings imply that maturation of specific parts of the brain is required before novel environments, unfamiliar stimuli, or threat displays will produce fear. Further, the capacity for these fears may not require much social experience.*

The rate of brain and body growth in the monkey is about three to four times that of the human infant. Hence, the comparable period in the child is between seven and fifteen months. This is precisely the interval when fear of strangers and of separation from the mother appear in most human infants regardless of their rearing. Hence, it is reasonable to suggest that the emergence of fear of events that are not immediately comprehensible is due, in part, to maturational changes in the central nervous system and not only to prior unpleasant experiences or specific forms of maternal care.

Also, during this interval, the infant becomes capable of inhibiting some strong reflexes that are inherent in the baby's commerce with the world. For example, if a toy is placed inside a transparent box that has only the left side open, a six-month-old will paw at the top of the box and not reach into the open side because he cannot inhibit the automatic tendency to reach for an object where he sees it. Even if an examiner gently puts the baby's hand through the open side of the box, permitting the child to touch the toy, on the very next trial the infant will return to banging the top of the box because he cannot help but reach for an object in a direction that is in accord with his line of sight. But by one year, maturation of the brain allows the infant to suppress this automatic reflex and to retrieve the toy through the open side (Diamond 1983).

These new phenomena—the fears as well as the ability to inhibit the reaching reflex—imply a significant transition in psychological functioning between eight and twelve months. As I noted, three components in this transition are the ability to retrieve the past, to detect a relation between the past and the present, and to attempt to predict consequences in the near future.† It is difficult to find the best set of adjectives to describe these changes, but phrases like

---

* Fear to the unfamiliar occurs in puppies at five weeks; in ducklings, as early as three days.

† Joseph Campos, of the University of Denver, believes that the onset of crawling during this period provides the infant with special experiences that facilitate some of these cognitive advances.

"thoughtful," "flexible," and "freed from reflexes" capture some of the essential qualities of the new talents that brain growth has made possible.

But acknowledging the role of biological changes is difficult— in part, because it requires explanation in two domains of discourse, the languages of psychology and of biology. Scientists do not like to explain phenomena with propositions belonging to two different vocabularies, each with its own network of unique associations. One can invent a logically commanding psychological explanation of separation fear based either on past frightening experiences or on attachment to a caregiver, each of which generates a sense of understanding. But acknowledging the role of the maturation of the central nervous system requires the theorist to begin the explanation of a phenomenon with psychological phrases and then to add sentences containing biological words. The shift in vocabulary flaws an aesthetic quality that makes an interpretation satisfying.

A COMPARISON WITH PIAGET'S VIEW

This description of cognitive growth over the first year has awarded emphasis to schemata and the enhancement of retrieval and active memory. Jean Piaget, who had a different conceptualization of the psychology of the infant, focused on the actions that aid the child's adaptation to the external environment. The central element of knowledge in Piaget's theory of the infant is the sensory-motor scheme. It is a representation of the class of motor actions necessary to obtain a goal, and it is acquired through active manipulation of objects. The belief that actions with objects are a more important origin of new cognitive structures than is a more purely cognitive comparison of past and present is partially traceable to two ideas that were regnant during the early decades of this century when Piaget was a young scholar: the first was the evolutionary biologist's concern with adaptation; the second was the mechanist's desire to externalize the forces for change so that they could be observed and measured. These two ideologies, which remain popular today, are present in Piaget's view of the bases for the growth and transformations of sensory-motor schemes.

Knowledge has multiple functions. It aids understanding, produces emotions, and permits adaptive behavior. Each theorist chooses the function most congruent with his or her perspective, based on unarticulated intuitions and more conscious intentions. Piaget hoped that observations of the infant would answer two basic kinds of question—one philosophical, the other central to nineteenth-century biology. The philosophical puzzles centered on the developmental course of the Kantian categories of space, time, causality, morality, and the existence of objects. The biological questions dealt with the mechanisms that changed structures over the course of evolution. I suspect that Piaget came to the infant with these ideas in the forefront of consciousness. Thus, he made the ability to retrieve an object hidden under a cloth a major victory of the first year—in part, because he wanted to know when the infant first appreciates that objects exist independent of an observer. Piaget proposed that a long history of interaction with objects was the basis for this victory, because he wanted both to externalize and to smooth the bases for psychological growth.

I came to the infant with preoccupations that were less philosophical and more narrowly psychological. What representations do infants have of their environment? How does the relation between what they know and what they experience change both their knowledge and their behavior? I believe the eight-month-old's ability to find a hidden toy is due to a capacity to remember its location and to use the retrieved knowledge to initiate the act of reaching. Piaget interpreted the same behavior as reflecting the infant's belief that an object does not disappear when it is no longer visible.

How different are these two views? At one level, it must be true that the eight-month-old believes in the permanence of the hidden object, for the child would not search for the toy if she did not believe it was there. Whereas Piaget simply posited the slow emergence of the concept of a permanent object, I suggest this structure can occur only after the memory ability has matured. Thus, one can regard the eight-month-old's reaching for a covered rattle as reflecting the enhancement of retrieval memory, or the initial form of the concept of the permanent object, or both. The preferred description depends on whether one believes the child is concerned with the continued existence of objects or simply remembers the location of the toy he has just held.

Piaget also assumed connectedness and gradualness in growth. But it is not obvious that the child's ability to reach under a cloth to find a hidden toy began to grow eight months earlier when the newborn reflexively closed his fingers on his mother's thumb. Some functions can appear with short, rather than long, histories.

The fourth assumption in Piaget's conceptualization is more congruent with the views expressed here. Piaget claimed that increased intentionality is one of the major competences to develop during infancy. The two-year-old child is able to generate an idea of what he wants to do, select the objects he needs, and implement his plan with a resistance to distraction not possible in the opening weeks of life. Whereas Piaget argued that intentionality eventually emerges from the repetition of actions that produce change in the world—as continuous whipping turns cream into a frothy solid—I suspect that intentionality is inserted into the repertoire late in the first year as a result of the maturation of parts of the brain. Without those morphological changes thousands of hours of "action on the world" would never create the talent of intention.

The Infant's Attachments

The notions of schemata and the stage of active memory conjure up images of a solitary cerebral infant who, like an alchemist at his table, invents powerful potions from mundane elements. But the infant also has a social surface. From the first days the child is necessarily involved with others who administer to his needs and reciprocate his overtures. From the thousands of tiny interactions that define the caregiver-child relation, a special state evolves. Modern commentators have chosen to call that state *attachment*. Unlike the enhancement of active memory, the signs that announce the infant's attachment to a caregiver are more public. Three such signs are central to the notion of attachment: the infant is more easily placated by the adults who care for him than by those who do not, is less distressed by the unfamiliar when in the presence of these adults, and approaches these adults for play when his mood is gay and for solace when he is distressed. This trio of robust facts is as replicable as any in psychology and invites a term to name the properties of the infant that will explain why a small number of people can reduce the infant's uncertainty and be sources of pleasure and preferred targets for social behavior. The word *attachment* seems a good choice: it conveys the idea that the infant has acquired a special emotional relation with those who care for him, and experiences pleasure or serenity in their presence but anxiety and distress when they are gone. Although the physical presence of the mother is ameliorative, her psychological availability is even more so. An infant becomes more apprehensive in a laboratory room when his mother is reading a newspaper than when she is watching him (Sorce and Emde 1981). Apparently the mother's power to mute anxiety includes the child's assumption of her availability.

Although a few inanimate objects in an infant's environment can reduce distress—a favorite blanket, for example—no one would quarrel with the popular assumption that the people who care for the child have the greatest power to alter her emotional state. This is because an attachment is most likely to develop toward objects to which the infant displays species-specific responses, like clinging, vocalizing, smiling, holding, and playing. Adults are the best targets for these responses.

Although an attachment is established, in part, through pleasant experiences, occasionally unpleasant experiences can intensify an attachment in both animals and humans. One group of puppies was cared for exclusively by an adult who fed and played with them but did not create distress. A second group of puppies was fed and played with by the same adult who, on occasion, would strike a puppy on the nose when it approached. During a later test period, the puppies that were punished stayed closer to the caregiver adult than did those that had been treated more kindly (Scott and Fuller 1965). Similarly, infant monkeys whose mothers were often abusive (because as infants the mothers had been raised in isolation) persisted in seeking proximity to them, as did infant monkeys raised with an inanimate surrogate mother which periodically directed a blast of compressed air at the babies (Rosenblum and Harlow 1963).

Resolution of distress is a special class of pleasure; hence, the adult who both produces and resolves uncertainty might generate a stronger attachment, or at least a different quality of attachment, than one who provides the infant only with comfort. Perhaps that is why infants reared only at home, who experience more frequent restrictiveness and, therefore, more bouts of uncertainty than infants who spend most of the day in a nurturant day-care center, appear to be more closely attached to their mothers than day-care infants are to their caregivers at the center (Kagan, Kearsley, and Zelazo 1978). The possibility that experiences we normally evaluate as unpleasant (like restriction or punishment) make an attachment stronger may bother some readers, because we like to believe that all good experiences cluster together and have positive consequences, while unpleasant experiences should have bad sequelae. Some Americans may have difficulty assimilating the fact that in many Polynesian societies, where most adults profess love for children and mothers are nurturant and affectionate to infants during the first two years, there is an abrupt increase in parental aloofness, and even punitiveness, toward the child during the third and fourth years. Many families give the weaned child to a relative who had requested the baby during the mother's pregnancy. In earlier times, some of these societies practiced infanticide. However cruel these practices seem to a Western observer, they are not so regarded by the Polynesian community (Ritchie and Ritchie 1979). The assumption that an infant's attachment, which is presumably beneficial, should be aided only by pleasant experiences is part of a general Western conviction that all good things cohere if only we can find the proper formula.

QUALITY OF ATTACHMENT

If the state of "being attached" is established through interactions with caregiving adults—or, as in some societies, with older children—then attachments should vary in intensity, strength, or quality depending upon the nature of the interaction. The assumption that particular caregiving regimens can make both infant and older child more or less vulnerable to anxiety catapulted the concept of attachment to prominence. Although the basis for regarding an infant's anxiety as potentially toxic was not always specified, but left to the reader to construct, Western theorists implied that a fragile attachment to the biological mother renders the young child vulnerable to psychological symptoms for an indefinite time.

This idea has not been popular in most societies, either in the historical present or in the past. The Efe!, a semi-nomadic group in Zaire, believe that a child will grow best if a woman other than the mother is the first to hold and to nurse the newborn, and the Efe! infant is cared for by many different people during the first year (Tronick, Winn, and Morelli, in press). In eighteenth-century France, about one half of middle-class infants were sent to wet nurses who often cared for several infants over the same period. Although strong public reaction to the high mortality rates among these infants led to a decline in the widespread use of wet nurses toward the end of the nineteenth century, there is no evidence that French mothers worried about the effects of this experience on their infant's attachment or future vulnerability to anxiety.

Indeed, nineteenth-century European and American authors were concerned more with the mother's emotional involvement with the baby than with the baby's attachment to the parent. In an essay on motherhood, Elizabeth Evans wrote, "The strongest human tie is, understandably, that which binds a mother to her child" (1875, p. 7): but nowhere in this 129-page essay did its author ever say that the infant naturally binds itself to the mother. The famous German psychologist William Stern also questioned the intensity of the infant's attachment: "How quickly the little child gets used to a new nurse, even when it had great affection for her predecessor; how little the child misses—perhaps after short pain at parting—its parents when they leave home or a favorite animal" (1930, p. 531).

One author suggested that the function of infant helplessness was not to encourage an attachment to the parent, but to facilitate the emotional bonding between the father and mother (Fiske 1909). The cooperativeness necessary to nurture several children through adolescence would inevitably strengthen the relationship between the parents and, therefore, keep the marital bond strong.

The nineteenth-century observer saw the young infant as a collection of reflexes, instincts, and sensory capacities who developed a sense of self and a burgeoning morality by acting in and on the natural world. But, by the end of the second decade of this century, and with increasing frequency after Freud's writings became popular, *attachment, trust,* and *dependence* became the major descriptive terms applied to the infant, and the "proper" amount of parental love became an issue of serious concern. Frank Richardson, a physician who disseminated the implications of Freudian theory for parents, opened the first chapter of his book with the simple declaration, "Love is the greatest thing in the world" (1926, p. 3), and went on to warn parents of the dangers of expressing too little or too much affection toward their children. Insufficient love could injure the child, but excessive love might produce "unfortunate individuals who present a sorry sight ten or twelve years later. They are irritable, dissatisfied, wholly incapacitated for happy middle-age or later life" (p. 22).

JOHN BOWLBY AND SEPARATION ANXIETY

Perhaps the strongest statement on the significance of the love relation between child and parent appears in the final volume of John Bowlby's ambitious trilogy on attachment and loss (Bowlby 1980). *Loss* begins with a conclusion unlikely to appear before 1800 in any Western essay on human experience: "Loss of a loved person is one of the most intensely painful experiences any human being can suffer" (p. 7). Certainly high-caste Hindus would not agree with Bowlby for the Hindu tries to avoid a deep attachment to others. A Brahmin informant told a British psychiatrist:

Great Indian souls, they ignore the things of this world. A *tyagi,* he is a man who lives in the world, but does not let his spirit become attached to things of the world—if some close relation dies, even a wife or a son, he is not too much distressed, because he knows that this is the rule of the world. He lives in the world like a pearly drop of water on a lotus leaf—it moves about on the leaf but it is not absorbed. (Carstairs 1967, p. 231)

On the final page of *Loss* Bowlby celebrates the centrality of affectional relationships: "Intimate attachments to other human beings are the hub around which a person's life revolves, not only when he is an infant or a toddler, but throughout his adolescence and his years of maturity as well, and on into old age" (p. 442).

Bowlby, like most commentators on human nature, argues that each person has a private judge who approves or disapproves of each day's actions. Whereas Saint Augustine urged that God is that judge, and Emerson maintained that it rests with one's private conscience, Bowlby places love objects in the position of evaluator: "In the working model of the self that anyone builds a key feature is his notion of how acceptable or unacceptable he himself is in the eyes of his attachment figures" (Bowlby 1973, p. 203).

Bowlby argues that an attachment to another person is instinctive and endures from infancy to adulthood, and, most important, that an insecure attachment during infancy permanently affects future vulnerability to psychopathology. Although the first of these suggestions is likely to be true, the other two are more controversial. Because the infant's attachment was central to his views regarding healthy psychological development, Bowlby needed to find a sign of the infant's attachment. He decided that separation protest was that sign. The reason for that hunch is found on the first page of the first volume of *Attachment* (1969), where Bowlby suggests that the distress of separation in a one-year-old resembles the emotional upset of an adult following loss of spouse or sweetheart. Bowlby invented a connection between these two phenomena because both seemed to him to involve "distress to the loss of a love object." This is not a persuasive justification. The motor tantrum of a one-year-old following frustration resembles the aggression of a twenty-year-old; the seizure of a toy by a two-year-old shares some qualities with adolescent vandalism. Yet few modern scholars would suggest that a one-year-old who throws tantrums is likely to become a violent adult. Some of the nineteenth-century theorists who did argue for such a connection ignored the relation of separation distress to adult affectional loss. Twentieth-century observers have come to focus on the infant's cry following loss of the caregiver because of historical changes that have promoted love, trust, and security between child and mother to a position of prominence.

Although many nineteenth-century observers would have understood and probably agreed with Bowlby, few would have written three books on the theme of attachment because, like the blue of the sky, the idea was obviously true. Bowlby's conclusions are newsworthy in the last half of the twentieth century because historical events have led many citizens to question the inevitability of maternal devotion to the child and of the child's love for the family. Parental abuse and adolescent homicide of parents have undermined the nineteenth-century faith in the naturalness of familial love. Modern citizens have begun to question the universality of deep affection and continued loyalty, whether between adults or between parents and children, are saddened by the conclusions implied by that inquiry, and are eager to hear a wise commentator on human nature assert that the love between child and parent is an absolute requisite for psychological health.

There are good reasons why Americans in this century have become concerned with the potential hazards of childhood anxiety.* First, the geographical mobility that increased in the United States after the First World War forced many Americans to live in communities of strangers whom they could not trust. Second, the combination of an economic depression, the atrocities of the Second World War, and, later, possible nuclear catastrophe created in the average citizen serious apprehension about the future. I suggest that these uncertainties have been projected onto the infant. Adults want to understand why they feel anxious and prefer an interpretation that is rooted in experiences originating in the deep past.† Erik Erikson suggests that a capacity for trust and, by inference, adult self-confidence are established in infancy. Harry Harlow and his colleagues demonstrated that macaque monkeys raised with terrycloth mothers were less seriously distressed and more likely to explore their environment than were infant monkeys raised with wire surrogate mothers (Harlow and Harlow 1966). Harlow used the word *love* to explain why the terrycloth-reared monkeys were more secure—a term with connotations similar to Erikson's phrase "infant trust." Both theorists assumed that nature's intended buffer for the infant's anxiety was the attachment promoted by an emotionally close, gratifying interaction between infant and mother.

Every society needs some transcendental theme to which citizens can be loyal. In the past, God, the beauty and utility of knowledge, and the sanctity of faithful romantic love were among the most

---

* Fijian parents regard anxiety over adult reprisal as a sign of maturity in children and celebrate the four-year-old who is insecure about gaining the approval and affection of parents (Katz 1981).

† The modern concern with a "trusting relation" has also influenced scholars outside the field of human development. G. Morris Carstairs (1967) begins his ethnographic description of a Hindu community with a discussion of the mutual distrust he saw among the adult members of the town. I suspect that no nineteenth-century visitor to this community would have begun an essay with this theme.

sacred themes in our society. Unfortunately the facts of modern life have made it difficult for many Americans to remain loyal to these ideas. The sacredness of the parent-infant bond may be one of the last unsullied beliefs. The barrage of books and magazine articles on attachment and the necessity of skin-to-skin bonding between mother and infant in the first postnatal hours is generated by strong emotion, suggesting that something more than scientific fact is monitoring the discussion. If the infant can be cared for by any concerned adult, and the biological mother is expendable (this is not yet proven), then one more moral imperative will have been destroyed.

MARY AINSWORTH AND THE STRANGE SITUATION

Although absence of an attachment to any caregiver is rare, insecure or ambivalent attachments can be the result of caregiver practices that have failed to provide the infant with sufficient physical affection and predictability, especially when the child is in distress. Because infant monkeys, like human infants, become distressed when separated from their biological or surrogate mothers, it has seemed reasonable to conclude that the separation distress in both monkey and child reflects anxiety over loss of the attachment relationship. As a consequence, the infant's reaction to temporary separation from and reunion with the mother has become the most popular index of the quality of an infant's attachment.

Mary Ainsworth and her colleagues (1978) carefully standardized a set of procedures they believed would measure the degree of security inherent in the child's attachment to the mother. It has come to be known as the "Strange Situation." Infants between nine and twenty-four months are observed in an unfamiliar laboratory room during brief periods—each around three minutes long—when they are with their mother, with a stranger, with the mother and the stranger, or all alone. The two key episodes are those in which the mother leaves the child, once with the stranger and once alone, and returns several minutes later to be reunited with child. The child's immediate reaction to the mother's departure and his behavior upon her return are supposed to provide a sensitive index of the infant's quality of attachment (Ainsworth et al. 1978). Children who show mild protest following the departure, seek the mother upon her return, and are easily placated by her (about three quarters of a typical sample of middle-class, one-year-old American children) are regarded as the most securely attached. Infants who do not protest maternal departure, and who do not approach the mother when she re-enters (a little fewer than one quarter of middle-class American children), are regarded as less securely attached and labeled "avoidant." Finally, children who become seriously upset by the departure, and who—though seeking contact with the mother—resist her attempts to soothe them (about 10 percent of American children), are also insecurely attached and are labeled "resistant."

How can we tell if this procedure does indeed reveal the security of an infant's attachment? One way is to see if securely attached children are more likely than insecurely attached ones to develop qualities that are regarded as more adaptive. There is some evidence for this relation. Eighteen-month-old children who were classified as securely attached, using the Strange Situation, became more resilient, curious, and socially adroit with peers than did infants classified as less securely attached (Arend, Gove, and Sroufe 1979; Waters, Wippman, and Sroufe 1979). However, despite this assuring fact, there remain several serious problems that restrain an enthusiasm for the power of this method to disclose the nature of the bond between infant and caregiver.

The first troublesome fact is that the stability of the classifications "secure" and "insecure" is not high. Among children who were observed at both twelve and nineteen months, about one half changed their attachment classification across the brief seven-month interval (Thompson, Lamb, and Estes 1982). The two additional problems are best appreciated if one reflects on the key behavior evaluated in this unusual laboratory situation. A one-year-old in an unfamiliar room is left unexpectedly with a stranger or alone. Because the degree of distress and fearfulness shown by the child determines how he will behave when the mother returns and, therefore, whether his attachment will be "secure" or "insecure," let us ask what factors, other than the historic relationship to the mother, might lead a child to become very upset, only mildly upset, or minimally upset? One obvious factor is the child's temperamental vulnerability to becoming anxious in response to an unexpected experience in an unfamiliar situation. Infants who may have a very close relationship with their mother, but who are not easily frightened by the unfamiliar, may not cry when the mother leaves and, therefore, are unlikely to approach her when she returns. They may not even glance up at her. These children will be classified as "avoidant" and "insecurely attached." Infants who are moderately vulnerable to anxiety to the unfamiliar are more likely to cry when the mother leaves and approach her when she returns. Because they are not extremely upset, they will be easily placated and classified as "securely attached." Finally, children who are extremely vulnerable to anxiety will become very upset by the unexpected maternal departure, especially when they are left alone. Because they are in such an extreme state of distress, they often push the mother away as they continue to sob. They are classified as "resistant" and "insecurely attached" (Ainsworth et al. 1978; Thompson and Lamb 1983b). Indeed, the best predictor of seeking contact with the mother when she returns is the degree of upset and distress the child showed following her departure (Gaensbauer, Connell, and Schultz 1983).

There are good reasons for believing that vulnerability to anxiety is a quality of some infants from the openings days of life, long before the child has had an opportunity to establish an attachment to another person. Japanese newborn infants who would be classified as "resistant" at one year were more likely to cry intensely to frustration than newborn infants who would be classified later as "securely attached." This fact suggests that the former infants were born with a lower threshold for extreme irritability following an unexpected event.* When these same Japanese infants were observed in their homes at one and three months of age, those who would later be "resistant" cried more often and more intensely. When they were seven months old, they showed more fear to an adult stranger; and when they were two years old, they were more cautious and shy with an unfamiliar child than were the "securely attached" children.

In a comparable study in West Germany, newborns who were highly attentive and minimally irritable during the first ten days of life were more likely to be classified as "securely attached" at one year than were inattentive, extraordinarily irritable newborns

* K. Miyake, personal communication, 1983.

(Grossman and Grossman 1983). In two quite different countries with very different maternal practices, one-year-olds classified as "insecurely attached" in the Strange Situation were unusually irritable during the opening days of life. Because infant irritability seems to be influenced by genetic factors (Wilson, Brown, and Matheny 1971), it seems reasonable to conclude that the child's biological characteristics have some influence on his vulnerability to fear in the Strange Situation, and, therefore, on the attachment group to which he is assigned.

It is of historical interest that Mary Ainsworth's first book on attachment—*Infancy in Uganda,* published in 1967—also implicated the importance of temperament. Ainsworth classified her Ganda babies into sixteen "securely attached," seven "insecurely attached," and five "nonattached" infants and described the qualities of these infants in some detail. The "nonattached" infants were described as minimally fearful to the approach of strangers and to separation—one "nonattached" child, Nora, was described as "precociously independent." The "insecurely attached" babies were so named because they cried frequently whenever Ainsworth observed them. "They were designated as insecure according to the criterion of frequent crying. They were fussy babies, who cried not just when parted from their mothers, *but even when with their mothers*" (p. 391). Ainsworth's additional descriptions make it likely that the children's irritability was a function of their temperament or of frequent bouts of illness, rather than of the emotional bond to the mother.

In a classic study, cited frequently during the period when Mary Ainsworth was beginning her scientific career, Jean Arsenian (1943) of Smith College placed two-year-olds, who were living with their mothers in a woman's reformatory, in an unfamiliar room both with and without the mother. Arsenian noted that the children differed in how upset they became when the mother was gone; but, anticipating my argument here, Arsenian interpreted variations in distress as due to the children's personalities, and not to variations in the security of their relationship with the mother.

A second important factor controlling the child's behavior in the Strange Situation is the degree to which the mother, over the course of infancy, has encouraged her child to control his anxiety. A child whose mother has been otherwise attentive and loving, but has successfully encouraged self-reliance and control of fear, is less likely to cry when the mother leaves and, therefore, is less likely to approach her when she returns. This child will be classified as "avoidant" and "insecurely attached." By contrast, the child whose mother has been protective and less insistent that her child "tough it," is likely to cry, to rush to the mother when she re-enters the room, and to be classified as "securely attached." Mothers of one group of "securely attached" one-year-olds told a visitor to their home that their babies were not very self-reliant; these mothers felt that they were irreplaceable in the lives of their infants.

The mothers of babies who would have been classified as less "securely attached" had professional careers outside the home and were less accommodating to their infants' needs. Although some psychologists might regard these latter mothers as less nurturant, the mothers may have behaved as they did because they valued control of fear and sturdy self-reliance in their children. It may have been no accident that these infants were better able to cope with uncertainty when their mothers left them alone in the Strange Situation (Hock and Clinger 1981).

There are two ways to interpret these results. Some psychologists might say that the first group of protective mothers created more securely attached infants. On the other hand, the parental protectiveness may have produced infants who were less able to deal with the uncertainty created in the unfamiliar Strange Situation. This second evaluation suddenly modifies one's initially positive attitude toward the protective mother-infant dyads, for it implies that the babies who did not become upset in the Strange Situation had acquired adaptive coping strategies to deal with stress. These babies might be at greater advantage in later childhood, at least in our society, than those who cry when the mother leaves. It is likely that both groups of infants are attached, but one is better able to deal with the uncertainty created by the testing procedure (Hock and Clinger 1981).

The attractiveness of this suggestion is enhanced by the behavior of the middle-class West German children mentioned earlier. In sharp contrast to the norms for Americans, where three fourths of one-year-olds were classified as "securely attached," only one third of the German children behaved in the Strange Situation as if they were securely attached, and close to one half were classified as "avoidant" because they did not greet the mother when she returned to the room.

Should we conclude from these data that many more German than American children are "insecurely attached"; or, rather, that the German children were taught to control their fear when their mothers left because, in this particular region of Germany, an emotionally independent child who does not cling to the mother exemplifies the ego ideal?* The investigators noted that "the children in the geographic region of our investigation are exposed to a strong push in the direction of affective reserve as a cultural mode of adaptation" (Grossman et al. 1981, p. 179). I believe that some young children are classified as "insecurely attached" either because of temperamental qualities that influence the ease with which they become anxious, or because they have experienced a regimen of socialization that teaches them to suppress their fear in an unfamiliar place. It is probably an error to assume that either group of children has a weaker bond to the mother than those who cry at maternal departure and rush to her when she re-enters the room.

An additional flaw in the logic of the Strange Situation is seen in the reactions of infant squirrel monkeys who were removed from their mothers after an attachment had been established. When each monkey was put in an unfamiliar place following the separation, it showed both an increase in disturbed behavior and a rise in the level of cortisol in the blood—two reliable signs of emotional upset. However, if an infant monkey was put in a similar environment with familiar animals, it did not show the behavioral signs of distress, but continued to show high levels of cortisol. The high cortisol levels mean that the infant in the familiar environment was reacting emotionally to the absence of the mother, even though its behavior implied that it was not very upset by the separation (Levine 1982). The implication is clear. Even though an infant behaves as if he or she is not upset by the loss of the mother, that fact alone cannot be regarded as evidence of an "insecure attachment."

Finally, there is the argument based on reasonableness. The classifications of "secure" and "insecure attachment" are based primarily on the child's behavior during two three-minute episodes in the Strange Situation. Is it reasonable that a history of interaction between mother and infant comprising over a half-million minutes

---

* K. Grossman and K. E. Grossman, personal communication, 1983.

62

in the home would be revealed in six minutes in an unfamiliar room? Perhaps that is why two groups of psychologists, following exhaustive reviews of investigations that use the Strange Situation, concluded that this procedure is not a sensitive index of security of attachment (Campos et al. 1983; Lamb et al., in press). One group stated simply, "None of the currently popular claims regarding the validity and reliability of this procedure are well founded" (Lamb et al., in press, p. 1).

But even though the child's behavior in the Strange Situation might not provide a sensitive index of the quality of a child's attachment, the concept of attachment remains useful and should not be abandoned. The quality of maternal care given the infant does predict later behavior. Children who have spent their opening year or two in institutions where care is not consistent cling more frequently to adults than do children brought up in families, and, when older, have emotionally distant relations with other children (Tizard and Rees 1975; Tizard and Hodges 1978). These facts can be understood by calling upon the concept of differential attachment during infancy.

I believe that the major consequence of an attachment is to make the child receptive to the adoption of parental standards because the child is reluctant to tolerate the uncertainty implied by anticipated signs of parental indifference or rejection. If the standards promoted by the parents are in accord with the society's normative values, all will be well. But if these standards are not normative, the attached child will be at a disadvantage at a later age. A closely attached infant girl whose mother promotes passivity, fear of boys, and a noncompetitive attitude toward schoolwork will be vulnerable to conflict and anxiety when she becomes an adolescent. Thus, it is not obvious that a secure attachment at one year will be beneficial for an indefinite period of time.

Finally, I suspect that a unitary concept of attachment is less useful than a set of related concepts that specify the nature of the continuing interactions that produce the emotional bond to the caregiver. Consider the typical child in Third World villages in parts of Central America or Africa who is physically close to his mother for most of the day, is nursed on demand, but is rarely played with or spoken to during the first twelve months of life. Because this child's distress rarely mounts to intense levels, and is relieved quickly when it does, most observers would regard this child as closely and securely attached to the mother. Compare such a child with one from an upper-middle-class urban American family whose mother is reliably nurturant when the child is in distress, and plays with the child about two hours a day, but has the child play and sleep in a room apart from her for most of the day. Although both infants are likely to become securely attached, other qualities of their attachment may well differ.

Psychologists are in an unfortunate position. They are convinced that the idea of attachment has substantial utility, but are unable to make any firm statements about the sequelae of different qualities of attachment because they do not yet possess sensitive ways to evaluate the subtle variations that exist in this complex human bond.

Temperamental Variation among Infants

It is apparent to the least sophisticated parent that infants vary in vigor, lability of mood, and reactions to people when they are hungry, tired, bored, or simply playing. It is possible to create annoyingly irritable or delightfully happy babies simply by handling them in particular ways. But there are also reasons for believing that a small group of infants are born with a strong bias that favors certain moods and styles of reacting. These biases are called *temperamental properties.* All such temperamental qualities can be changed by experience, and all require certain experiences in order to be actualized. The very few temperamental properties that have been studied by scientists in an objective frame—activity, fussiness, fearfulness, sensitivity, attentiveness, and vigor of reaction—were selected because they are all relatively easy to observe and seem to be related to a child's future adaptation. These are reasonable criteria to employ when a new area is being explored.

The words chosen to name a baby's temperamental qualities are a function of the methods used by the investigator. Alexander Thomas and Stella Chess (1977), who are among the most influential scientists to explore temperament in depth, interviewed urban middle-class parents and recorded their descriptions of their children. Hence, the dimensions these investigators chose were based, in part, on the qualities that were of concern to these parents. American parents worry most about their infant's fussiness, ease of feeding, regularity of sleep, fearfulness, and reciprocity with others. It is not surprising, therefore, that the investigators created three types of children: "easy to handle," "difficult to manage," and "slow to warm up to other people." Suppose that, in the eighteenth century, Linnaeus, in his efforts to categorize animals, had asked informed people to describe all the animals they knew. Although his informants would probably have correctly put roosters and turkeys into the same category, they would have incorrectly placed the whale and the shark in the same category and the squirrel and seal in different ones. Likewise, although parents' descriptions of their children are useful initially, these descriptions should be replaced by methods that are not seriously colored by the language and preoccupations of the observer.

WATCHFUL INHIBITION VERSUS FEARLESS EXPLORATION

Of all the temperamental qualities that have been studied—activity, irritability, and fearfulness are the most popular—an initial display of inhibition to the unfamiliar (what parents call "shyness," "caution," or "timidity") and its opposite (what they call "sociability," "boldness," or "fearlessness") are two qualities that seem to persist from the first birthday to late childhood. Inhibition to the unfamiliar can be seen in the eight-month-old but is displayed most clearly after the first birthday. Most two-year-olds will stop playing and become quiet to many events that are very surprising or puzzling. But infants and children differ in how easy it is to elicit these reactions and in how consistently they display inhibition across many different situations. About 10 percent of American two-year-olds consistently show an extreme degree of inhibition to nonthreatening, but unfamiliar, events—for example, an unfamiliar woman talking to them. They will stop playing, become quiet, and assume a wary expression. Other infants will smile, talk to the adult stranger, and allow her to play with them. The inhibited child may recover after ten or fifteen minutes and talk and play with the stranger with considerable zeal. But even though the inhibition is temporary, it is a reliable reaction during the second and third years. Among a group of children selected as extremely inhibited at twenty-one months, three fourths had retained this quality through their fourth birthday. Among the group selected as extremely uninhibited, not one had become inhibited at age four (Garcia-Coll et al. 1984).

When each four-year-old child played with an unfamiliar child of the same age and sex, the formerly inhibited children rarely approached the peer and typically were passive to attack from the other child. The uninhibited children made frequent overtures, occasionally seized toys, and were generally gleeful and active; some ran around the room wildly.

More of the inhibited than uninhibited children had frequent nightmares, unusual fears, and, because they were sensitive to parental reprimand, were generally obedient to parental requests. When tested by an unfamiliar woman, the inhibited children rarely made interrupting comments, looked at the examiner frequently, and spoke in soft, hesistant voices. One inhibited boy did not speak at all during the ninety minutes of testing. By contrast, the uninhibited children interrupted the examiner with questions and irrelevant comments, laughed frequently, and spoke with confident, vital voices.

In searching for concise adjectives to capture the differences between the two kinds of children, recognizing that any word distorts what is observed, the words *restrained, watchful,* and *gentle* come close to capturing the essence of the inhibited child, while *free, energetic,* and *spontaneous* capture the style of the uninhibited youngster. When the inhibited child throws a ball, knocks down a tower of blocks, or hits a large toy clown, the act is monitored, restrained, almost soft. The same act performed by the uninhibited child seems relaxed and free.

To unfamiliar or challenging situations, the inhibited children show physiological reactions suggesting they are easily aroused by mild stress. One of these reactions involves the heart. Almost one half of the inhibited children, but only 10 percent of the uninhibited ones, show higher and more stable heart rates when they are looking at pictures or listening to sounds or stories that are a little difficult to understand. When a child or adult is watching pictures or listening to speech under relaxed conditions, the heart rate displays a cycling that is in phase with the child's breathing. As the child inspires, the heart rate rises; as he expires, the heart rate drops. The decrease in heart rate is mediated by the vagus nerve, which is under parasympathetic control. However, when a child or adult is psychologically involved in a mental task, the accompanying physiological arousal can inhibit vagal control of heart rate; and as a result, the heart rate rises slightly and becomes much more stable. This fact suggests that children who usually have higher and more stable heart rates while attending to information that is difficult to understand are physiologically more aroused. If these children also become easily aroused in real-life situations that are unexpected, unfamiliar, or difficult to understand, they might show an initial caution. This tendency to become easily aroused by the stresses of daily life was also present during the first year. For, as infants, the inhibited children were more irritable during the early months of life, and more susceptible to frequent constipation and allergic reactions—symptoms that reflect a higher level of physiological arousal to everyday events. This behavioral quality can be stable for many years.

One group of eighty-nine children was studied from birth to age fourteen and again as young adults. In this group were seven boys who were extremely inhibited during the first three years of life. They remained different from the extremely uninhibited boys throughout childhood, adolescence, and adulthood. The inhibited males avoided traditional masculine sexual activities, chose less masculine vocations in adulthood, and, as adults, were introverted and very anxious in new social situations (Kagan and Moss 1983).

Throughout his first ten years, one of these boys was described as shy, timid, and anxious. Observers used phrases like "insecure," "gentle," "delicate," "meek," "vulnerable," and "a shrinking violet." When he was sixteen years old, he told an interviewer, "I'd like to be more forward, I mean, to be able to meet people and talk. . . . I like to feel I could take on responsibilities. . . . I don't feel self-confident. That's it in a nutshell, self-confidence" (Kagan and Moss 1983, p. 179). When this young man returned to be interviewed four years later, he complained of his extreme anxiety in social situations: "I'd like to go up and be able to talk to people that I don't know, but I can't" (p. 181).

Because this longitudinal study is one of the few sources of evidence that implies preservation of this quality from infancy to adulthood, it should be viewed with some caution. But it does invite the speculation that this temperamental bias, which can be seen clearly during the second and third years, may influence later behavioral choices.

However, the behavioral surface of the inhibited child can be changed if parents gently encourage a less fearful approach to unfamiliar people and situations. Because most American parents prefer a bold to a timid child, they consciously try to make their inhibited three-year-old less cautious. And they are often successful. But if the basic temperamental quality were preserved, such children might reveal it in subtle ways under special circumstances and might show signs of conflict.

One four-year-old boy fits this description. Although he was behaviorally inhibited and showed the heart-rate pattern characteristic of high arousal at twenty-one months of age, his mother wanted a bold, fearless child. When he was four, his behavior resembled that of an uninhibited child. He was relaxed, playful, cooperative, and laughed with great energy. However, two reactions seemed to give him away. First, he was afraid to permit the examiner to put on the small, dime-sized electrodes necessary to record heart rate. It is rare for an uninhibited child to show any apprehension over the electrodes. Second, when he was playing with an unfamiliar boy in the playroom, his behavior seemed hostile rather than relaxed. Most children who seize toys or tease a peer do so in a playful manner, or as a counterattack following aggression. This boy's aggression was neither playful nor in the service of self-defense but seemed mean-spirited. When the other child finally became dominating and aggressive, this boy became frightened and retreated to his mother's side.

An initial tendency favoring inhibition or lack of inhibition to the unfamiliar may be one of the few behavioral dispositions that is preserved in children, because it probably has a partial base in the child's biology (Scarr 1969). One of the basic principles of physiology is that each animal species is characterized by a few complementary systems that compete for dominance. The competition between the two cerebral hemispheres is one example. For most humans, the temporal lobe of the left hemisphere is dominant over the comparable area of the right hemisphere; but for a few children, the dominance relation is reversed. And once reversed, it is difficult to change.

The competition between the sympathetic and the parasympathetic nervous systems is another example of competing systems, and it is possible, though not yet proven, that genetic or prenatal influences create conditions that, in some children, promote the sympathetic system to a position of dominance over the parasympathetic in uncertain situations. Such children might be prone to become the extremely inhibited children I have been describing, if their early environments were somewhat stressful. Identical, one-year-old twins are much more similar in their tendency to be inhibited or uninhibited than are non-identical twins—a fact that implies genetic influence (Plomin and Rowe 1979). And the adult tendency to be shy and introverted always shows strong evidence for the operation of heredity (Scarr 1969). Further, longitudinal observations on groups of laboratory-reared macaque monkeys reveal that the only one of three qualities that persisted over several years was absence of fearfulness to novel situations (Stevenson-Hinde 1980a, b, Stillwell-Barnes, and Zunz 1980). But a biological vulnerability to inhibition may not be actualized if the home environment is unusually benevolent; for example, the child has sensitive parents and is protected from bullying by an older sibling.

Unlike extreme aggressiveness or consistent nonconformity to authority, initial inhibition is more tolerated by adults. A few parents are pleased with their children's caution because it means they will not rush impulsively into dangerous situations. Additionally, the shy school-age child is likely to devote more time to academic mastery and, as a result, may develop the intellectual skills that invite adult approval. The perfection of such talents will preserve the original disposition. Finally, unlike most behavior, the conditions for inhibited or uninhibited behavior toward others are present continually. Many moments of every day are punctuated by interactions with other people that require a decision to withdraw or to participate. Each time one chooses either course, the relevant habit is strengthened, making this disposition an intimate part of each person's character.

Parents react differently to inhibited and uninhibited infants. Because inhibited children are likely to accept socialization more easily—they achieve bladder control earlier (Kaffman and Elizur 1977)—these children will initially please their parents and should have less strained relations with adults than uninhibited children. However, peers are less kind to inhibited children; hence, they experience greater difficulty adjusting to playmates. The combination of a close relationship to parents and a more conflicted relationship with peers would, at least in this society, draw the inhibited children toward adults and the adoption of adult values. But if an inhibited child were born to a mother or father who was extremely threatened by this characteristic and reacted to the child with hostility, the child might grow into an aggressive and disobedient five-year-old. The final profile is a joint product of the child's temperament and the adult reactions.

Although this principle seems obvious for most environmental experiences—a father's frown or a mother's protectiveness—it even holds for experiences that seem blatantly traumatic. Closely related species of macaque monkeys are not affected in similar ways by such a profound experience as being reared in total isolation for the first six months of life (Sackett et al. 1981). One might think that isolation from all living things for the first half-year should affect all animals in a similar way. Yet rhesus monkeys emerge from isolation with seriously deviant social behavior, crab-eater monkeys show minimal disruption, and pigtail monkeys display intermediate levels of disturbance in social behavior. Similarly, the dominance behavior of beagles is seriously influenced by twelve weeks of isolation, while terriers are relatively unaffected by the same experience (Fuller and Clark 1968). These surprising facts provide dramatic confirmation of the principle of interaction between the infant's biological qualities and its experiences. Apparently, genetic differences among species of monkeys and dogs create temperamental dispositions that transduce the isolation in different ways. The temperamental variations among young children imply that there will be few uniform consequences of a particular class of experience. Each child's temperament leads him or her to impose a special frame on experience, thus making it difficult to predict the consequences of a particular home environment.

Conclusion

Three ideas have dominated this discussion of the human infant. The first provides substance to the earlier suggestion that maturation of the central nervous system makes possible a sequence of intellectual abilities that include recognition and retrieval of the past, the ability to compare past and present, and inhibition of the primitive and automatic reflexes that humans inherit from their primate ancestors. As each of these new competences matures, like new organs in the growth of the embryo, reorganizations occur in the bases of behavior, thought, and emotion. The fears of a stranger and of loss of a mother cannot occur until the infant is able to compare the known with the unknown, but is still unable to put the recognition aside when comprehension fails. Although nineteenth-century observers appreciated the importance of maturation, they shared the twentieth-century commitment to the catalytic power of social experience. What modern science is discovering, however, is that some of these competences are so deeply engrained in the human genome that they require less interaction with others than we have wanted to believe:

> Those who contend that knowledge results wholly from the experiences of the individual, ignoring as they do the mental evolution which accompanies the autogenous development of the nervous system, fall into an error as great as if they were to ascribe all bodily growth and structure to exercise, forgetting the innate tendency to assume the adult form.... The gradually increasing intelligence displayed throughout childhood and youth is more attributable to the completion of the cerebral organization than to the individual experiences.... Doubtless the child's daily observations and reasonings aid the formation of those involved nervous connexions that are in process of spontaneous evolution ... but saying this is quite a different thing from saying that its intelligence is wholly produced by its experiences. (James 1981b [1890], p. 1221)

The attachment of infant to caregiver is also an inherent capacity that is difficult to suppress. Even though we cannot measure with sensitivity the variations in the emotional quality of an infant's attachment, there is good reason for believing in the theoretical utility of this idea, for most infants living in neglecting environments are more fearful, more labile, and less gleeful than those who have the benefit of predictable and loving care.

The second idea represents the return of an old and popular conviction. Most cultures acknowledge the distinctive temperamental styles of infants, and most parents accommodate to these inborn biases. It is probably not an accident that modern research finds differences in fearfulness to be a persistent quality, for the essence of this characteristic is present in most of the homespun personality theories that can be traced to Plato and Aristotle.

Finally, I have relied heavily on the assumption that a state of uncertainty is a major incentive for mental work, emotion, and action. Discrepant events provoke prolonged attention and either understanding or anxiety.* I have used the term *uncertainty* to describe the state that monitors the infant's behavior because this word seems hedonically neutral. The eighteenth-century scholar assumed that the infant and child acted to maximize *pleasant* feelings and to minimize *painful* ones. These words have a misleading connotation, for the one-year-old who carefully puts his finger on an odd-looking toy looks neither happy nor unhappy but puzzled. Benjamin Franklin (1868) wrote in his autobiography that uneasiness was the central human motive. After biological needs are cared for, children and adults seem to spend much of their time and energy in a narrow, psychological space bounded on the right by boredom with the familiar and on the left by terror of the bizarre.

* It is of interest that developmental changes in the young embryo are often provoked by a tiny asymmetry, or lack of uniformity, in the chemical composition of the cells in a particular area.

3

Connectedness

The great tragedy of science—the slaying
of a beautiful hypothesis by an ugly fact.

THOMAS HENRY HUXLEY,
"Biogenesis and Abiogenesis"

FROM THE BEGINNING OF HISTORY, human beings have longed to
know something of the future and have searched for signs of it in
nature. They have looked to the color of the rising and setting sun
to predict the weather, to the thickness of a squirrel's fur to guess
the harshness of the coming winter, to the presence of a thin mem-
brane on the face of a newborn girl to know whether she is destined to be a midwife. Although most societies believe in some
special sign that foretells a child's future, contemporary American
parents are unusual in the depth of their commitment to the view
that the psychological qualities of the infant, inborn temperamental characteristics as well as those shaped by experience, might be
preserved for an indefinite time. A lusty cry, low tolerance for
frustration, and hyperactivity at twelve months are possible signs of
athlete or criminal, while gentleness and timidity might mark the
beginnings of artist or anxious adolescent. Exposing the infant to
many caregivers is assumed to create permanent emotional insecurity; physical affection and reliable care by a single caregiver, especially the biological mother, are supposed to inoculate the young
child against an easy vulnerability to later threats.

Faith in a connection between early childhood and the succeeding years also permeates our views of the growth of those qualities that are characteristic of all children, for most theorists believe that each of the universal milestones grows out of earlier competences. But there is another way to view the changes that characterize psychological development. One can maintain that, even though all children pass through the same sequence of milestones—for example, babbling, speaking single words, and then complex conversation—there is no dependent relation between successive abilities: that is, the capacity that underlies the speaking of sentences might not require a prior capacity to speak single words. This view is not as preposterous as it sounds. All children crawl before they stand, but a child would stand at about one year of age, even though he was prevented from crawling. In a classic experiment, salamander larvae were anesthetized and prevented from practicing any swimming movements. When the anesthetic was removed and the larvae were transferred to fresh water, they swam as well as those that had never been anesthetized. The swimming movements require only maturation of the central nervous system; they are not dependent upon the opportunity to practice the immature swimming movements that occur in normally growing larvae (Carmichael 1927). Thus, the fact that one behavior always occurs before another does not mean that the earlier behavior is necessary for the later one.

This more loosely connected conception of growth has never been as popular as its complement, which assumes a fixed series of increasingly complex competences, occurring at similar ages, that are sequentially related to each other so that a later capacity cannot occur without an earlier one. The quieter intervals between the appearance of new competences are called *stages,* and the transition from one stage to the next is supposed to be provoked by a combination of maturing functions and information that is extracted from conditioning experiences, discrepant events, reflective thought, and active interaction with people and objects.

Development as a Sequence of Stages

The course of a life, like the cycle of the seasons, consists of a set of inevitable, genetically determined phenomena which, depending on time and place, are exhibited in a local script whose surface details can take on remarkable variety. The Eskimo infant living near Hudson Bay remains physically close to its mother for most of the first year; the infant born on an Israeli kibbutz is cared for by a hired caregiver; the Mayan infant of northwest Guatemala, wrapped in tattered pieces of woven cloth, spends much of the first year sleeping in a hammock hung from the roof of the house. But—despite the differences in affectivity, alertness, and maturity of motor coordination produced by these varied rearing conditions—by three years of age, children from these three cultures share the capacity to recognize the past, to become frightened by the unusual, and to understand the significance of an adult prohibition—a trio of talents that emerge in that order.

The hypothesis that the transformation of a babbling, poorly coordinated newborn into a loquacious ballerina involves a set of hidden stages unites three separate assumptions—a special organization, slow growth, and connectedness. The quintessential criterion of a stage is that it consists of a special constellation of necessarily related qualities. Biology supplies many exquisite examples. When the original fertilized egg becomes two cell layers thick, a stage in which half the cells are outside and half inside, subsequent growth of the cells is determined by the spatial relation between the two layers. The cells on the outside grow to become skin and brain; the cells on the inside become stomach and lungs. Thus, all the neurons of the newborn's brain are derived from the outer layer of cells that emerged at a stage of development nine months earlier.

There are good reasons for positing stages in psychological growth, in addition to the rationales put forward by Freud (1964 [1938]) and Piaget (1951). As I indicated in chapter 2, around eight to ten months of age, the infant becomes capable of retrieving the past and relating past and present and, as a result, shows obvious signs of fear in response to the same events that were innocuous a few weeks earlier. One way to interpret the changed reaction is to assume that the maturation of a new competence permits the infant to retrieve the past and to work at understanding unfamiliar or unexpected experience (the stranger and the unexpected maternal departure). Failure to understand provokes a special emotional state.

During the era Piaget (1950) calls the concrete operational stage of intelligence, which emerges in a majority of European and American youngsters by seven years of age, children appreciate that the quantity of clay in a ball does not change despite a major alteration in its shape. The child knows that she can pound the same ball of clay into a broad, flat pancake and put it back into its original shape. Additionally, the child knows that names for objects can be nested into categories that have a logical relation to each other. Dogs are members of the category pets, pets are animals, and animals are living things. Piaget claimed that these new talents are due to the emergence of the ability to manipulate the relation between an event and its category, and the relation between categories.

A new psychological organization need not require the maturation of new functions. The loss of loved one, a drug experience, or repeated school failure can produce deep insights and changed moods that permanently reorganize beliefs. The popular idea of "stages of adulthood" rests on this phenomenon. Historians and sociologists use the idea of stage in a similar way. A new idea, invention, or law changes the relations among people, groups, or institutions. The introduction of factories and machine labor led many men and women to leave their rural agricultural settings in order to live in the cities. In time, this practice led to new social structures, including a large group of middle-class, nonworking mothers committed almost entirely to raising their children, and—in the contemporary West—of fathers who were away from their families for many hours every day.

I shall use a restricted definition of *stage:* namely, a changed set of relations among psychological dispositions resulting from the maturation of a new competence. But even this definition implies the possibility of many more stages than Freud or Piaget imagined. Why, then, did these two theorists single out the second year, the sixth year, and puberty as being transitional to new stages and ignore equally significant changes that occur at other times?

Connectedness

The consensus that the second year marks a special transition is not surprising, for language, pretend play, self-awareness, and the appreciation of right and wrong all appear at this time. Even cultures without formal knowledge of human behavior regard the two-year-old as qualitatively different from the infant. The transition at six years is more subtle. Piaget used changes in reasoning to mark this era; while Freud generated the idea of the oedipal stage from the fact of sex-role identification and from the appearance of guilt over violation of standards, which begins to rival fear of parental punishment as a basis for socialization.

There is a possible relation between the cognitive competences of Piaget's concrete operational stage and the emergence of guilt and identification with the same-sex parent. The emotion of guilt requires a conscious appreciation that one could have acted other than the way one has acted. In order to recognize this possibility, the child must be able to reverse in thought an act issued in the past and to consider an alternative script. This is precisely the ability Piaget posits as being central to the concrete operational stage. Identification with other members of one's biological sex requires the ability to appreciate that one is a member of a set of categories—boy or girl, male or female—that nest into each other. According to Piagetian theory, the appreciation that categories are related to each other in a hierarchical way emerges in most children between five and seven years of age.

A boy's fear that the father might retaliate in response to the child's hostility toward the parent, which is the heart of the oedipal conflict, requires that the child put himself in the mind of another and imagine how the father might feel if he knew the boy's thoughts. Although two-year-olds are able to appreciate some of the psychological states of others, these states are typically feelings produced by external events and not motivational ideas conditional upon the child's behavior. According to Freud, the six-year-old is in conflict because he believes the father knows his motives. But equally important, the child believes he can mute the father's hostility and reverse the course of the parent's resentment by becoming similar to him. In each of these examples, cognitive advances are the bases for new emotional phenomena, not the other way around. As we saw in chapter 2, the universal fears of infancy are due, in part, to enhanced retrieval memory. Hence, new emotional and motivational states, especially those that mark a stage, often follow the emergence of new cognitive abilities.

But the idea of stage in Western writing on development usually contains two additional assumptions that are not necessary to a change in organization: the first is that the movement into a new stage is always gradual; the second posits a material connection among the elements that compose successive stages.

NEW STAGES: GRADUAL OR ABRUPT?

Most theorists assume a slow, continuous growth of the structures that define a stage, with gradual transitions between successive stages. Although the infant's spontaneous smile to a human face appears rather suddenly at about three months of age, psychologists believe that the structures and processes that make this smile possible have been changing in tiny steps since birth. The velocity of growth of the qualities that characterize a new stage is a matter of perspective: the suddenness of an event is always relative, be it the first snow or a dogwood's first blossoms. Although no one denies that some events intrude abruptly into conscious experience, controversy centers not on the subjectively perceived event but on the suddenness of the inferred, underlying processes hidden from unaided perception that are described in the objective frame. Although a wave breaking on the beach is relatively discrete and short-lived, an engineer measuring the changes in hydrostatic pressure a hundred yards out from the beach would note a gradual, continuous phenomenon. Analogously, although the one-year-old's first word—"Bye-bye"—seems to appear without much prior warning, its display is assumed to depend on an association between the word and the gesture established slowly and imperceptibly from the first days of life.

The degree of gradualness in the growth of structures represents a specific instance of the general, and historically ancient, thema discussed in chapter 1 regarding the wisdom of reducing all qualities to quantities. Although a fair proportion of qualities that appear with suddenness must have taken a long time to grow, it is as reasonable to suppose that many equally abrupt characteristics have a shorter history. Reproductive fertility, for example, emerges between twelve and fourteen years of age in most well-fed girls when the brain's sensitivity to blood-circulating estrogen is changed, and the normal inhibition of pituitary secretion of gonadotrophins by the hypothalamus fails. As a result of these relatively abrupt events, sex hormones are released and the visible signs of puberty appear.

Modern historians have become friendly to the idea of sudden societal change. War, natural catastrophe, or a technical innovation may have only a brief preceding aura that is not always traceable to the deep past. For example, some historians claim that the disillusion among European intellectuals over the failure of political and economic reforms after the First World War made it easy for fascist ideas to take root quickly in the decade after Versailles (Wohl 1979).

Even evolutionary biologists, who traditionally have claimed that changes in the morphological characteristics that define species are slow and gradual, now entertain the possibility that, on occasion, a major alteration in the environment can lead to relatively rapid changes in a species. For example, as a result of a major drought on one of the islands in the Galapagos in 1977, a species of finch that did not breed that year suffered an 85-percent decline in population, presumably due to a serious reduction in the availability of seeds. One year later, the ratio of males to females had changed from parity to six males for every female. Further, the birds that survived were considerably larger than those that had disappeared. In only one year, an infinitesimal interval of time on the scale of evolution, a dramatic change had occurred in the character of the finch population on this island (Boag and Grant 1981).

In August 1980, a Caribbean hurricane severely damaged the shore and coral reefs on the northern coast of Jamaica. Biologists were surprised by the amount of change in plant and animal species:

the effects of Hurricane Allen on the reef populations were impressive for their magnitude, speed, and patchiness. Organisms were unevenly affected, and the reefs are now a mosaic of areas that differ in the amount of open space and in the relative abundance of surviving species. . . . Overnight, Hurricane Allen created patterns of distribution and abundance of organisms that are strikingly different from pre-existing states. (Woodley et al. 1981, p. 754)

It has been argued that the mass protests against the Vietnam War in the 1960s had a serious, long-lasting influence on high school youths' attitudes toward authority and, by extension, toward the purposes of educational institutions. Those cynical attitudes were established over just a few years, not even a decade.

But despite these examples of serious change with a fast onset, the majority of psychologists have preferred gradual, continuous transitions. Consider some popular concepts that assume slow growth to lie behind psychological novelties. The famous nineteenth-century "law of practice" was invented to extend the time it took for will and self-consciousness to emerge; the gradual relocation of libido, through the mechanisms of fixation and regression, smoothed the sudden appearance of an adult phobia; the "law of effect" removed the surprise from the child's first words; and Piaget's stages of intelligence transformed the abrupt display of conservation of mass into an extended, seamless, achievement that originated in the play of the infant. The distinguished biologist C. H. Waddington has written:

The orderly minded orthodox biological world closed its ranks against [the] suggestion that revolutionary processes may happen. It became accepted that the only respectable doctrine is that evolution never involves any thing but step-by-step Fabian gradualism, plodding along a weary way similar to that by which the annual milk yield of dairy cows or egg yield of hens has slowly improved. (1969, pp. 123–124)

CONNECTIONS BETWEEN STAGES

The preservation of a structure across stages is perhaps the most controversial property of a stagelike conception of human development. This Aristotelian idea, amplified by medieval scholars and present in modern essays, declares that each natural state contains within it the seeds of the next higher state. One obvious advantage of assuming such a material connection is that one can preview what is to come by examining only what is.

The possibility of a connection between early and later developmental phases takes two related forms. One involves only a dependence of one structure or process upon an earlier one, as fingernails require the prior existence of fingers. Does the appearance of language by two years of age, for example, depend upon the prior capacities for symbolism and enhanced memory that are present by one year? Piaget, together with many contemporary psychologists, believed the competences of one phase to be closely interdependent with those of preceding and succeeding ones. Although this form

Connectedness

of connectedness between stages occurs, one should remain open to
the possibility that some competences may be relatively independent of earlier functions.

A second stronger meaning of connectedness assumes not only
interdependence but, in addition, the belief that a particular structure is preserved through succeeding stages, as the same forty-six
chromosomes are preserved from the original fertilized egg to the
end of life. Are the schemata that a three-year-old has created of
the mother's face preserved in any form, or are they replaced completely by the many different exposures to the mother between
three years and adolescence? Because the profile of manifest characteristics changes dramatically over the first dozen years, all psychologists agree on the impossibility of finding preservation at the
level of the phenotype. If it is present, it must be found in hidden
essences that undergo transformation at the surface. Thus, it is
assumed that the insecurely attached infant who becomes a delinquent twelve-year-old has done so because fear and hostility to
parents have remained as deep qualities from infancy to
adolescence.

William Stern, a nineteenth-century observer of children, believed in a connection between the babbling of the five-month-old
and the speech of the two-year-old (1930). Other scholars suggested that a person's aesthetic sense is dependent on early exposure to attractive toys (Rand, Sweeny, and Vincent 1930). Modern
authors have argued for a connection between the harshness of
toilet training during the second year and conformity during adulthood, or between multiple caregivers during infancy and a fragile
emotional security in adolescence. Some observers even believe
that the five-month-old's ability to detect the difference between
two and three black dots is the first sign of a future appreciation of
the concept of number (Starkey and Cooper 1980).

The assumption of connectedness imposes a significant bias on
what is observed and described. An observer who believes that a
hidden structure is preserved between two points in time is likely
to look for actions that can be classified (usually on the basis of
physical resemblance) with ones manifested earlier. Piaget, for example, grouped the newborn's grasping of a finger placed in her
palm with the eighteen-month-old's imitative opening and closing
of the hand: that is, some residue of the act displayed on the first
day is participating in the later response. Piaget's insistence on the

preservation of remnants of old structures can be traced to his first scientific papers on the classification of snails written before he was twenty years old (Vidal 1981). The young Piaget defended the hypothesis that morphological changes can be induced slowly by the organism's continued commerce with the environment, and disagreed sharply with those naturalists who defended sudden mutation as the primary basis for evolutionary change (the genus in question was *Limnaea*). These morphological changes, according to Piaget, occur gradually over time and eventually become hereditary and preserved.

These views of snails, written in 1913, remained key premises in his later writings on the origins of intelligence in children:

Thus, when we studied the beginnings of intelligence we were forced to go as far back as the reflex in order to trace the cause of the assimilating activity which finally leads to the construction of adaptive schemas, for it is only by a principle of functional continuity that the indefinite variety of structures can be explained. (1951, p. 6)

Following the spirit of Piagetian theory, Jonas Langer suggests that the origins of adult logic can be detected in the object manipulations of infants six to twelve months old. When a six-month-old raises an object to her face with the left hand while her right hand slides a second object to the right, Langer writes, "The most advanced binary mappings produced at this stage consist of two-step sequences of simultaneous but different transformations" (1980, p. 29). A child who bangs a block three times on a table is displaying a "three unit equivalence which is an instance of two distinct proto-responding reproductions" (p. 136).

These strong claims for preservation of structure are reasonable only if one already believes in connectedness. When Freud's writings were more popular, many scholars accepted as probable the suggestion that the verbal aggression of a twenty-two-year-old woman toward her professor rests on structures whose establishment began with premature weaning from the breast at nine months of age. Faith in a connectedness between the distant past and the present remains an essential premise in theories of development, as it has been since the beginning of formal study of the child in the decades following Darwin's great work. All theorists assumed a structural link between all phases of development and wrote in affirmation of Bertrand Russell's bold assertion, "The chain of causation can be traced by the inquiring mind from any given point backward to the creation of the world" (quoted in Hanson 1961, p. 50). Many theorists implied that no part of the child's past can ever be lost; that every psychological property in the adult can, in theory, be traced to a distant origin:

But there seems to be no manner of doubt, among those whose studies have best qualified them to speak with authority, that the mind of any person, child or adult, is made up of the sum total of all of the experiences through which he has passed since birth, plus every impression that has ever touched him in passing, no matter how fleeting and transitory some of these may have seemed. That is to say, that every thought, feeling, experience, or image that has ever impinged upon one's consciousness becomes, once and for all, a component part of a great, constantly growing, indestructible body, his mind,—which is to say, his real self. (Richardson 1926, pp. 33–34)

In one of the most popular psychology texts of the first decade of this century, Edward L. Thorndike (1905) ended his final chapter with a ringing affirmation of the permanence of early acquisitions:

Though we seem to forget what we learn, each mental acquisition really leaves its mark and makes future judgments more sagacious; . . . nothing of good or evil is ever lost; we may forget and forgive, but the neurones never forget or forgive. . . . It is certain that every worthy deed represents a modification of the neurones of which nothing can ever rob us. Every event of a man's mental life is written indelibly in the brain's archives, to be counted for or against him. (1905, pp. 330–31)

P. H. Mussen, J. J. Conger, and I suggested, in an early edition of our text, that there is a connection between harsh toilet training in the second year and later conformity: "Excessive timidity and over-conformity may also stem from unduly severe toilet training" (1969, p. 264); and, "Toilet training is a learned situation . . . in which the mother-child relationship may deteriorate, handicapping subsequent, healthy emotional and social adjustment" (p. 265).

All of the preceding statements contain the same premise evident in John Locke's writing several centuries ago:

The little, or almost insensible, impressions on our tender infancies, have very important and lasting consequences: and there it is, as in the fountains of some rivers, where a gentle application of the hand turns the flexible waters into channels, that make them take quite contrary courses; and by this little direction, given them at first, in the source, they receive different tendencies, and arrive at last at very remote and distant places. I imagine the minds of children as easily turned, this or that way, as water itself. (Quoted in Mandelbaum 1971, p. 151)

Most of the declarations of a connected relation between a quality of early childhood and one seen later in development have been based on a single element of possible similarity between the behavior of infants and actions seen in older children or adults. Humans are remarkably adept at inventing a theoretical reason for a relation between fundamentally different phenomena simply by detecting one feature that is shared, or seems to be shared, by two events. Such inventions are so easy that they cannot be sufficient to prove or even to imply a true relation. The pseudopod of amoeba is as similar to the newborn's penile erection as the infant's grasp reflex is to Silas Marner's grasping of coins. It is only the culture's assumptions that make the former assertion far less credible than the latter. A century ago, the protesting cry of the one-year-old following maternal departure was classified as similar to the willful disobedience of the adult. Today the same act is linked with the anxiety and sadness that follow loss of sweetheart, spouse, or parent.

As this century began, Havelock Ellis postulated a similarity between a nursing infant and adult sexual intercourse—to which Freud later referred in "The Three Essays on Sexuality":

The erectile nipple corresponds to the erectile penis: the eager watery mouth of the infant to the moist and throbbing vagina, the vitally albuminous milk to the vitally albuminous semen. The complete mutual satisfaction, physical and psychic, of mother and child in the transfer from one to the other of a precious organized fluid, is the one true physiological analogy to the relationship of a man and woman at the climax of the sexual act. (1900, p. 250)

Why is this analogy, which seemed reasonable in 1900, much less compelling today? Why has the event of nursing become, in this generation, analogous to adult trust rather than to sexual passion? The reasonableness of an analogy between two disparate domains requires, first, a heightened mood of uncertainty over the larger category of experience to which the analogy points; and, second, an *a priori* belief in the root basis of the similarity between the two phenomena. To many scholars at the turn of the century, sex and hunger were closely related by virtue of being the two major human drives around which all of society was supposedly organized. Hence, the mind of the community was prepared to regard an infant nursing as a partially sexual act.

Contemporary theorists award sex and hunger less importance and regard the individual's needs for a trusting, loving relationship and for control of anxiety as more potent forces in human behavior. Lack of trust between adults has become, in this century, a major source of uncertainty. Hence, to contemporary minds, Erik Erikson's suggestion that the act of nursing contains elements resembling the bond of trust between adults is more attractive than is Ellis's equally poetic idea. All current theories that posit a structural connection between early childhood and adult life are essentially hypotheses about possible histories. They are sentences that attempt to make a coherent story out of a multitude of events and, therefore, resemble both *On the Origin of Species* and *The Rise and Fall of the Roman Empire*.

But in developmental psychology, as in history and biology, the biases of the observer determine the details selected for the story that is told. Between any two points in time lie many more events than can be seen or recorded; of these the scholar selects a few and ignores many others. Between 1900 and 1978, the automobile, the television, the nuclear warhead, the laser, and the contraceptive pill were invented; the Germans lost the First World War; there was an economic depression; Germany was divided following the end of the Second World War; the Peoples' Republic of China was created; there was a long, bitter struggle in Vietnam; an American president resigned; the prices of oil and postage increased dramatically. Which of these events are part of a coherent sequence, and which are not? Only theory can produce an answer to that question. The same problem confronts psychologists. Between one and fifteen months of age, most infants will smile at a face, show anxiety toward a stranger, sit, stand, walk, run, reach for a toy they have seen hidden under a pillow, engage in symbolic play, and begin to speak single words. Which of these phenomena are connected, and which are not? The theorist determines which phenomena are structurally related by the plausibility of the reasons given for the relations noted. But these reasons, as well as the initial selection of phenomena, are guided by assumptions that are not always made explicit.

ARGUMENTS FOR CONNECTEDNESS

There are good reasons, sentimental as well as rational, for assuming connectedness in development. First, this doctrine renders original forms useful and rationalizes the maxim that one must prepare for the future. Ministers and statesmen in the early American colonies urged mothers to care for their young children, and implied that a conscientious attitude toward the infant was not unlike gathering wood in August to prepare for December's frigid winds. If the origins of adult properties occur during later childhood or adolescence, then the first years of life would appear to have no special purpose. However, if a person's future is determined by early experience, then the future is, to some degree, knowable through careful attention to each day in the infant's life. It is a parent's responsibility to provide the proper environment for the young child, and the earlier the better.

Second, arguments for connectedness have the illusion of being mechanistic. When each new function is preceded by another that makes a substantial contribution to it, one is better able to state the cause-effect sequence than if a function emerges relatively rapidly as a result of a new endogenous change. In the latter instance, the mind is left with an explanatory gap, as it was for early nineteenth-century biologists who had to deal with the suggestion that there was spontaneous generation of new life forms—an assumption that was troubling to minds who insisted on knowing the mechanisms that generate new forms. Similarly, the hypothesis of the egg as the origin of the fetus created theoretical problems, for no one could see the bodily organs in this tiny cell, and the organ, not the cell, was the primary theoretical entity. It was not until the cell as a unit and mitosis as a process were accepted that the continuous view became ascendant once more, and the nineteenth-century microbiologist and minister William Dallinger could write that there is a "continuity—an unbroken chain of unity—running from the base to the apex of the entire organic series" (quoted in Farley 1974, p. 149).

Connectedness

Many scientists believe that a mechanistic account of development is easier if one assumes that all psychological experience involves changes in neurons and synapses. The facts that experience can affect the weight of the brain, and that early stimulation can add tiny spines to brain cells or alter the sensitivity of the visual cortex to vertical lines, have led many scientists to regard the central nervous system as a malleable surface which accepts material marks that are difficult to erase. The belief that experience produces a permanent change in the brain, wedded to the premise that the brain directs thought and behavior, implies that since the structures first established are likely to direct the later ones, early experience must be important, even though most modern research on the brain also indicates inconstancy. Many synapses vanish; some are replaced; and new ones are being established throughout the life span (Stein, Rosen, and Butters 1974). Indeed, the waxing and waning of synapses in the canary's brain, which accompanies the annual song cycle, has been likened to the growth and shedding of leaves in May and October.

A third source of the persuasiveness of connectedness is more speculative. During each historical period, there is a dominant philosophical view that most scholars try to avoid confronting—an intellectual electric fence. From the Renaissance to the nineteenth century, philosophers and scientists were reluctant to deduce or infer propositions that would refute or contradict biblical statements on man and nature. Although few contemporary scientists worry about the implications of their results for Christian teaching, many social scientists are concerned, often unconsciously, with the implications of their data and ideas for the doctrine of egalitarianism. The criticisms of Arthur Jensen, Richard Herrnstein, and E. O. Wilson have less to do with the data they discuss than with their implications for the idea of equality.

The assumption of connectedness in the growth of human characteristics is in greater accord with egalitarian principles than is the possibility of discontinuous growth, for the latter is likely to be due to maturational changes in the central nervous system. Emphasis on the role of biological changes in the brain implies that an individual's biology has formative force. Since each person is biologically unique (except for one-egg twins), scholars are forced to assume different rates of psychological growth which have their roots in biological processes. This conclusion is regarded by some theorists as inconsistent with egalitarian premises, although it need not be. By contrast, the assumption of continuous development is taken to imply the formative action of experiences that gradually establish new properties. Because most psychologists believe that the life experiences of children are potentially controllable, the connected view implies, but does not prove, that one can arrange similar experiences for all infants. Legitimizing discontinuity in development—due to biological maturation, genetic variation, or revolutionary social arrangements—implies that the benevolent products of early experience might be abrogated by peer groups, quality of schooling, social unrest, or changes in physiology. Awarding power to the latter forces is regarded by some theorists (incorrectly, I might add) as inconsistent with egalitarian suppositions, for it seems to make it more difficult to arrange similar benevolent experiences for all young children.

Fourth, the belief in the permanence of characteristics is sustained by our language habits, for English contains a bias favoring continuity in an individual's qualities. The adjectives used to describe young children rarely refer to the age of the actor or to the context of action. Like the names of colors, they imply a permanence over time and place. Adjectives like *passive, irritable, intelligent,* or *labile* are applied to infants, children, and adults as if the meanings of these terms were not altered by growth. This is not the case in all languages. In Japanese, for example, a different word is used to describe the quality of intelligence in a child from that in an adult. On the island of Ifaluk in the Western Carolines, the emotion called *fago,* which only approximates our word *compassion,* is never applied to children under six years of age.

There is always a strong temptation to assume that entities with the same name are of the same essence: hence, sixteenth-century herbalists classified wheat (a grass) with buckwheat (which is not a grass), because both had *wheat* in their names. Thus, use of the same word to describe a characteristic in children and adults makes each of us receptive to believing in a hidden disposition which survives, unchanged, over the years.

Fifth, the appeal of connectedness to Western minds may be due, in part, to the significance of formal, written knowledge in our lives, as compared with the daily experiences of most humans for whom many significant events are transient or cyclical. Hunger and satiation, pain and pleasure, rain and drought, illness and health, anger and grief are salient in the consciousness of those who live under conditions where survival is the immediate and primary requirement. In technological societies, reasoning and written knowledge assume a greater importance in daily life. Knowledge printed in books generates a feeling of permanence, unlike the continually changing flux of human moods and desires. The knowledge that influenza is caused by a virus that will run its course imposes some stabilizing certainty on what is an unpredictable sequence of changes in feeling tone. To put it more plainly than is proper, living in a world of scientific explanations composed of abstract ideas that are printed on paper imposes on experience a sense of stability that may be less compelling for those who live closer to events.

A sixth argument for the belief in the connectedness of earlier experience is based on our ranking of children on valued traits both in and out of school. This practice sensitizes every parent of a preschool child to the fact that the child will be ranked at the end of the first grade, and that that evaluation will influence the quality of education the child will receive from that time forward. Few societies practice such a severe grading of children with such zeal. American commitment to a meritocratic system forces us to select candidates from the best trained—a decision that is made early, perhaps by age ten or eleven. Most parents know this sequence, or sense it; hence their goal is to guarantee that their child is ahead early in the race. Most people believe that a seven-year-old who is more talented in reading, art, or mathematics than other children of the same age is more likely to remain more skilled, rather than to plummet. This belief is true to some extent; the school-age child who gets off to a good start is likely, other things being equal, to remain ahead. Parents assume that the half-dozen years prior to school determine that initial evaluation, and interpret the child's characteristics at age seven as a complex derivative of all that has gone before.

ARGUMENTS AGAINST CONNECTEDNESS

Despite the appeal of connectedness, modern biology supplies substantial counter examples. The development of the embryo contains frequent discontinuities in which some structures disappear after their mission has been accomplished, leaving no structural residue. In the metamorphosis of the tadpole, for example, a particular class of sensory cells in the dorsal spinal cord vanishes, to be replaced by the more typical dorsal root ganglion cells. Similar examples have led some biologists (see Oppenheim 1981) to suggest that each life stage requires special temporary structures and functions that facilitate maximal adaptation for that specific developmental period. (See also Lerner 1984.) When the next stage is reached, and these adaptive functions are no longer needed, they are inhibited, replaced, or lost. In most modern psychological writing, for example, the crying of the one-year-old at separation from the caregiver is treated as an index of the infant's attachment to that adult, a state that is assumed to persist indefinitely. The infant's attachment is regarded neither as a temporary process that serves to keep the mother close during the helplessness of the first year, nor as an accompaniment to the maturation of new cognitive talents that have produced separation anxiety as a consequence. In neither of these latter scripts does the phenomenon called separation distress have an important future role. It is similar to the reflex actions of birds that are about to hatch. The special behavior accompanying hatching is used once, and once only, and has no future function. The hatching behavior is like the stepping reflex of the fetus whose presumed function is to ensure normal positioning of the head for delivery (an improperly positioned fetus "walks itself" around the uterus until its head is against the cervix). During the first year of life, the helpless infant needs to have the caregiver near. Absence of the caregiver is dangerous, at least until the second and third years. Thus, separation distress may occur toward the end of the first year because children are crawling or beginning to walk and may need a way to recall a caregiver when they move away and confront a dangerous situation. But by age three, when children are more self-reliant, there is no need to cry if a caregiver is not present. In this script, the separation anxiety of the one-year-old is adaptive for that period of development and has no future function. It might even be omitted from the experiences of the first year with no untoward consequences. The normal suckling of young rat pups appears to be of no consequence for the efficiency or the quality of the adult rats' feeding habits. Infant rats prevented from suckling (by being fed artificially) do not differ from normally reared rats in eating or in appetitive learning for foods (Hall 1975). Similarly, even though the initiation of play behavior in juvenile squirrel monkeys is believed to facilitate later social behavior, the absence of play in some troops of juvenile squirrel monkeys does not prevent the appearance of normal social behavior (Baldwin and Baldwin 1973).

Each life phase makes special demands, and so each phase is accompanied by a special set of qualities. Succeeding phases have a different set of demands; hence, some of the past is inhibited or discarded. The new pattern may contain none of the elements of the earlier, but often functionally similar, competence.

Faith in the material preservation of human qualities across the life span resembles the pre-Darwinian belief in the fixity of species. Darwin's great insight was to see the history of animals as dynamic, with some species vanishing and new ones emerging. If the analogy between evolution and ontogeny is fruitful, a structure or a process is likely to be preserved if it is adaptive. The demands of the first two years are so different from those of later childhood and adolescence that one might expect many of the qualities of the early period to disappear and leave no trace of their temporary ascendency.

All aspects of growth are not analogous to a relay race where batons are handed in sequence from one runner to another. Rather, some developmental sequences are more like the creation of a painting in which an artist decides when and where a new figure will be added to the canvas. The presence of a row of trees on a canvas does not give rise to the later insertion of a figure reclining by one of the trees, even though the latter follows the former. Despite the attractiveness and seeming utility of regarding development as being composed of slowly growing, connected stages, we should remain open to the velocity of the transitions and the degree of connectedness among them.

I do not claim that there are no structurally preserved elements in development—there must be some; I suggest only that it is unlikely that every actor in the first scene of the play has a role in the second act.

Paul Baltes of the Max Planck Institute in West Berlin has invented a useful heuristic conception of the balance of both early and late forces that monitor the development of a life. He suggests that if one were to study the behavior of a single person every day for fifty years—cognitive talents, social behavior, emotional reactions—one would discover times of transition when the person's behavior changed in a major way. Each of the four major conditions for change assumes differential potency during successive periods of development.

The first set of conditions is a product of the genetically programmed changes in the central nervous system I described in chapter 2. As the effect of maturation slows during later childhood, changes in behavior will be more obviously correlated with environmental demands. Hence, a second set of conditions resides in the normative regimens of a particular culture. All American children go to school between five and six years of age; that normative event produces a major change in the child's behavior. Most youths learn to drive a car, and about half go on to college at sixteen to eighteen years of age. And each of these socially normative events leads to significant changes in a person's behavior. Although such norms persist through early adulthood, by the third decade they have become weaker. For new normative constraints are imposed on the behavior of a thirty-year-old.

A third set consists of historical events that affect the entire society but are most influential on adolescents and young adults. These historical events include economic depression, war, revolution, natural catastrophe, or inventions, like the automobile, radio, or television. It is argued that the children who were five to fifteen years of age when television was introduced were more influenced by that medium than were younger children or adults. Similarly, it is believed that Americans who were between fifteen and twenty-five years of age during the Vietnam war were more seriously influenced by the anti-war demonstrations than Americans who were younger or older in the 1960s. The children who are now between seven and seventeen years of age will be influenced more profoundly by the widespread use of computers than their parents will be.

A fourth set of forces are unexpected or unpredictable events, like a divorce, illness, accident, or the meeting of a certain person. Although these rare events are always potent, they become increasingly significant in controlling change in a particular person's behavior after age thirty, when the other three factors wane in significance, and behavior, beliefs, and moods have become relatively fixed.

The Preservation of Individual Qualities

The theme of connectedness assumes a much different meaning when we consider the preservation of those special psychological qualities that distinguish one child from another. Extreme inhibition to the unfamiliar, which I discussed in chapter 2, is an example of one such characteristic. This meaning of connectedness is of great interest to parents who wish to know whether their child's personality provides a preview of his or her adult character. Before we can answer this question, there first must be some agreement on the individual qualities that might enjoy the privilege of preservation.

Unfortunately psychologists do not have the benefit of consensus on primary theoretical entities. Biologists begin each day's work with that advantage: at the core of the three major theoretical ideas in biology—inheritance, growth, and evolution—is a different hypothetical entity or unit. The gene is the major unit in inheritance; the cell, in growth; and the individual organism, in evolution. Each of these three entities has different qualities and functions.

The major theoretical entities in psychology are not things, like genes or cells, but processes. Hence psychologists must make nouns out of predicates, as do physiologists who write, "Respiration aerates the blood." Although psychologists have not yet discovered any theoretical entities comparable in significance to the gene or the cell, it may be helpful to suggest some candidates. As in biology, the primacy of a theoretical entity is a function of the use to which it is put; and the candidates I shall nominate are most useful for descriptions of the preservation of psychological qualities. These entities may be less helpful in theoretical discussions of language or reasoning, for example.

I also recognize that the primacy of an entity is a function of the

discipline's level of progress; and, therefore, its status is imperma-
nent. In the eighteenth century, the organ, not the cell, was a
primary entity in biology; and earlier in this century, the nucleus of
the atom, not the quark, was a primary entity in physics. Perhaps a
century from now, neither the cell nor the quark will be as fundamental as each is today. Considering the current immaturity of
psychology, there is little risk in predicting that none of the five
units I suggest will be fundamental a century from now.

The units invented to explain preservation have to accomplish
five important psychological functions. First, we need a unit that
stores an experience in a form sufficiently faithful that a person can
recognize most events encountered in the past. The *schema* fills that
function. As I noted in chapter 2, a schema is the infant's way to
represent an event, whether it be the father's face, an internal feeling, or the anticipation of the mother. Schemata allow older children and adults to recognize that a voice, a room, a melody, or a
fragrance that is now in the perceptual field has been encountered
previously.

But schemata do not lend themselves well either to linguistic
description or to logical reasoning; hence, we need a more discrete
unit that can be communicated easily and is amenable to manipulation in thought. A *category,* defined as the symbolic representation
of the qualities shared by a set of events, fills that function. Each
person has a large number of schemata for the distinctive qualities
of separate adult females, but the category *woman* is a stabilizing
force permitting the person to talk about the whole class of previously encountered women. When schemata are sorted into the
symbolic categorical bins of food, justice, and joy, the concrete
differences among the originally varied experiences are muted.
Some schemata become equivalent, while others become part of
something larger. When I place my schema for my ten-year-old
green Volvo into its appropriate category *car,* it loses its color,
dents, and squeak from the rear wheels; when placed in the category
vehicle, it even loses its shape and size.

Categories are the essential components of beliefs, for a belief is
a relation between categories. The belief, "Boys are tough," for
example, represents the relation between the categories *boy* and
tough. Linguistic philosophers and psychologists treat beliefs as part
of a larger class of units called *propositions.* Because many beliefs are

preserved, some for long periods of time, it would seem wise to make propositions basic units. Such a decision would not be an error. However, I can avoid positing this extra unit by suggesting that a belief like, "Boys are tough" can also be regarded as meaning that the category *boy* has toughness as one of its salient qualities. And most propositions can be treated as statements about one or more salient attributes of a concept. When a person's belief changes, the salient attributes of the underlying categories change too. A girl whose attitude of hostility toward her mother is transformed to one of respect alters a salient attribute of the category *mother*. There are few propositions that cannot be transformed this way. For this reason, I treat *category* as the basic entity and *proposition* as derivative.

Schemata, categories, and propositions are mental units, and we need to provide the person with entities that will allow him or her to stay alive and out of danger. Thus, a third primary unit is an *action* which produces some change in the environment. Smiling, talking, hammering, and conforming to a command are potential examples, but dreaming is not. I do not wish to minimize the psychological significance of processes like dreaming, but I suspect that these acts are less significant because a behavior that produces a change in the environment provides the person with information that can be used to perfect the action so that the behavioral surface can move toward adaptation. I suspect that the *operant,* defined by behaviorists as an action that produces a change, has been behaviorism's most important idea (Skinner 1938,. Herrnstein 1970).

Each person, however, possesses many actions, schemata, and categories, and we need to invent a unit that selects the relevant few from the larger array. The nineteenth-century scholar nominated *will* to serve this function. But will is purely cognitive in its connotation; and chronic emotional states, or moods, which control the selection of behavior, can be preserved for a long time. Thus, a *state of consciousness,* which includes perceived feeling tone and the intentions that dominate awareness at a particular moment, is a fourth unit. Although specific states of consciousness are more transient than schemata, categories, or actions, a state of consciousness is the executor, or executrix, of a large but limited proportion of an individual's behaviors, desires, and emotions.

Finally, psychologists find it useful to invent categories for coherences of schemata, categories, acts, and states of consciousness. These four elementary units form clusters that are regarded as *classes of persons,* our fifth entity. An adolescent who feels anxious in test situations, and avoids situations that contain intellectual challenge, is classified by the scientist as "one who is afraid of failure." One who generates schemata in which one is in a higher status than another, who categorizes most interaction as either facilitating or blocking one's access to status, and who experiences pleasure from dominating another, is classified as a "person with a motive for power." Because investigators who study preservation of human qualities theorize about such coherences, we need to posit a class of person as a fundamental unit.

Almost all the available studies concerned with the preservation of human qualities from childhood forward have concentrated on actions and classes of persons because psychologists do not yet have sensitive ways to measure schemata, categories, or states of consciousness. As we shall see shortly, when actions and classes of persons are the primary units, long-term preservation is minimal until late childhood. But it remains a possibility that when scientists are able to evaluate with greater sensitivity the other three units—schemata, categories, and states of consciousness—they may find evidence for the folk belief that some early memories and intense emotional states are preserved from infancy to adolescence and adulthood. We will have to wait and see.

HOW TO MEASURE PRESERVATION

Evaluating whether a psychological quality is preserved over time is much more difficult than it may seem on the surface. One reason for the difficulty is that no living creature remains exactly the same; hence, all statements about degree of preservation must be relative. But relative to what or to whom? An example will clarify the problem. Imagine that, for one hundred successive mornings, we have filmed a woman's behavior in her home for the first hour after she awakens, and wish to know if her actions during this hour are preserved across the one hundred days. That is, does the woman perform the same acts in the same order on a majority of mornings? But we cannot know whether the woman's behavior is preserved to a significant degree unless we have some point of comparison; that comparison might be her behavior during another part of the day, her behavior in another place, or the early-morning behavior of another person. If we study only her behavior during the first hour, it is likely that we might find that, on one morning, she makes her bed, bathes, dresses, and then eats breakfast. But, on a second morning, she dresses and eats breakfast but neither makes her bed nor bathes; and, on a third morning, she does not eat breakfast at all. If we demand a repetition of the same acts or the same acts in the same order, on every morning, we might come to the counterintuitive conclusion that the woman's behavior is not stable from day to day. But her morning behavior will seem stable if we compare her actions during the first hour with her actions at another time of the day, or her behavior at another place, like a hotel resort in the middle of summer. Now we find that bathing, dressing, and eating breakfast are much more likely to occur in that order during the first hour at home than at any other time of day, and that these three acts are more likely to occur at home than at a holiday hotel. Thus, once we supply a comparison time or place, we see that there is considerable preservation of her behavior during the first morning hour. But in actuality our conclusions refer to the preservation of *differences in behavior* between times and places.

A third point of comparison might be a less frequent action that occurs during the first hour—let us say, listening to the radio. If the woman was always more likely to bathe than to listen to the radio, we would conclude that the former act was better preserved than the latter. This way of assessing stability—that is, comparing the relative frequency of one behavior with another—is often used by parents when they reflect on the consistency of their child's personality. For example, children either obey or disobey maternal commands. One might reasonably ask whether a particular child's tendency to obey rather than to disobey is preserved over time. If, for each set of one hundred maternal requests, a child obeys 75 percent of the time and disobeys 25 percent of the time, we could conclude that the child's preference to obey, rather than to disobey, is preserved. But note that the frequency or form of the obedience or disobedience might be very different over time and situation. The child might protest on one occasion, ignore the mother on another, or delay acquiescence on a third. Parents who say that their ten-year-old has always been obedient do not mean that their child has consistently conformed to their requests or is more conforming than other children. I suspect they mean that their child's tendency to obey is usually stronger than the counter tendency to disobey.

The most frequently used comparison is the behavior of another person or persons in the same context. When other persons are the referent, the psychologist draws conclusions about the preservation of differences in behavior among a particular group of persons. But the selection of the "other person" is extremely important. A comparison of the morning routine of our woman with a neighbor's routine will reveal small differences in behavior, while comparing her with an Eskimo wife living at Hudson Bay will reveal dramatic differences. Once again, depending upon the comparison chosen, the conclusion drawn about the degree of preservation will vary.

The vast majority of scientific investigations of preservation of human qualities over time rely on differences among persons in some attribute or set of related attributes. For example, if the statures of one hundred children are assessed every six months from one to five years of age, the correlation between height at age one and height at age five is likely to be 0.5, and the scientist concludes that relative height is a stable attribute of children. However, this statement does not mean that a child's height does not change, or that height is better preserved than another attribute, like weight. Rather, it means that the differences in the heights of the one hundred children have remained somewhat constant. When textbooks state that children's intelligence is stable from five to ten years of age, they do not mean that a child's basic intellectual abilities are stable—they are not—but that the differences in I.Q. test scores among a group of children are preserved, despite dramatic changes in the intellectual talents that accompany growth. A serious problem with drawing conclusions about the stability of an abstract quality from the results of such a strategy is that it is easy to invent a hypothetical quality that might account for the differences among individuals in two markedly different behaviors observed at two different times, especially when many years intervene. As I noted in chapter 2, Alan Sroufe (1979) believes that the positive relation between behavior in Ainsworth's Strange Situation at one year (some children cry at maternal departure but greet the mother upon her return) and a three-year-old's tendency to explore new toys in a novel environment reflects preservation of the quality that Sroufe calls a "secure attachment."

Although this hypothesis about what disposition is preserved might be correct, it is neither intuitively obvious nor empirically certain. Indeed, the positive relation between two classes of behavior at two points in time is likely to be the result of many intermediate changes that occur between the two measurements. A middle-class three-year-old with an unusually large vocabulary is more likely to become a successful lawyer than is a working-class three-year-old who has just begun to speak. But it is as reasonable to suggest that these different outcomes in adulthood are due to the maintenance of their respective environments for three decades, as it is to suggest that the differences in each child's original cognitive abilities were preserved from the third year to adulthood.

The Evidence for Stability of Differences

Scientific study of the preservation of psychological qualities has a short history, fragile facts, and is typically based on comparisons among children. Hence, conclusions must be viewed with great caution. Additionally, as I noted earlier, the primary psychological entities typically studied have been actions and classes of persons, not schemata, categories, or states of consciousness.

In general, the differences among children in specific action profiles—like aggression toward or dominance with peers, dependency upon parents, sociability or shyness with unfamiliar people, and intellectual accomplishments—are preserved from age five or six through adolescence (Kagan and Moss 1983; Olweus 1981). The very shy, timid six-year-old is likely to become an adolescent who is tense and quiet with strangers (Kagan and Moss 1983), and an adult who prefers a secure job to one that entails risk (Morris et al. 1954). When a group of extremely shy, withdrawn three- to eight-year-olds boys were interviewed as adults twenty years later, the vast majority were working for large institutions, and few had chosen an entrepreneurial vocation with its attendant risk. These men stressed the importance of job security, and many more had married outgoing women who complemented their personality than women who were shy and retiring like themselves.

The aggressive seven-year-old is likely to be an adolescent bully. Over fourteen different longitudinal studies, from both American and European laboratories, reveal stability of aggressive behavior over periods of two to three years, especially among boys. Although there is a gradual drop in the degree of preservation of aggression as the age interval increases, even for intervals as long as twenty years, the differences in aggressive behavior are preserved (Olweus 1981). There is, therefore, preservation of some acts and classes of persons from childhood to adulthood.

However, the existing data, albeit vulnerable to criticism, are far less supportive of the belief that the characteristics displayed during the first two to three years of life, with the exception of the temperamental qualities of inhibition and lack of inhibition, provide a sensitive preview of the future (Moss and Susman 1980). Although the results of each investigation are too weak to bear the burden of proof alone, the findings of many related studies can be woven into a more persuasive fabric.

After the Second World War, an international social service agency arranged for middle-class American families to adopt homeless children who had led uncertain lives in Europe during the war. When the children arrived in the United States, they ranged in age from about five months to ten years. A group of thirty-eight of these children were followed in their new homes. About 20 percent of the children initially displayed severe signs of anxiety, like overeating, sleep disturbance, and nightmares. But, over the years, all of these symptoms vanished; the vast majority of the children made good school progress; and there was no case of academic difficulty among them. The authors of this study wrote:

The thing that is most impressive is that with only a few exceptions they do not seem to be suffering either from frozen affect or the indiscriminate friendliness that Bowlby describes. As far as can be determined their relationships to their adopted families are genuinely affectionate. . . . The present results indicate that for the child suffering extreme loss the chances for recovery are far better than had previously been expected. (Rathbun, DeVirgilio, and Waldfogel 1958).

In a later but similar study, 229 Korean girls who—when they were between two and three years of age—had been adopted by middle-class American families were followed for at least six years. At the time of admission the children were divided into three groups based on their degree of malnutrition and were studied again about six years after admission to their foster homes, when all were in elementary school. The average I.Q. of the severely malnourished group (I.Q. of 102) was forty points higher than the scores reported for similar Korean samples who were returned to their original home environments. This degree of recovery of intellectual skills, as well as of physical health, does not occur among malnourished children who are returned to their originally poor environments after a period of rehabilitation (Winick, Meyer, and Harris 1975).

Even children with symptoms serious enough to lead to their referral to a child guidance clinic at nine years of age can become adequately adjusted young adults. The authors of a relevant study wrote:

Except for extreme personality deviations, that is, psychoses and extreme anti-social behavior, there seems to be little continuity between child and adult disturbances. Most children . . . can be expected to improve in adjustment into adulthood with or without therapy. (Cass and Thomas 1979, p. 121).

It may be that the difficulty in predicting from childhood characteristics to adult adjustment is due at least in part to the influence of certain life experiences intervening between the two points in time. As research evidence accumulates, however, to cast doubt on previously favored theories of the continuity of personality development and of the great importance to be attached to the experience of the first three years of life, the issue of the effects of intervening events, particularly of trauma and stress, has also been open to debate. It now seems probable that life experiences intervening between early childhood and adulthood may counteract or reinforce earlier positive and negative experience and thereby influence adjustment in complex ways. (p. 142)

Psychologists have been following the development of a girl named Genie who at thirteen and one-half years of age was removed from a home where she had been immobilized, isolated from contact with others, and physically beaten for most of the first thirteen years of her life. When discovered, she was malnourished, unable to stand erect, and without language, an unsocialized victim of extreme deprivation. After only four years in a normal environment, she developed some language, learned some social skills, was able to take a bus to school, and began to express some of the basic human emotions. On some of the scales of a standardized intelligence test, she obtained scores close to those of the average child. Although she is still markedly different from an average California eighteen-year-old, Genie has grown remarkably in a short time (Curtiss et al. 1975).

Studies of normal children reveal that most behavior normally undergoes alteration with development. The results of several longitudinal investigations of working-and middle-class American children, most of whom were growing up in relatively stable and supportive homes, indicated that variation in psychological qualities during the first three years of life was not substantially predictive of variation in culturally significant and age-appropriate characteristics five, ten, or twenty years later; while variation during the early school years, especially five to ten years of age, was predictive of adolescent and adult profiles. For example, children from working- and middle-class parents living in the Boston area had been evaluated extensively four times during the first three years of life. In the first part of the study, the infants' attentiveness, vocal excitability, activity level, tempo of play, irritability, and disposition to smile were evaluated at four, eight, thirteen, and twenty-seven months of age. With only one exception, variation in these classes of behavior prior to one year was not highly predictive of a small set of theoretically related qualities at twenty-seven months of age. These children were evaluated again when they were ten years old, in order to determine if variation in the infant qualities would predict intelligence test scores, reading ability, or a tendency toward reflection-impulsivity at that age. The educational level of the family—and therefore the family's social class—was the only robust predictor of a child's I.Q. and reading skill. When children from the same social class who were markedly different on both reading ability and I.Q. were compared, there were no major differences between them during the period of infancy.

A major long-term study of seventy-one children who had grown up in southwestern Ohio between 1929 and 1957 revealed little relation between variation in activity, dependency, tantrums, or aggression during the first three years of life and variation in a variety of culturally related and relevant qualities during adolescence and early adulthood. Infants who were extremely irritable did not differ in a major way from those who were less irritable when they were of school age; active infants did not turn out differently from less active ones. The only hint of preservation held for the quality I call "inhibition to the unfamiliar": some infants initially withdraw from the unfamiliar, from threat, and from obstacles, while others are more disposed to approach, attack, or retaliate to threat (see chapter 2, pages 65–69). When the inhibited infants were of school age, they displayed behavior that seemed to reflect the same quality. They avoided dangerous activities, were less aggressive with peers, and were more withdrawn and less spontaneous with other people. The adult males who had been the most inhibited infants chose vocations that minimized competitiveness and were less traditionally masculine. By contrast, those men who had been the least inhibited infants chose more competitive and traditionally masculine occupations (athletic coach, salesman, and engineer) (Kagan and Moss 1983).

But even if there is a biological contribution to this behavior, these qualities will not persist if they are totally maladaptive. This statement finds support in the fact that about one third of a group of extremely inhibited twenty-one-month-old children were less inhibited when they were four years old, while no uninhibited twenty-one-month-old was markedly inhibited at the older age (Kagan et al. in press). As most American parents do not like timid, fearful children, they promote courage and boldness and consistently discourage timidity. A child can change from being inhibited to uninhibited, even though such a change might be more difficult for a child whose behavioral inhibition rested, in part, on biological constitution.

Similarly, most school-age children who are extremely aggressive or withdrawn, and who are therefore subject to both anxiety and social rejection, are likely to grow toward less extreme behavior. Fewer than one third of three thousand children, six to thirteen years of age, who were nominated by their classmates as being unusually aggressive or withdrawn, remained as extreme three years later. That fact does not mean that the extremely aggressive children were no longer aggressive, but it does imply that the majority were *less* aggressive than they had been three years earlier (Ledingham and Schwartzman 1983).

A similar investigation studied thirty-year-old adults who had been nominated by their peers when they were eight years old as either minimally or maximally aggressive. Although the extremely aggressive children, compared with the less aggressive ones, became adults who described themselves as aggressive and had more criminal offenses, the correlation between the degree of childhood aggression and these two indexes of aggressive behavior at age thirty were low: only about 0.3 for men and 0.2 for the women. Apparently, most aggressive children became less aggressive, and many minimally aggressive children became more aggressive, over the intervening twenty-two years (Huesman et al. 1983).

Each child's tendency to acquire the qualities the social environment demands, in spite of an earlier history that might be inconsistent with adaptative abilities, has a nice analogue in evolution. Biologists suggest that those morphological features that are involved in the animal's adaptation are poorer guides to its phylogenetic history than are those qualities that are minimally or only indirectly, related to its adaptation. Thus, the shape of a bird's beak, which is important for the acquisition of food, is a less useful sign of its closeness of relation to other avian species than are its internal organs or biochemistry. A sociable and easy manner with strangers is a desirable human characteristic in modern society; hence, similarity among adults in this quality may not be a sensitive index of similarities in earlier histories. But school failure and extreme timidity, which are not adaptive, are likely to be more revealing signs of a person's past.

Even among laboratory-reared animals, there seems to be minimal stability from infancy to adulthood of individual differences in qualities like aggressiveness, activity, or excitability. For example, the differences among young monkeys in excitability or social interaction were not stable over periods as short as eighteen months (Stevenson-Hinde, Stillwell-Barnes, and Zunz 1980b); and differences in dominance behavior among a group of laboratory rats were not preserved over twenty months of observation (Ewer 1968).

After an extensive review of the evidence on preservation of behavioral differences in animals, R. B. Cairns and K. E. Hood (1983) concluded that the preservation of differences in behavior only became obvious as the animal neared reproductive maturity:

The findings offer meagre support for the idea that significant features of social interactions at maturity are fixed by experiences in early development. . . . The qualities that are predictable are not in the organism but in the developmental context; its relationships and its likely course of subsequent development. (p. 53)

The young organism is remarkably plastic, and much of what is acquired "from the social environment is transient and is relevant primarily for the organism's immediate adaptation" (p. 55).

Preservation of a quality over a shorter period—one to two years—occurs often. For example, some infants who were extremely irritable and hard to quiet during the first month of life remained harder to placate at three months (Crockenberg and Smith 1981). But it is likely, from all the evidence reviewed, that if these children were seen again at five years of age, they might not differ in irritability or in related behavior.

Some psychologists and psychiatrists resist this conclusion, arguing that infants who are extremely irritable at six months should remain different in some way from those who are less irritable, because the basis for the initial behavior cannot vanish. These theorists suspect that certain schemata or vulnerabilities to anxiety—units that are difficult to measure—are preserved, even if the surface actions have changed. This belief is at the heart of the controversy on connectedness. One can always claim that if scientists measured these subtle properties, they would find theoretically appropriate differences between irritable and non-irritable infants ten years later. This is a possibility, but I am suggesting it is also reasonable that no such difference would occur because the bases for the infant irritability may have vanished. Some babies are irritable because of transient conditions, like colic or a temporary allergy to milk. As each of these conditions disappears with growth, so, too, does the tendency to be irritable. There is no more reason to assume that irritability during the first six months will leave persistent structural residues than that a child who has perspired a lot during her first three months, because she was born in North Carolina in the middle of July, will take with her into late childhood psychological remnants of the bouts of excessive perspiration. Every quality need not leave structural heirs.

A second reason that we might not see derivatives of early irritability is that parents do not react in the same way to highly irritable or to minimally irritable babies. Some mothers ignore irritable infants. Other mothers become overprotective, thus creating different dispositions in these children. Similarly, some parents react to non-irritable infants by letting them play alone for long periods; others interact with them a great deal.

The behavioral profile created in children by differential treatment invites special reactions from other people. By the time the child is ten years old, it is unlikely that there will be any common outcome of the simple fact of extreme irritability at three months, even though it is possible, if the entire child's history were known, to create a story that seems to explain why a particular quality of a ten-year-old—say, shyness with peers—has been influenced by excessive irritability during the opening year of life (Moss and Susman 1980).

In contrast to the difficulty of using an infant's qualities to predict his or her future, a family's education, vocation, and income are excellent predictors of many aspects of a child's behavior at age ten. Thus, discovery of a relation between variation in a quality during infancy and one seen in a five- or a ten-year-old need not mean that some aspect of the original quality has been preserved; rather, it could indicate that the same forces that produced the behavior in the first year continued to operate for the next decade. For example, infants who are very attentive to discrepant stimuli have higher I.Q. scores five to ten years later than do less attentive babies (Kagan, Lapidus, and Moore 1978). This finding appears to imply that a quality related to intelligence has been preserved; it is assumed that the "intellectual ability" of some children led them to detect the discrepant events and to look longer in order to understand them. However, both prolonged attention during infancy and a higher I.Q. are more often characteristic of infants from better-educated families. Many inattentive infants born to middle-class families will have a high I.Q. when they are ten years old.

Consider an analogy. Well-nourished, physically healthy infants play with more vitality than malnourished or sickly infants, and healthy adults are likely to engage in more athletic tasks than ill adults. Yet no one would suggest that there is a quality called *playfulness* that is stable from the first year through adulthood. Rather, if a sickly child stays in an environment that does not support health, he or she will be ill and weak as an infant and unlikely to engage in athletic activity later in life. The relation between the two qualities is due to the continued operation of a specific external influence, not to the uninterrupted possession of the property of playfulness. If a marble placed in a narrow trough rolls in a straight line, one does not attribute a sense of direction to the marble but appropriately concludes that its linear roll is fixed by the environmental constraint of the trough. In most areas of the world, children born to parents in poverty grow up to be poverty-stricken adults, not because they possess an inherent incapacity to acquire property, but because they cannot escape their villages.

In general, about 10 percent to 20 percent of adolescents in a typical modern community fail to adjust to the demands of the school or to other local norms for socialized behavior. The best predictor of these apparent failures in adaptation is continued rearing in a family that is under economic stress and believes itself powerless to change its status. Children who grow up in such settings are less well prepared for school mastery and, as a result of identification with their social class, grow to doubt their potency. Hence, they lower their expectations and create defenses against middle-class standards. A child's social class constitutes a continuing set of influences on development. It is this constancy in the envelope of daily events that determines the degree of stability of a psychological quality. The more stable the environment, the more likely the preservation of those properties that are adaptive in that context. It is claimed that, over the last one hundred thousand years, clams have changed far less than terrestrial animals because there have been fewer serious changes in the ecology of the clam compared with that of the horse (Stanley 1982). Thus, one should not view the infant as possessing a set of prerecorded tapes embedded deep within the brain labeled "intelligent," "irritable," "dependent," "labile, or "passive." Although children present different behavioral surfaces to their environment during the opening years of life, each accommodates to the pressures imposed from without and is altered in accord with those forces.

When a behavior persists it is often a silent attempt to communicate a wish, a resentment, or a request, either because words are inadequate or because the person is unaware of the message he feels pressed to declare. Many of the adolescents who vandalize stores, smear paint on statues, or steal purses are trying to tell the community they are angry. The scribbled note that warns of a suicide is a request for help; the twelve-year-old girl who refuses to eat is trying to say she does not want to grow up. Of course, each culture imposes special meanings on an action. Among a group in New Guinea, a sudden display of unprovoked aggression by a twenty-year-old man is not a sign of anger, but an announcement that the new burdens of adulthood are too heavy (Newman 1960).

Thus, a behavior is preserved if the underlying message remains urgent. With growth, many messages lose their urgency. Although some stubborn habits resist replacement, many more are symbolic greetings, which, we know, are altered when conditions change.

The existing corpus of data is not firm enough to permit the conclusion that the early experiences or the qualities of infants are of no consequence for later childhood. But the evidence does imply that if the profiles created by early encounters are not supported by future and current environments, change is likely. Some parents resist this conclusion because they want to believe that a particular recipe of experiences in the home is an elixir young children need in order to grow up healthy and happy. Many citizens fear that if the experiences of infancy do not contribute substantially to the future, parents may become indifferent to the needs of their young children. Because the way infants are treated does affect their mood and behavior, some clarification is needed.

There is probably a broad range of early environments that have similar effects on infants. As long as caregivers provide food, protection from pain, and playful interaction with children on a regular schedule, it is likely that the small differences among two-year-olds raised on such regimens will have little predictive consequences for differences among them five or ten years hence. But there is no question that infants who frequently experience prolonged periods of distress, and do not enjoy playful interaction with adults, will be more fearful, irritable, and perhaps more aggressive and less cognitively proficient at age three than children treated in more benevolent fashion.

Consider an analogy to colds. It is reasonable to suppose that infants who contract only two colds during the first year will not, other things being equal, be healthier at age six than infants who contract six colds. But children who have had chronic respiratory infection throughout the first year will probably be less healthy at age six. And, indeed, the evidence indicates that the number of acute bouts of self-limiting illnesses in early childhood is not very predictive of the future health of middle-class children. There seems to be a threshold function: up to a point, quality of experience is of minimal importance for the future. But once that threshold is crossed, the consequences are more serious. Because most American parents provide adequate care for their infants, they may not need to worry excessively about the potential impact of every missed hug or impulsively administered punishment. But that suggestion does not condone indifference, aloofness, or lack of love.

Infants whose experiences have created pathology are likely to continue to grow anomalously only if they remain in the same environment. However, two-year-olds are receptive to change if their neglecting environments become benevolent and facilitate more desirable development. Nature has supplied a nice example of this hypothesis. If a pregnant mother is tense or ill for most of the pregnancy, the probability of a premature birth is increased. And infants born prematurely are different psychologically during the first year or two of life. But if the environment is supportive of growth, psychologists are unable to find any differences between six-year-old children born prematurely and those born at term. The experiences of the intervening six years are able to repair or change the psychological profile of the premature infant.

Another example of this principle is seen in a long-term study of over six hundred children growing up on the island of Kauai in the Hawaiian group who were followed from birth to eighteen years of age to see whether infants born with perinatal complications were at risk for later academic problems or psychiatric disorders (Werner and Smith 1982). Only a small group of fourteen infants were born with serious perinatal stress. Of this group, four were mentally retarded at age ten, two had mental health problems, and three were delinquent. Thus, serious perinatal stress does place an infant at risk. But, of the sixty-nine infants born with mild perinatal stress, the occurrence of mental retardation, schizophrenia, neurotic symptoms, or delinquency was not greater than it was for infants born without risk, because a supportive home environment can ameliorate the vulnerabilities imposed by perinatal stress. More important, the stressful nature of the home environment was more predictive of later psychological problems than was risk status at birth. Children growing up in homes that had minimal psychological stability or economic disadvantage were more likely to have problems during adolescence than were those born with some form of biological risk.

When these children were ten years old, about sixty—10 percent of the original group—were anxious, had neurotic symptoms, or were in need of psychiatric treatment. But these problems proved temporary, especially for the adolescents who came form economically secure families. The combination of biological stress at birth and an economically stressed family environment was the best predictor of later psychological problems; either condition alone was far less potent. The authors wrote: "As we watched these children grow from babyhood to adulthood we could not help but respect the self-righting tendencies within them that produced normal development under all but the most persistently adverse circumstances" (Werner and Smith 1982, p. 159).

Conclusion

This discussion of the two forms of connectedness challenges two favorite assumptions in Western views on human development. Many observers want the past to seriously constrain the present through material links that join the universal milestones of growth into a forged chain. Each child must step on every link—no skipping permitted—as he or she journeys into maturity. It is odd that, in a society that celebrates originality, many social scientists prefer psychological novelties that are so dependent upon the past they seem almost determined.

The second popular assumption, captured by the motto "Well begun is half done," holds that the qualities acquired first will be the last to go. Hence, by looking at an infant, we not only obtain a preview of what is to come, but we are also justified in explaining a particular adult's personality as a necessary product of the distant past. These two suppositions ignore the power of the many social forces and maturing abilities that appear later in life.

The evolutionary tree may be a good metaphor for psychological development. Biologists do not explain the appearance of man by pointing to protozoa, even though in the remote past the existence of protozoa made humans a little more likely. Rather, scientists point to the entire evolutionary sequence. Similarly, one cannot explain a ten-year-old's phobia of horses or Proust's aestheticism by listing their respective experiences as infants. Each person can be understood only as a coherence of many, many past events.

The satisfying quality of an explanation that relates two psychological qualities separated by a long period of time depends on the degree to which the theorist can fill the temporal space with possible mechanisms. The older the child, the less satisfying are explanatory propositions that rely too heavily on early experience.

Each developmental journey contains many points where one can move in any one of several directions. Each choice modifies, in however small a way, the probability of a particular outcome. A perinatal trauma alters the probability of future academic failure by some very small amount. The affection of the mother, the arrival of a sibling, the authoritarian quality of the father, and the degree of success in first grade comprise successive events that move a child toward certain choices and away from others. Once a choice is made, the child will resist being detracted from that path.

The embryological development of the neural crest cells provides the most informative analogy. Early in the growth of the nervous system, the cells surrounding the future spinal cord begin to migrate to various locations in the tiny embryo. Some of these cells will end up serving the eye; some, the gut; some, the heart. Their final fate is determined by the cells they will encounter in their journey; it is not inherent in their intrinsic structure before their migration begins (Le Douarin 1982). But once the cell reaches its destination—whether eye, gut, or heart—it assumes a form that eventually becomes impossible to change. This principle seems to apply to psychological development. I suspect that it is only when the child interprets experiences as having implications for his talent, gender, virtue, and acceptability that his dispositions become more resistant to change. As we shall see in the next chapter, the first components of a sense of self do not emerge until late in the second year.

4

Establishing a Morality

Metaphysics is the finding of bad reasons
for what we believe upon instinct.

FRANCIS HERBERT BRADLEY,
Appearance and Reality

THE CAPACITY TO EVALUATE the actions of self and others as good
or bad is one of the psychological qualities that most distinguishes
Homo sapiens from the higher apes. Chimpanzees are capable of
symbolic communication, even though their talent falls far short of
the language ability of the human three-year-old, and they behave
as if fear, joy, and sadness were within their experience. But there
is not the slimmest shred of evidence to suggest that these animals
possess the ideas of good and bad and apply these categories to their
actions or those of others. Admission of the idea of standard into
the working vocabulary of psychology is based on the fact that
some ideas and actions are classified as good or bad, and each evaluation is related to specific feeling states. Children will readily acknowledge that "hitting another" is bad, but look puzzled if asked
whether "eating potatoes" is bad. They will regard "hitting a
home run" as good but not know how to evaluate "opening a
door." The fact that evaluative language is selectively applied to
thoughts and acts that can provoke anxiety, shame, guilt, or pride
implies the existence of a special class of ideas. I shall call this class
a *standard,* with the understanding that membership in this class
can be temporary.

112

The Meanings of Good and Bad

This essay is not the occasion to consider in detail either the continuing philosophical debates over the meanings of good and bad
or the relation of their meanings to the moral propositions that
form the basis for deciding what one should do in times of choice.
Before discussing the child's acquisition of moral standards, however, it is useful to articulate three major, unresolved issues: the
meanings of *good* and *bad;* the beneficiaries whose states of well-
being are to be awarded priority by a person considering an action;
and the possibility of defending a set of universal standards for
human action on logical, empirical, or phenomenological grounds.

Even though the English philosopher G. E. Moore (1959 [1922])
insisted that the meanings of *good* and *bad* are given intuitively and
cannot be defined in objective terms, most philosophers, as well as
everyday citizens, are unhappy with such elasticity, and the former
have tried to defend a definition on purely rational grounds. But
opinion is divided as to whether the criteria of good and bad
should emphasize a person's knowledge, rationality, feelings, intentions, actions, or the consequences for another of an agent's
freely willed behavior. None of these criteria is logically flawed,
empirically unsupportable, or intuitively unattractive. Each has
components that can be—and have been—evaluated as good or
bad. The disagreement is over which criterion is to be awarded
priority in the construction of a prescriptive morality that can control the disruptive behavior of persons in a society. For most philosophers have wanted to persuade others that aggression, exploitation, stealing, and arbitrary coercion, which interfere with the
harmonious functions of society, are bad, and that restraint on
these acts is morally binding on all citizens.

A significant historical change in Western morality occurred
when a group of seventeenth-century scholars, influenced by the
new respect for naturalism, individualism, and empiricism, promoted the view that each person's privately felt pleasure or displeasure should be the primary criteria for good and bad. David Hume,
responsive to the desire to base morality on natural law, declared
that each individual's feelings were to guide moral evaluation:

pleasant feelings were good; unpleasant ones were bad (Hume 1969 [1739–40]). But this basis for moral obligation has obvious flaws, especially in large societies consisting of unrelated people who differ in privilege, for it permits exploitation of and aggression toward those with less power by those with more.

Hume's position set the stage for a conflict between an emerging group of libertarians who prized personal freedom and self-interest, and proponents of the traditional ethic who urged subservience of desires for power, wealth, and beauty (Hume's three virtues) to a willingness to conform to the rules of benevolent authority, usually framed as *universals*. By the end of the eighteenth century, this ideological division had polarized scientists against humanists, bourgeoisie against the working class, agnostics against Christians. The consequences of unrestrained self-interest by those with the power to act on their will revealed the inadequacy of the simple but attractive suggestion that liberty and pleasure are natural definitions of good, and set the occasion for Kant's invention of the categorical imperative (Kant 1959 [1785]). This powerful idea, which stated that a standard was morally binding on any person who wished that standard to apply to all, accomplished three goals at once. It refuted Hobbes's pessimistic ethics, allowed morality to rest on a person's free but reflective choice, and—most important—permitted the rational defense of a small set of universal standards, including, of course, control of aggression toward others.

But humans are so skilled at disguising their true intentions the categorical imperative failed to solve the social problems that philosophers had taken as their obligation to resolve. Hence, nineteenth-century scholars shifted to a pragmatic criterion that might cope with these problems more directly. They declared that good and bad actions should be defined in terms of consequences, regardless of the feelings, the intentions, or even the behavior of an agent—not unlike the recent demand by minority groups for equality of outcome rather than of opportunity. The preferred outcome was one in which the largest number of people are made happier or put in a state of less discomfort. It is more difficult for a person than for a legislative body to apply this utilitarian criterion because no one can predict the sequelae of an action. A narrow interpretation of the utilitarian view for an individual action holds that a man who jumps in the sea to save a child whom he believes to be drowning, and, as a result, kills both the child and himself, has not committed a morally praiseworthy act.

Regardless of whether consequences, feeling states, intentions, or acts are nominated for moral priority, the hierarchy of the various choices within each of these classes remains undecided. If feeling states are primary, should priority be awarded to an agent's sensory delight or to feelings of loyalty and devotion? If intentions define what is good, does the desire to be just take precedence over the desire to enhance another's sense of esteem, or even over the wish to be truthful? If actions form the ethical axis, should aggression, dishonesty, coercion, or sexual exploitation be the most abhorrent behavior? If consequences are the monitor, should primacy be given to another's feelings of dignity, health, psychological serenity, economic security, or freedom of action? And whose feeling states are most important if there is a conflict—those of spouse, kin, any individual at risk, the members of a community, or the maximum number of people in the world?

For reasons that are partly understandable, modern Western scholars have awarded special ethical status to individual freedom and the intentions to be just and honest. Among the contemporary writers promoting this position are Lawrence Kohlberg (1981), Charles Fried (1978), John Rawls (1971), and Alan Gewirth (1978). Although the claim that freedom is a primary good and its loss the most serious wrong is implicit in the Christian assumption of a will free to choose between right and wrong actions, this moral premise became transformed during the Enlightenment to mean freedom to enter into contracts with others, to hold personal property, to speak and to think without fear of reprisal, and to act in the service of one's self-interest. The validity of these definitions of individual liberty would not be as obvious to many societies— including the fourth-century Athenians who felt no guilt over enslaving barbarians, or sixth-century French monks who declared their total loyalty to God. Nonetheless, the moral primacy of this view of individual freedom has a ring of validity to almost all citizens in our society because, despite ideological pluralism on many issues, there is a consensus that there should be minimal restraint on one's willed efforts to improve one's talents and to attain wealth and status. However, the axiom that freedom to act in the service of one's self-interest is an absolute, primary good follows from neither logic nor observation. It is not transparently true that such freedom is friendlier to human nature or more conducive to social harmony than the ambivalent acceptance either of an obligation to care for a sick relative or of an invitation to participate in the cooperative creation of an object of beauty.

To a princess who had asked about rules of conduct, Descartes answered "Although each of us is a person distinct from all others . . . we must always remember that none of us could exist alone . . . the interests of the whole, of which each of us is a part, must always be preferred to those of our individual personality (cited in Goldmann 1973, p. 27). The virtue of justice toward non-kin whom one has not wronged directly, which is at the center of most arguments for social and economic equality (Rawls 1971), is also a more necessary ideal in the contemporary West than it is in small villages in Latin America and Africa. The inhabitants of most of these subsistence farming communities, composed of households that are relatively homogeneous with regard to economic resources and ideology, do not believe that the less advantaged in the larger community should be the primary beneficiary of each agent's actions. In a hamlet of three hundred people belonging to half a dozen families, it is usually the individual act of gossip, aggression, stealing, or adultery that is quintessentially bad because it is disruptive to another person and his or her extended family.

Charles Fried's defense of the virtue of honesty is based on the premise that one is free to make the best self-interested choice only if one has access to the total truth. Despite the popular folk belief that a little delusion helps one to make decisions that will eventually benefit the self, Fried believes that those who deceive another, despite the best intentions, will not enhance the other's self-interest (1978). This moral imperative has even seeped into the essays of linguistic philosophers, for, in an otherwise analytically objective analysis of language, John Pollock suddenly declares, "You are not supposed to state something unless you believe it is true" (1982, p. 239).

Cultures vary in the degree to which a standard on honesty toward others is broadly inclusive or context-specific. In Western society, standards for honesty and dishonesty in reporting facts and intentions have typically not specified the situation in which the agent behaves. Any act of lying is bad, without regard to the target person to whom the lie is told. In Japan, it is ethically acceptable to avoid telling the truth in many social situations in order to maintain social harmony. Exemplars of this class of behavior, called *tatemae,* are not evaluated as morally wrong. Lying to a member of one's inner group, however, is wrong because it violates the standard of *honne.*

The concern with lying among Western parents is unusual when viewed against the total spectrum of cultures. I suspect that one reason for this preoccupation is the deep premise that a child's character, like his intelligence, is an indivisible unity which, if flawed in any part, is sullied completely.

The Western preference for highly abstracted standards, minimally constrained by occasions or targets, is one more instance of the addiction to abstract ideas that was considered as our fourth theme in chapter 1. Most social scientists prefer a single category like *intelligence* to name many distinctly separate cognitive competences, or *fear* to classify distinctive affect experiences, or *ambition* for separate classes of motivation. Theorists like Piaget and Kohlberg have a large following, in part, because they posit stages of moral development that are indifferent to the specific situation in which the moral competence is operative. It is supposed that all the major decisions of a twenty-year-old in stage six of Kohlberg's (1981) scheme for moral development stem from a coherent, consistent arrangement of premises and standards—a private moral theory. In such a scheme, to tell a lie to a stranger who is lost has as profound an implication for the status of one's character as has stealing from a close friend. Few cultures conceptualize human morality so abstractly. Even though psychological growth is accompanied by both differentiation and synthesis, Western scholars celebrate the latter over the former because it allows them to describe the ideal adult as one whose daily decisions are faithful to a small set of abstract principles, rather than as a person who accommodates to local demands. Thus, what the Japanese might call "properly sensitive accommodation to the situation" is called "hypocrisy," "insincerity," or "inconsistency" by Americans in order to announce the community's prejudice against a person whose standards shift with the special requirements of a situation. William James captured the tension between these two attitudes: "Life is one long struggle between conclusions based on abstract ways of conceiving cases, and opposite conclusions prompted by an instinctive perception of them as individual facts" (1981b, p. 1266).

Can There Be Universal Standards?

The typical argument against universal moral standards relies on the fact that a historical comparison of the qualities nominated as virtues reveals remarkable variety in the actions promoted to moral status because the criteria for judging an action as morally proper or repugnant reflect, in part, changing social facts. Loyalty to one's place of residence was a central virtue in the Greek city-state; this standard is far less binding on citizens living in a modern metropolis. The right of each citizen to better his or her life is a salient feature of modern Western ethics; it was not so in most ancient societies. The Jacobin virtues of liberty, fraternity, and equality would not be understood by sixth-century Mayan villagers in southern Mexico. In order to deal with the local sources of tension that are ascendant during a particular historical era, the surface qualities of a proscriptive morality are altered, a fact that has led Alasdair MacIntyre (1981) to note that the courage Homer praised in the *Odyssey* refers to actions that are not realizable for a majority of adults in modern America. The restraint Aristotle urged would not be understandable to the majority of adults in Los Angeles, who also seek the comfortable feeling of virtue. Because the moral status of an act or an intention, even of killing, is usually judged in a particular context, the fact that contexts change with time and location implies the absence of consensus across cultures in the everyday definition of a good person and in the explicit hierarchy of good acts. This state of affairs has led many citizens to accept begrudgingly a philosophy of moral relativism.

AFFECT AND UNIVERSAL STANDARDS

I believe, however, that, beneath the extraordinary variety in surface behavior and consciously articulated ideals, there is a set of emotional states that form the bases for a limited number of universal moral categories that transcend time and locality. An adult in a Kipsigis community in Western Kenya tries to explain this emotional feeling of conscience:

> You remain unhappy because you have something in your heart that will draw you to a shadow of being afraid of something that you have done to someone else. Because you will charge yourself according to your heart that you were not right at that time. (Harkness, Edwards, and Super 1981, p. 600)

David Hume asserted the same thought two centuries earlier. "When you pronounce any action or character to be vicious, you mean nothing, but that from the constitution of your nature you have a feeling or sentiment of blame from the contemplation of it" (1739, p. 520). The human competence to experience a small number of distinctive emotional states can be likened to the preservation of basic morphological structures in evolution—the eye is an example—each of which is expressed in varied phenotypes but descended from an original, fundamental form. Let us suppose, first, that the pattern of economic, political, and social conditions within a society determines the surface virtues that will be required in abundance—whether physical courage, loyalty to the community, honesty in communication, thrift, industry, charity to strangers, self-understanding, or a dozen other standards that have dominated discussions of morality. The virtues awarded the highest praise during any historical period will require effort but will be within the capacity of all citizens. Assume further that the virtues easiest to promote in others, and to defend to oneself, are those that prevent the unpleasant feelings accompanying temptations to violate a standard, that mute the discomfort following a violation, and that generate pleasant emotions through practice of the virtue.

The unpleasant emotions are provoked by specific conditions that occur with different probabilities across communities. Five potential candidates are: anticipation of the different varieties of "anxiety" in response to possible physical harm, social disproval, or task failure; the feeling of empathy toward those who are in need or at risk; the feeling of responsibility that follows the recognition that one has caused distress or harm to another; the feeling of fatigue and/or ennui following repeated gratifications of a desire;

and the feeling of uncertainty accompanying encounters with discrepant events that are not easily understood, or the detection of inconsistency among one's beliefs or between one's beliefs and actions. Because people do not like to feel afraid, to feel sorry for someone less privileged, or to feel guilty, bored, fatigued, or confused, these unpleasant states will be classified as bad; and people will want to replace, suppress, or avoid them. The acts, motives, and qualities that accomplish these goals will be good and, therefore, virtuous. But the specific concrete conditions that provoke these unpleasant emotions will differ with time and location; and so, too, will the specific acts and qualities that suppress them. If the anticipation of losing a leg while defending the polis is a frequent source of anxiety, physical courage will be a central virtue. But if a common incentive for anxiety is anticipated social rejection for holding an unpopular belief, then loyalty to private conviction will be a celebrated virtue. If the culture has a small number of impoverished citizens, it will appear to many that it is possible to eliminate poverty; and charity toward the poor will be promoted. However, if there are too many disenfranchised, as there are in India and Tibet, success will seem unattainable, and concern for the poor is likely to be replaced with celebration of a mood of detachment. In Tibet, practice of the virtue of detachment from people and material things protects each poor person from the unpleasantness of chronic envy, while the few with property avoid provoking jealousy in others by disguising their wealth.

Each of the four virtues of fifth-century Athens—courage, justice, wisdom, and restraint—had a special actualization in Athenian life that would be difficult to simulate in nineteenth-century Boston, where the comparable virtues might have been called: loyalty to personal convictions, charity toward the poor, insight into one's intentions, and moderation of ambition. Peter Geach (1977) nominates faith, hope, charity, and prudence as the basic modern virtues. Faith and hope allay the depression, sadness, and apathy that follow recognition that one cannot attain a desired goal; charity mutes sympathetically induced disquiet; and prudence is an effective prophylaxis against worry over the possible loss of wealth and reputation. Thus, each culture and historical period presents a unique profile of provocative conditions for a few unpleasant feeling states, and special opportunities for actions that prevent or alleviate these states. As a result, the concrete, morally praiseworthy characteristics that are encouraged will assume different forms.

Recognition of the relation of feelings to morality may help to explain the useful distinction between a conventional and a principled standard, because only the latter is tied to strong emotion.

Five-year-olds realize that rules of dress are conventional; but when asked whether it is all right for a particular school to allow children to hit others, they reply, "No, it is not OK." "Why not?" "Because that is like making other people unhappy. You can hurt them that way. It hurts other people; hurting is not good" (Shweder, Turiel, and Much 1981, p. 293). When an individual's affective reaction to violation of a principled standard vanishes, the standard becomes conventional. Consider, for example, the recent trend in North American films to legitimize prostitution and adultery by implying that standards for sexual behavior should be conventional. An American television play, which began with each spouse discovering the other to be unfaithful, ended happily when each forgave the other for the minor transgression. In the French film *The Return of Martin Guerre* (1983) a married woman's love for an imposter she knows is not her husband is given moral precedence over the village's loyalty to the standard on adultery. The National Film Board of Canada produced a movie about a married prostitute with a loving husband who regarded his wife's work as an honest trade—a way for her to earn a living and "pull her weight." The movie is so sympathetically done that it may change some people's feelings about prostitution. I suggest that, half a century ago, few Canadians or Americans would have regarded as conventional the standard for a married woman's sexual behavior because there was a strong affective reaction to illicit sexuality, not because that standard rested on a persuasively rational argument derived from premises about right and wrong. When the community's emotional reaction to violation of a standard is weakened, the rational argument against it also becomes fragile, and the standard can slip into conventionality, as the Brahmin's principled standard on contact with an untouchable is slowly being converted to conventionality in contemporary India.

Parents who protest violence on television sense that continued exposure to aggression will numb their children's emotional reactions, and that, as children stop feeling strong revulsion or fear toward acts of aggression, the principled standard on violence will become more conventional.

There is, therefore, a difference of opinion over the criterion for deciding whether a standard is principled or conventional. The rationalists, who were and still are in the majority among philosophers and psychologists, make the decision on the basis of the logic of an argument that defends a standard as universally applicable because of the rightness of certain moral axioms and the rationally derived ethical deductions that follow. Rawls (1971) argues that a person's sense of justice is a mental capacity involving thought and deliberation; it is definitely not an impulsive sentiment.

The classic example is that hurting another is wrong because: (1) I should not act in any way that I would not want for myself; or (2) human life and happiness are the most basic goods and, hence, any act that interferes with life and happiness must always be wrong. One or both of these arguments is usually offered as the criterion for a universal standard.

But I suggest that the average citizen, although far less articulate, relies more on feelings to come to the same decision. Parents in most societies believe that what a child sees and hears form the most significant socialization experiences. Although parents may not be able to explain why they believe in the correctness of certain standards, deep probing would, I suspect, reveal the conviction that the child who witnesses too much aggression, dishonesty, sexuality, and destruction will stop experiencing the emotions of fear, anxiety, and repugnance that sustain the standards for these acts. Most adults fear—correctly, I might add—that when emotional reactions to socially undesirable responses cease, the standard will become arbitrary and less binding.

The two arguments are complementary. Because humans prefer—or demand, as some psychologists would say—a reason for holding a standard, they invent the arguments that rationalists regard as essential. The rationalization of a standard does have inhibitory force and is not simply a gloss, for humans do not enjoy recognition of inconsistency between what they believe and what they do. But without the original emotional reaction, the standard might never have gained persuasive power. Indeed, psychologists and psychiatrists who worry about parental cruelty to children argue zealously—though on other grounds—that a child who is a target of such abuse will grow up to be a cruel parent.

Establishing a Morality

One reason many scholars have preferred to base morality on logic, rather than on feeling, is that most Western philosophers have assumed human nature to be basically selfish, cruel, and deceitful. As a result, they could not trust a person's emotion as a basis for ethical choice and had to insert the idea of will between a person's strong desire and his behavior. Will is a planful, reflective executive amenable to reason. However, because the Chinese regarded human nature as more benevolent, they could be more trusting of human instincts and did not need to rely on a rational will to ensure that children and adults would behave in a civilized manner. Additionally, the Chinese awarded greater significance to each person's awareness of his or her feeling states, while the West, especially after the Renaissance, emphasized each person's actions and their consequences.

The philosopher Bernard Williams (1971) has suggested that Kant was reluctant to acknowledge the influence of emotion on moral conduct because he supposed that adults differed biologically in their capacity for emotion; hence, they could not be equal in moral sense. But the capacity to reason, Kant insisted, was available to all persons. Finally, by insisting on the rational justification of a moral principle, philosophers hoped to make it possible to judge a moral standard as correct or incorrect. Such an evaluation cannot be applied when feelings are the basis for judging moral ideas.

I recognize that to be more persuasive this speculative argument requires better examples and closer reasoning. But if the human potential for certain feeling states is a nonrelativistic platform upon which a set of universal, or principled, moral standards can be built, then Hume was correct in his insistence that morality draws its force from sentiment, not logic, even though Hume suggested that only one emotion—sympathy—was necessary to explain all the "artificial virtues," including justice, modesty, and etiquette. Although Wittgenstein also believed that morality is based on a sense of the aesthetic, he did not want unobservable private feelings to be the basis for social consensus on ethics, apparently persuaded that some individuals might regard worry and confusion as desirable states they wished to preserve (Janik and Toulmin 1973).* Pascal's comment in *Pensées* is relevant, "We know the truth not

*Stuart Hampshire, in his recent essay, *Morality and Conflict* (1983), admits to giving up his former belief that reason is primary in morality and argues for the significance of conflict—which implies emotion.

only by reason but also by the heart. It is from this last source that we know the first principles and it is in vain that reason, which has no part in it, attempts to combat it" (Kline 1980, p. 134).

Although moral philosophers have tried to write a coherent and logically tight defense of good and bad that would deal with their society's major uncertainties, contemporary psychologists have taken a different assignment: they are more interested in each person's evaluation of self than in the evaluation of an agent's separate acts, intentions, and feelings. The evidence used to judge self's virtue is the degree to which its acts, intentions, and feelings are congruent with its personal standards. This difference in locus of concern is at the heart of a central, and still unresolved, tension.

If the priority for a moral evaluation lies with each person's loyalty to his or her personal standards—no matter what they are—then one may, on occasion, justifiably hurt others, as terrorists deeply committed to an ideology do. If, on the other hand, weight is given either to particular acts or to their consequences, one may be pressed to behave in ways that violate one's personal standards, as when a neighbor—even though reluctant—helps another at risk and, by that act, accepts ambivalently a limitation on personal freedom and makes the self vulnerable to the unpleasant feeling of moral conflict. Moral philosophers have tried, unsuccessfully thus far, to make the second criterion of morality follow rationally from the first. Perhaps each of us is persuaded of the moral rightness of an idea by two different, incommensurate processes. One is based on feelings; the other, on logical consistency with a few deep premises. When a standard derives its strength from either foundation, we find it difficult to be disloyal to its directives. When it enjoys the support of both, as it does for torture and unprovoked murder, its binding force is maximal.

The Emergence of Standards

Sometime after the middle of the second year, children become aware of standards. They will point to broken objects, torn clothing, and missing buttons, revealing in voice and face a mood of concern. A child will point to a crack in a plastic toy and say, "Oh-oh" or "Broke." When fourteen- and nineteen-month-old children were brought to a laboratory playroom that contained many toys, some of which were purposely torn or flawed (a doll's face was marked with black crayon, the head of an animal was removed), not one of the younger children, but over one half of the older ones, showed obvious preoccupation with the damaged toys. They would bring a flawed toy to their mother, point to the damaged part, stick a finger in the place where the animal's head had been removed, or, if they had language, indicate that something was wrong by saying, "Fix" or "Yukky." The two-year-old does not respond this way to all deviations from the normal, but only to those events that might have been produced by actions or events the child classifies as improper or bad. If more buttons had been added to the blouse or more bristles to the broom, or the shirt was cleaner than it had been before, the child would have responded differently or not at all.

In order to explain this new concern, we must assume that the child is beginning to make inferences about the causes of events. A child who reacts emotionally to a shirt without a button is assuming that the missing button was not an inherent property of the shirt, and that some event created the altered state. If the child infers that the missing button was produced by actions that she knows are disapproved by parents, she will become upset. The adult disapproval—be it frown, verbal chastisement, or slap in the face—elicits a state of uncertainty that becomes associated with the idea of the improper action. Thus, when the child infers that someone tore the button from the shirt, she becomes concerned. Hence, one source of standards originates in the acts that adults disapprove or punish.

The philosopher W. V. Quine, loyal to the tenets of behaviorism, insists that standards are inculcated through "slaps and sugar plums" (1981, p. 57). Quine, therefore, maximizes the power of an association between feeling and action to change ordinary ideas into moral ones:

The transmutation of means into ends ... is what underlies moral training. Many sorts of good behavior have a low initial rating on the valuation scale, and are indulged in at first only for their inductive links to higher ends: the pleasant consequences or the avoidance of unpleasant ones at the preceptor's hands. (1981, p. 57)

An alternative interpretation of the concern with a missing button assumes that the child creates representations of how events should be in their ideal state as a function of how they normally appear. Shirts should have all their buttons, toys should be without cracks, curtains should have no rips or stains. Worry, concern, or a dysphoric mood is a probable reaction to transmutation of the ideal. Although this interpretation of the child's concern does not require prior parental disapproval—an assumption that is counterintuitive and difficult to prove—I recall a two-year-old girl in a playroom who searched through all the toys looking for a small bed on which to place a small doll. The girl's parents did not tell her that small dolls should sleep on small beds; she generated that standard on her own. Similarly, a boy learning Estonian at home and English in his day-care center began to use each language in its appropriate context soon after his second birthday, despite the absence of any sudden increase in parental or teacher punishment for speaking English at home or Estonian at the center (Vihman 1983). It is as if the child suddenly appreciated which language was proper in each setting.

Further, two-year-olds react with interest, and occasionally with anxiety, to pictures of people who have distorted faces or bodies (Kagan 1971). Both American and Mayan Indian two-year-old children from villages in the Yucatan peninsula look longer at a picture of a human face with distorted features than at a normal face. The children's verbalizations ("What happened to his nose?" or "Who hit him in the nose?") imply a concern with the causes of the damaged face and contain inferences about the events that might have produced the distortions. These observations suggest that children are ready to react with anxious concern to events that violate their understanding of the normal appearance of things.

A second basis for standards comes from the capacity for empathy with another (Hoffman 1981). Most two-year-olds have experienced the discomfort that comes from being hit, spanked, or bruised. When the child becomes capable of inferring that others also experience discomfort in the same situations, actions that hurt another will be treated as violations of standards. Jerome Bruner (1983) notes, "It is a primitive that other minds are treated as if they were like our own minds" (1983, p. 122). We know that two-year-olds are capable of inference; for, by the middle of the second year, they will infer that a nonsense word—"zoob" for example—might be the name of an unfamiliar object, and their speech and behavior imply an ability to infer the private feeling states of others (Novey 1975; Zahn-Waxler, Radke-Yarrow, and King 1979). An observation of two three-and-a-half-year-old boys who were playing in our laboratory provides a persuasive illustration of empathic understanding. One of the boys had dominated the other for the first thirty minutes of play. But when the intimidated boy put on the single Batman costume, the other boy immediately wanted the costume but was sufficiently socialized not to seize it. The formerly passive child suddenly realized that he had achieved symbolic power, and paraded around the room showing off his prize. And then, as if he understood the jealousy he was generating in the more aggressive boy, said, "You can hate me if you want."

A third source of standards emerges when the child realizes that he can or cannot attain a goal through use of his talents. Two-year-olds become very upset if they are unable to meet a standard for mastery imposed by another person. When a woman approaches a child, picks up some toys, acts out some brief sequences that are difficult to remember or to implement, and then returns to her chair, children from diverse cultural settings will immediately cry or protest (Kagan 1981). It is unlikely that these children had been punished for failing to imitate either their parent or another adult. Therefore, we can eliminate a conditioned or acquired fear of punishment as a basis for the distress. I believe that the child invents an obligation to duplicate the adult's actions and, additionally, knows that she is unable to do so. The combination of awareness of a standard for a performance to be met with an inability to meet that standard is the basis for the crying and protest. However, children who do meet a self-imposed standard will show signs of joy: the two-year-old typically smiles spontaneously after spending several minutes building a six-block tower or finishing a difficult puzzle. The child does not look at anyone as she smiles; it is a private response reflecting the recognition that she has met the standard she set for herself. If an adult should try to take over the puzzle before its completion, the child is likely to resist.

Many years ago, while walking on the outskirts of a small Indian village located in the sparsely settled highlands of northwest Guatemala, I came upon a three-year-old molding some moist clay into what seemed like crude tortillas. As I came closer, the boy looked up, then looked down at the clay, and blushed in embarrassment as if acknowledging that he knew his misshapen tortilla was an imperfect replica. Once the child is capable of an idea of a terminal state to be attained through effort and is aware of his ability to initiate actions that might attain that state, the experience of attainment is good, as long as the action has not been subject to adult disapproval and does not harm another. The last two caveats are necessary, for no child regards the careful tearing of a shirt as good, even though it requires a plan and effort; and the capacity for empathy with another forms a universal foundation for regarding restraint on aggression as good.

The recognition of a future state of affairs that can be gained through the use of one's abilities—what psychologists call *mastery*—creates an obligation to attempt to actualize that state. Because success is accompanied by a pleasant state and failure by an unpleasant one, the representation of the future goal meets my earlier definition of a standard. Unlike the standards on destruction or dirty hands, the standard on mastery is not an obvious product of tutoring or of a prior association with pain or comfort, but seems to be as endogenous a process as hunger or walking.

The evaluation of an act as bad is extended to the self during the third and fourth years. A mother in one of our studies found her three-year-old boy pinching himself with force. To her request for a reason for the self-inflicted pain, he replied, "I don't like myself." It is relevant to add that this boy was aggressive with other children in the neighborhood and was aware that both the children and their parents disapproved of his behavior. Many parents have noted that their four-year-old children deliberately misbehave in order to be punished and often ask their parents, "Do you love me? or "Am I good?" By age four, children treat their dreams as bad or good. A four-year-old girl told her mother she had done something naughty. When pressed to explain, the girl confessed to dreaming that her infant brother had died after being stung by a bee.

How is it possible for a child to classify dreams or thoughts as bad or good when they are private and, therefore, insulated from approval or disapproval? Why is the thought "I hate my mother" evaluated as bad, while "I think about my mother" is neither good nor bad? One possibility is that, early in development, the child believes that thoughts and acts are equivalent. This assumption is supported by the four-year-old who was upset by the dream of her brother's death. But the assumption is rendered less likely by the fact that a four-year-old will, without equivocation, tell an interrogator that thinking of ice cream is not equivalent to eating it, or that thinking of wrestling with a friend or kicking a ball is not the same as entering into either activity. Because the child does not believe in the equivalence of thought and action in such contexts, why should the child regard "dreaming" or "just thinking of hurting" as bad?

A more likely possibility is that the child believes others can detect some of his thoughts, especially hostile ideas. The child learns to diagnose anger in a parent through frown, gesture, action, and voice and may assume that if he can diagnose anger in another, the parent must be able to diagnose anger in him. Because the three-year-old can empathize with the feelings of another, he realizes that the person he dislikes privately would feel distressed upon discovering that fact. Thus, hostile thoughts can hurt another and, therefore, are bad.

The evaluation of self as bad is not a welcome categorization, and the child is motivated to avoid recognition of that fact. Hence, the potential to classify self as bad is a source of inhibition on the violation of standards. Because this dynamic is operative early in development, I suggest that the inhibition of aggressive behavior in young children is not based solely on fear of adult punishment but is supported by self-condemnation, even though few four-year-olds would say so if a parent asked them why, when frustrated, they did not strike another person.

Parents from diverse cultures recognize that, by the third birthday, children are aware of standards on prohibited behavior and are expected to regulate such behavior by their seventh birthday. The Utku Eskimo of Hudson Bay call this awareness *ihuma* (translated as "reason"); the Fijians call it *vakayalo* ("sense of what is proper"). Both cultures believe it is futile to punish children until they have acquired the ability to recognize the difference between right and wrong. Around the world, two- and three-year-olds begin to reflect on the correctness, the competence, and the appropriateness of their actions before, during, and after execution. They compare their behavior, thoughts, and feelings against the standard and try to keep in close accord with the standard, as a space vehicle's program corrects its course in flight.

The relation between close monitoring of the correctness of one's behavior and a vulnerability to distress following violation of a standard can be observed during the period when this new ability is being elaborated. Three- and four-year-old children were asked to draw a familiar object (a tree, an animal, or a person). One week later, they were shown four drawings of a particular object, only one of which was their own (the other three, similar in appearance, were drawn by other children). Each child was asked to point to the drawing he or she had completed one week earlier. Additionally, each child's play was observed before and after an experience of failure, when the examiner showed a child a toy airplane constructed of blocks and requested him or her to duplicate the object with an identical set of blocks. The task was beyond the children's capacity, and none completed it. The disruption in play after the experience of failure was regarded as an index of the degree of uncertainty generated by failure to meet the standard imposed by the adult. The children who were best at remembering their drawings, presumably because they reflected on the quality of their performance at the time, were most upset by their failure to meet the adult standard, as revealed in a large decrease in play following failure. Some children said later, "I could do it now," or "I want to try it again" (Nolan 1979).

The behaviorists' explanation of a new action relies on the psychological consequences of that action. But this force for change, although operative on many occasions, does not seem helpful in accounting for the smile following mastery or the distress after task failure. It is unlikely that the three-year-old's upset after being unable to finish a puzzle is a generalized response traceable to parental punishment for failing to finish breakfast or to complete a sentence correctly. Rather, as nineteenth-century theorists suspected, the child is biologically prepared to acquire standards. I do not suggest that exposure to adults who praise the proper and punish the improper is irrelevant, but I believe that all children have a capacity to generate ideas about good and bad states, actions, and outcomes. Hume regarded moral sentiments as "so rooted in our constitution and temper, that without entirely confounding the human mind by disease or madness, 'tis impossible to extirpate and destroy them" (1969 [1739–40], p. 526). Why should an appreciation of standards emerge so early in development, long before language and motor coordination are mature, and a decade before reproductive fertility? One possibility is that a sense of right and wrong, an awareness of one's ability to hurt another, and the capacity to empathize with a victim are accidental accompaniments to the more fundamental competences of retrieval memory, symbolism, planfulness, and language. But it is also reasonable that these distinctly human characteristics appear early in development because they are necessary for the socialization of aggressive and destructive behavior. In most parts of the world, mothers give birth to the next infant about two to three years after birth of the previous child. The three-year-old has both the strength to inflict injury on a younger sibling and, more important, is able to retain hostile ideas long after a brief bout of anger has subsided. The aggressive behavior that can be the product of jealousy a three-year-old feels toward a younger sibling must be held in check. It would be adaptive if all three-year-olds appreciated that certain behaviors were wrong, and were aware of their ability to inhibit such actions. Without this fundamental human capacity, which nineteenth-century observers called a *moral sense,* the child could not be socialized.

Faith in the inevitability of conscience was lost during the fifty years between the First World War and the end of our Vietnam involvement—a period when Locke's view of an unprejudiced child was revitalized and promoted by the disciples of behaviorism. During this period, many psychologists declared that all children had to learn the meaning of good and bad; and that if environmental experiences were not properly orchestrated, it was possible for a person to be without any understanding of right and wrong—to be a moral imbecile. The psychiatric diagnosis of *psychopath* is applied explicitly to persons who commit acts of aggression unaccompanied by remorse or guilt, and implies the possibility of adults, neither mentally defective nor insane, who do not know that rape, torture, and murder are wrong. But, as the British writer James Sulley noted in 1896, all children must, because they are human, realize that causing hurt to another is immoral. Such knowledge can never be lost, regardless of any subsequent cruelty the child may have experienced. The child does not have to be taught that hurting others is bad; that insight accompanies growth.

It was necessary, however, to have a psychological mechanism for transforming the competence contained in the appreciation of right and wrong into the capacity for proper behavior. Will played that role for the nineteenth-century theorists. According to William Preyer,

All muscular movements of man may, in fact, be distinguished as willed and not willed, voluntary and involuntary. . . . The development of will . . . and the development of non-willing . . . in the inhibition of frequently repeated movements furnishes the foundation for the formation of character. (1888, p 193)

Will is the union of a mental representation of a goal with the behavior necessary to attain that goal. Will is active, deliberate, and selective and assumes an executive able to choose among alternatives. Will was so central to late nineteenth- and early twentieth-century writers that it was occasionally given a place in the explanatory equation equal to, and independent of, both heredity and environment. The author of one popular text on child psychology implied that will is a special organ every child possesses to a sufficient degree to oppose or to enhance the influence of both biology and family (Forbush 1915).

Thus, through the first decade of this century, the child's character was conceptualized in an absolutist frame. The disposition to adopt a uniform set of proper actions was rooted in biology and universal experiences and implemented by an autonomous will. But, surprisingly, by 1920, this view had vanished. Pragmatism, moral relativism, and conditioning theory had created a profound alteration in the explanation of a child's ethical stance. The new theorists emphasized interactive experience within the family, replaced free will with motives and habits, and became preoccupied with individual differences in the child's adjustment.

The emphasis on social experience as the source of important psychological qualities affected theories on the establishment of standards. Textbooks in child psychology written just before the First World War began to modulate the earlier emphasis on the maturation of a moral sense and awarded greater potency, but not yet total power, to specific experiences with adults. Gabriel Compayré, rector of the University of Lyons and author of a two-volume treatise on the young child, argued that, although imitation, which was an inherited competence, was the basis of socialization of values, the adults to whom the child is exposed determine what responses the child will imitate and acquire. Compayré rejected the assumption of an innate moral sense and asserted that morality is acquired gradually, with pleasure and pain as the necessary catalysts:

This is why it is not an anachronism to think from the cradle of the responsibility, the moral obligations, that will one day rest on the head of the little child, smiling now in his unconscious innocence, his ideas and his feeling only the reflections of those of his parents; just as his left cheek or his right cheek, when he has finished nursing, like one side of a peach gilded by the sun, remains very red for several minutes, warmed as it is by the touch of the mother's breast. (1914, p. 185)

Following the dissemination of Pavlovian theory at the end of the First World War, the child's morality became just another habit that might not appear if conditions were not arranged properly: "Unless a good many habit systems are gradually built into a child's conduct he cannot be expected to operate with any large degree of judgment and freedom. . . . Moral behavior . . . is not an innate tendency. . . . it is a by-product of social living" (Chave 1937, p. 164).

By the middle of the third decade, the doctrine of moral relativism was so firmly entrenched in American schools that articles in the *Journal of the National Educational Association* legitimized the confusion teachers felt over the character traits they were supposed to encourage. Essays typical of this period asked, "How can a teacher know what habits should be formed by children? How can she know the relative importance of these habits? How can she know whether progress is being made in the development of these habits?" Teachers were told to consult inventories of character traits written by experts, as though pedagogical guidance in this domain could be obtained with the same strategy used in geography and history.

By the Second World War, there was no waffling on the theme

of moral relativism. The best child was the one who had been trained to meet the local environmental demands of achieving educational, vocational, and social success and, above all, freedom to actualize his or her special set of motives and talents. The assumption of a core set of uniform moral directives that every child was disposed to practice had become hopelessly obsolete, because all moral standards and the disposition to act morally were acquired through careful titration of reward and punishment.

Thus, half a century after The First World War, in an essay on moral values, Quine could write, "In language as in morality the uniformity is achieved by instruction (1981, p. 61); and, "It is hard to pick out a single distinguishing feature of moral values, beyond the vague matter of being somehow irreducibly social" (p. 58).

CONSISTENCY BETWEEN BELIEF AND ACTION

In addition to punishment, disapproval, and the capacity to feel empathy, to recognize deviations from norms, and to generate ideal outcomes, two other mechanisms, operative later in development, mediate the acquisition and maintenance of standards. One is a need for cognitive consistency among beliefs, actions, and the perceived demands of reality. The second is identification with others.

During the years just before puberty—the developmental interval that Piaget calls the *concrete operational stage*—children develop standards for judging the validity of propositions. The primary meaning of *true* for the seven-year-old, as well as for the adult, is consistency in the application of a certain symbolic description to an event: it is false to call a tree a piece of cake. But the degree of logical consistency among related propositions, and the consistency between a belief and related behavior, also invite a validity check whose outcome implies the goodness of the belief. For the ten-year-old, actions that are inconsistent with beliefs provoke feelings of uncertainty. "Keeping one's clothes clean" is a standard for a three-year-old because failure to do so is a violation of a learned prohibition. But ten-year-olds perceive that they have a choice that three-year-olds do not, and some older children need cognitive support for holding the standard on cleanliness because it is inconsistent with another standard for personal autonomy. Some children find it intolerable to regard the self as being afraid of parental displeasure; obeying a parental command because of fear of a parent violates an important age-role standard. When the child believes he or she has a choice—a competence that emerges before the fourth birthday—a new standard arises: consistency among beliefs and between beliefs and behavior.

If the child keeps her clothes clean regularly, she wants to believe that the habit is proper. The child regards the action as good simply because she must perform it, and that evaluation meets the standard for consistency. If an act is required by the inferred demands of reality, the child is likely to invent reasons for its propriety. The child goes to school, sits at a desk, and is quiet in the library because violations of those rules are not permitted. The child is persuaded to believe in the goodness of such behavior, even if she never violates those rules and, therefore, never experiences adult disapproval. Most eight-year-olds regard obedience to parents as a good quality, while many adolescents regard it as immature. The difference between the two groups is due, in part, to the fact that the younger children cannot avoid an obedient stance and so accept it. Adolescents can avoid that posture and, therefore, need to defend it. Forcing a child to practice particular behavior is one way to tempt the child to evaluate it positively.

There is no general principle that predicts what will happen when there is a conflict between a standard based on a need for consistency between belief and behavior and a standard based on prior prohibitions by authority. The consequences of that tension depend on the specific action and context. After puberty, when the ability to detect logical discord in the total system of beliefs is amplified, detection of inconsistency among beliefs leads youth to work on the inconsistent elements and change them. Thus, one function of knowledge is to change standards so that they are in better accord with what is perceived as fact.

The original founders of the Israeli kibbutzim believed it was good to put children in nurseries, because the relation with the caregiver was supposed to prevent both an overly close tie between mother and child and excessive dependence upon the parent later in development. Two generations later, the standard is weaker, because young mothers now believe it is good to have a closer emotional tie to their infants. One factual basis for the change in standard was a loss of status in the vocational roles of women on kibbutzim.

Profound changes in standards can occur later in life when cumulative experience condenses on facts that went unrecognized earlier. The forty-five-year-old woman who believed it was good to subordinate her personal autonomy and desires to the needs of her husband and children confronts the invalidation of that idea when both her children and husband abandon her in the same year. As events make it difficult to hold current standards, new ones are generated. In his autobiographical essay Jean-Paul Sartre (1964) said that as a young man he believed his essays were morally good because of their benevolent effects on an anguished community. When he lost faith in that idea he realized that he wrote because he was unable to do otherwise.

CONCEPTUALIZATION OF SELF

During the second through the sixth year, the child establishes an increasingly articulated conceptualization of the self as an object. Like the concepts *animal, eating,* and *justice,* the concept of self rests on two complementary sources of evidence. The intrinsic base consists of qualities that have an absolute character and do not derive their meaning primarily through comparison with others. These qualities involve the conscious awareness of feelings and intentions; the sense of belonging to certain ethnic, religious, racial, age, and sex categories; and physical characteristics like color of hair and eyes. The realization "I am a happy, ten-year-old, brown-eyed, Catholic, Chicano boy" contains six of these dimensions.

The first signs of self-awareness appear at the same time as an appreciation of standards. One such sign is the active direction of others. The child puts a toy telephone to the mother's ear, indicates that he wants her to change her chair, asks for help with a problem, or requests the mother to make a funny sound. These directives to adults are not aimed at obtaining a specific material object—the child does not want a cookie or a toy. Rather, the child's goal seems to be simply to influence the adult's behavior. Because the child would not issue such commands if he did not believe the parent would obey, we assume that the child has an expectancy of his ability to effect a change in adult action and—as significant—an appreciation of his ability to alter the behavior of others.

The two-year-old can recognize a picture of himself; and if, while looking at a mirror, he sees a spot of rouge on his nose (placed there by his mother without the child's knowing), he will touch his nose as if he knows that the face reflected in the mirror belongs to himself (Lewis and Brooks-Gunn 1979).

When the child begins to speak predicates, usually after the second birthday, she begins to describe her own actions as she is performing them, often using pronouns like *I, me,* or *mine* to refer to the self. The child says, "Up," as she climbs up on a chair; "Go out," as she runs outside; "I fix," as she tries to rebuild a fallen tower of blocks; or "Mary get cookie," as she goes to the kitchen. Because the child is more likely to describe her own activities than the same behavior in others, we assume the child has become preoccupied with her actions. Several months earlier, when the child first began to speak, she was likely to name the objects whose words she was just mastering, as if the realization that she knew the name of a toy excited her enough to produce the spontaneous utterance. The two-year-old's insight is that she has become aware of her ability to act, to influence others, and to meet her own standards. These are such exciting experiences that she describes her actions as she performs them. It is probably not a coincidence that deaf children who are learning American sign language begin to display signs that refer to the self at the same age hearing children begin to describe their actions (Petitto 1983). This remarkable temporal coincidence suggests the maturation of a competence that permits a conscious awareness of self as an entity.

By the third birthday, the sense of self has become extended to include a sense of possession. The following interaction between two three-year-old boys who were total strangers to each other provides an example of this characteristic. On four separate occasions during the first twenty minutes of a play session, child B took from child A some toy in the latter's territory. Child A did nothing to each of the four seizures: he did not protest, cry, whine, retaliate, or retreat to his mother for help. But a few minutes after the fourth seizure, he walked deliberately across the room, took a toy that child B had been playing with earlier but had just pushed aside, and brought it back to his territory. Several minutes later, while child A was playing with a wagon, child B came over and tried to take it. On this occasion, child A held on to it and successfully resisted child B's attempt at appropriation.

We have to explain first why child A retrieved the toy child B pushed aside; and, equally important, why child A resisted child B on the fifth occasion when he had not done so on the first four. Most of the time the best prediction of one's future action is one's previous behavior in the same situation. But that rule does not work all of the time. The reason for child A's resistant reaction must lie within him, for the external situation had not changed at all. What had changed as a result of four prior losses of his toys? The answer requires some idea of a sense of possession—a feeling that one has the control of and access to certain objects, even though the child may be encountering those objects for the first time. Uncertainty is generated when the sense of possession is disconfirmed by the seizure and loss. One reaction to the uncertainty is an attempt to reaffirm the sense of possession; hence, the child resists additional seizures and tries to take the other child's toys in order to prove that he is able to maintain possession. These descriptions imply the existence of a *self* that can possess objects and maintain control over them.

This first phase in the establishment of a sense of self consists essentially of a conscious awareness of intentions, feelings, standards, and the ability to attain a goal. A second, different basis for the conceptualization of self becomes important a few years later and is the result of comparative evaluations of self in relation to others, especially other children. Now the child ascribes to self a position on a psychological or a physical dimension that reflects a perception of the degree to which he or she possesses that quality in relation to other children. As confidently as a girl will say that a dog is bigger than a fly, she will say that she is kinder than her brother but not as brave as her sister. Some comparative qualities, like intelligence, may eventually come to be treated as absolutes. An adult may classify the self as intelligent and courageous in an absolute sense, although earlier the classification has been based on a comparison with others. The belief that a set of absolute and comparative qualities is part of the self's repertoire is acquired through several mechanisms—inferences based on the regular consequences of one's actions, comparing qualities of self with others, and identification. I now consider identification as a mechanism with implications for the acquisition of standards.

Establishing a Morality

By the fourth year, children have an unconscious appreciation of some of their psychological qualities, and an identification begins with the belief that some of the distinctive qualities of another person belong to the self. The other person can be parent, sibling, relative, friend, or even a fictional character. A boy realizes that he and his father have the same family name and the same bright red hair, and is told by relatives that he and the father both have a warm hearty laugh. In time, the boy comes to believe that he is similar to the parent in distinctive ways. The child goes beyond those facts and assumes that the self must have other psychological qualities that belong to the parent, even though he has no objective evidence for that inference. This inference, so critical for the consequences of an identification, is an example of the universal human tendency to assume that if two objects share some qualities, they probably share others that have not been observed directly.

When the belief in psychological similarity to another is associated with the experience of a vicarious emotion that seems appropriate to the model, the child is said to have established an identification. A girl who is identified with a mother whom she regards as intelligent will experience the pride that might occur if the girl had objective evidence of her own ability, based on her own performance. By contrast, if a girl whose parent is dishonest assumes that undesirable quality belongs to her, she will feel ashamed. In these examples, the child's emotional state is more appropriate to the parent than to the self.

A group of pre-adolescent boys who either had serious academic problems, or were rejected by most of their classmates, denied possessing these qualities when asked directly, because they knew these characteristics were undesirable. However, when these boys watched a film depicting a contest between a boy who had been described as popular (or academically competent) and one described as unpopular (or academically incompetent), they showed greater empathic, emotional involvement with the boy in the film who possessed their undesirable characteristics (Kagan et al. 1982).

Identification and the Acquisition of Standards   The child typically classifies as good a model who commands desirable characteristics—like nurturance, kindness, competence, and power—and wishes to establish or strengthen an identification with that person. One strategy is to maximize similarity to the model by adopting the model's standards. This mechanism is most obvious for those standards that are not usually subject to direct sanctions. Consider a six-year-old who hears his admired father state emphatically, "Always stand up to a bully," or, "Never give money to a stranger." Both standards might be accepted because they persuade the child that he is similar to an emulated model, not because the child fears punishment for their violation. The model's attractiveness lends persuasive power to the standard, as a Madison Avenue testimonial transfers attractiveness to a particular brand of skis.

As with standards established initially through adult approval or disapproval, standards adopted through identification can be transferred later to more abstract sponsors. The young child may acquire a standard for kindness through identification with the father and, in adolescence, amplify that role to a standard that regards all killing as immoral. The readiness with which this form of transfer occurs will depend on the child's relation to, and admiration for, the model. With development, all models lose some glamour, and a standard can become fragile when models develop clay feet. A young Catholic college student from the rural southwest, who had been deeply religious since early childhood, began to question his faith after attending mass for nine months in a large northeastern city because he perceived the priests as indifferent and uncommitted and therefore as violating his standards of religiosity.

Identification and Sex-Role Standards. As children come to recognize the age, sex, and ethnic categories to which they belong—partly as a result of identification—they assume that they should match their qualities to the proper category. If an object is a member of a category, it should have all the characteristics of that category. If it does not, feelings of disquiet are generated. The child believes that what is true about me is proper for me. Thus a boy assumes, "If boys do not cry, and I am a boy, then I should not cry." Similarly, a girl will experience uncertainty if she does not behave in accord with her definition of what is feminine.

Although many of the qualities that compose the standards for masculine and feminine behavior are communicated to the child directly, it is likely that some are invented. Carol Gilligan (1982) suggests that women treat socially supportive relationships as taking priority over those defined by hierarchy or power. Most cultures assume that aggression and domination come easier to men than to women, and children as young as four years of age agree with these characterizations of the sexes (Maccoby 1980). It is possible that because pregnancy and infant care, which are nurturant and life supportive, are uniquely associated with women, all children invent the idea that concern for the feelings and welfare of others is central to femininity, and that hurting and violating the trust of another are more serious violations of the standard for femaleness than of that for maleness. Hume used a variation of this argument to explain sex differences in modesty and control of licentiousness, stating that while courage is the primary standard for men, avoidance of social disapproval is the more pressing standard for women.

Every class of human activity is potentially vulnerable to being linked to the standard that describes culturally appropriate sex-role behavior. Even the work of the school can fall within this sphere. Because teachers in the primary grades of most American classrooms are women, the young child may conclude that the objects and the acts associated with school are feminine rather than masculine. Second-grade children in a small midwestern town were taught to label obviously masculine objects with the nonsense word *dep* and obviously feminine ones with the nonsense word *rov*. After the children had learned to apply these words quickly and correctly to pictures of men and women's clothing, baseball bats, and lipstick, they were shown pictures of objects that normally appear in school classrooms. The majority of both boys and girls applied the feminine *rov* to pictures of a blackboard, a book, a page of arithmetic, and a picture of a boy and a girl sitting at a school desk, but the masculine *dep* to a boat and a navigator's map (Kagan 1964).

Age and Role Standards   Children as young as three years have acquired some idea of the qualities appropriate to different ages. Four-year-old children were shown drawings of scenes and asked to decide how the person in a scene might feel. The children indicated their answer by pointing to one of eight schematic faces that were drawn to indicate mild or intense anger, sadness, fright, or happiness. In one scene, a person had grabbed a shovel from a baby, a child, or an adult. A second scene illustrated a baby, a child, or an adult in the middle of a large puddle. Over three quarters of the children reported that a baby would feel sad in these situations, but that the adult would be mad. (Lusk 1978).

Four-year-olds categorize the infant as vulnerable to anxiety, distress, and impotence. Adults, by contrast, are viewed as powerful agents who become angry rather than frightened in response to threat. One reason that children want to move toward maturity is that the adult role is attractive to them.

Thus, by the third birthday, children are aware of the age categories of infant, child, and adult and, further, recognize that it is good to behave in ways appropriate to the older age. Hence, the child wishes to adopt the standards adults want socialized. An anecdote is instructive. A three-year-old girl who still used a pacifier was regularly asked to give it up because it was inappropriate. One month before her third birthday, she told her mother, "On my birthday I'm going to throw my pacifier into the garbage." The mother forgot about the child's promise. On the morning of her birthday, she called her mother to her room and, pointing to the wastebasket, said proudly, "Look." In the bottom of the basket lay the pacifier. Three-year-olds appreciate different age roles, evaluate the younger role as undesirable, and are able consciously to plan to adopt behavior definitive of the more mature role. Further, meeting the standard for an age role is associated with a pleasant affective state. The same girl, who had been chastised earlier for smearing her feces in the bathroom, told her mother the next day, "I'm sad and happy. I'm sad because I made a mess. I'm happy because I'm not going to do it again."

The imperative quality of any standard can be based on more than one mechanism. The standard of kindness, for example, can be based on identification, on approval of authority, and on empathy with another. All three mechanisms are operative by seven years of age, and the balance among them depends on cultural conditions. The reason for differentiating among the sources of a standard is that it is likely that the emotion generated by violation of a standard, as well as its resistance to change, will depend both on its origin and on contemporary sustaining forces. Adult sanctions and identification with parents are formative during the first decade. Peer approval becomes ascendant during pre-adolescence. During late adolescence and adulthood, after formal operations have emerged, logical consistency between standards and the facts of experience becomes salient. Adults in Western society find it easier to ignore a standard based only on social approval because they place a high value on a private, autonomous conscience. Standards based on an identification are more difficult to alter, especially those that spring from membership in sex, age, class, or race categories. However, the consciousness raising among women in America and Western Europe during the last decade has had dramatic effects on existing sex-role standards. Thus all standards are at risk; none is assured permanence.

Standards as a Source of Motives

Standards are an important source of motivation because the child wants to reassure the self of its moral goodness. The concrete events that inform a child that he or she has met a standard become goals to attain. The child who believes it is good to be obedient has a motive to obey the parents; the child who believes it is good to be intelligent has a desire to obtain high grades. Thus, for some children and adolescents, the desire to obtain a sign that one is valued by parents is based on the belief that one ought to be loved. The experience sought is not contained in any particular parental act or sensory experience, for a kiss, a smile, a gift, or permission to go to a movie might satisfy the motive. Among the Inuit, for example, teasing of young children is common, and five-year-old Eskimo children want to be teased because they regard this form of adult attention as reflecting their importance in the family.

Because each person is motivated to validate a morally positive evaluation of self, individuals seek to find signs of moral flaw in those who have the power to award to self the desired prizes, but have failed to do so. The discovery of moral taint in another makes it easier for the individual to devalue the goals that have been difficult to obtain. A person who cannot gratify a motive he regards as highly virtuous will try to replace the unattainable goal with a more attainable one that also devalues the one that was missed. It is possible, for example, to interpret the ancient Hebrew insistence on the values of morality and wisdom, in contrast to wealth and secular power, as an ideological solution to the stark comparison of the Hebrews' nomadic, impoverished existence with the material advantages of their neighbors on either side, the Egyptians and the Mesopotamians. Thus, some of human motivation is partly a moral enterprise and, as such, provides a way to understand a person's changing hierarchy of motives.

Many Western philosophers concerned with the roots of goal-directed action have recognized that hedonism often loses to morality, and they have tried to solve this apparent paradox in different ways. John Stuart Mill assumed that the pleasures of mind were more salient than those of the senses. The utilitarians glossed over the problem by letting happiness be whatever the individual decides it should be, implicitly allowing uncritical readers to assume sensory pleasure to be the basis of all happiness.

Freud solved the problem by awarding primacy to the motives derived from the id, which he believed to be biological in origin. Motives related to standards were seen as inhibitory, rather than initiatory, of goal-related behavior and were assigned to the superego. The combination of materialism and Darwinian evolutionary theory, which dominated late nineteenth-century thought, rendered reasonable the suggestion that, because human motives had a phylogenetic basis, they should be classified by quality and intensity of affect. Sexuality and aggression are two classes of purposeful behavior that meet these criteria in an obvious way. The potential flaw in Freud's theorizing was the assumption that the sensory pleasures that come from the gratification of hunger and sexuality have a natural priority over the desire to regard the self as good. But these two goals need not be opposed, and are not when sensory pleasure is part of the community's definition of virtue, as it is for many modern Americans. The desires for sensory pleasure and the wish to perceive the self as good are complementary, rooted in biology, and emerge early in development.

The Violation of Standards

The quality of the emotional experience that follows behavior inconsistent with a standard is influenced by at least two factors. The first is whether the child believes other people know or will learn of the violation. The second is the assumption of personal responsibility for the violation: How much choice does the agent perceive he had after committing an improper act that hurt another? Combinations of these two factors create four outcomes differing in experiential quality. The agent feels what, in English, we call *guilt* when he perceives a choice of actions and believes that no one knows about the violation (the child broods on his hostility toward the parent). The agent who believes that she has no choice, and that others know of the violation (the child accidentally trips another), is likely to feel shame. The agent who senses no choice, and knows that no one knows of the violation (the child dreams of murdering a parent), is likely to feel anxiety. Finally, the agent who believes she has a choice, and that others know of the violation (the child purposely upsets the family dinner), feels a combination of both shame and guilt.

It is not useful to quarrel about the specific names given to these emotional states. Psychologists, as Hobbes said of Aristotle, often confuse the study of the meaning of words with study of the things for which the words stand. The words only lull us into thinking we have explained something. What is important is that the emotional experiences following these conditions are different. Children hold standards they know others share before they realize they have control over, and are responsible for, related actions. Hence, shame normally precedes guilt in development. But, by the fourth year, all children appreciate that they have some power of choice for many actions.

Coincident with this recognition is the appearance of self-blame. A three-and-a-half-year-old girl traveling in a car with her mother lost a toy balloon through the open window of the car. The mother offered to stop the car and return to find the child's balloon. The child surprised the mother by acknowledging that she lost it through her negligence and, therefore, it was not necessary to retrace the journey. The mother did return anyway, and the child was overjoyed when they found the balloon. A two-year-old would have screamed until the balloon was back in her tight fist.

Societies, too, differ in the degree to which their members believe they have a choice in ethical situations. In small communities where all villagers share the same values, and most deviations will be known by almost everyone within twenty-four hours, shame may be more frequent than in large urban areas where many violations are private. An adult man living in a Kipsigis community in Western Kenya told an interviewer (who was posing moral dilemmas to him), "When one hears someone talking about him, saying, 'Oh, why did he do that?', then his heart is frightened. . . . A person realizes that something is bad only when others have seen him" (Harkness, Edwards, and Super 1981, p. 602). Most American parents believe that children must come to realize that they are responsible for their actions, so that the older child will adhere to standards when family members are no longer present as sources of restraint. Hence, these parents award children more opportunity for choice than do parents in subsistence farming villages.

Although all adults are capable of experiencing both private self-condemnation as well as the feeling that accompanies anticipated criticism from others, societies differ in the balance between these two different bases for adhering to private standards and community norms. The reasons for the differences are likely to be multiple and complex. Diversity of values is one relevant factor. In order for anticipated social rejection over violation of a standard to be effective, there has to be consensus on basic values among most of the people one meets. The extraordinary heterogeneity of values among class, religious, and ethnic groups in the United States and Europe guarantees that each person can count on disapproval of his or her values from some people each and every day. As a result, each must rely on a personal ethic. The decision not to lie to a loved one, not to steal from a friend, or to ignore a sick parent, despite temptation, is likely to be due to a desire to avoid feelings of self-condemnation.

In other societies—Japan, for example—an important source of inhibition on the same temptations is the anticipation of criticism and social rejection by those with whom one wants to maintain a close relationship over an extended time. As I have indicated, Japanese parents encourage a state of psychological interdependence in their children and tell them that, in violating a standard, they will threaten their reciprocal relation to their family and to others outside the home. Japanese children are supposed to worry about angering people, for the guiding principle in social interaction is to avoid friction or hostility and to maintain harmonious relationships. Cicero, too, regarded as dangerous a conscience completely divorced from the opinions of others. "Greatness of soul," he wrote, "disunited from the company of men becomes a kind of uncouth ferocity." Spinoza regarded a person who lived according to the common laws of his society as freer than one who "obeys himself alone" (cited in Wolfson 1962, p. 260). But many American children are told that they alone must decide, through thought, what is right and what is wrong. The child is not to be afraid of social rejection for upholding an unpopular standard, for each person must do what he or she believes is right. This belief is not restricted to the middle-class family. A mother who left school in the tenth grade, and was living alone on welfare with her two daughters, told an interviewer about her wishes for her three-year-old: "I don't want her to be scared of anybody. She has to decide what to do and what to get on her own, not because someone wants her to do it."

It is not surprising that continued exposure to one of these two different regimens produces adults who differ in their profiles of anticipated guilt, shame, and anxiety for violating standards. The modern celebration of a private conscience, inoculated against all social opinion, appears to be a historic fact and not a profound insight about human nature or a statement of what should be a universally sacred good.

There may have occurred over the last three hundred years a change in the conscious feelings surrounding standards on desires for sexuality, power, aggression, fame, and wealth. Seventeenth- and eighteenth-century Puritans were tempted by the same desires that provoke modern American adults; but, among Puritans, the standard called for inhibition of excessive striving for these prizes. No adult was supposed to gain too much wealth, seek excessive recognition, or always gratify his or her sexual longings. As a result, each person could, through self-denial, reassure the self of its value and worth. More plainly, an adult who was tempted by, but nonetheless rejected, the initiation of a sexual liaison with a willing companion could feel a temporary sense of virtue by that act of restraint. It is more difficult for an adult in modern America to praise self for the same self-control because the culture values maximization of pleasure.

Each person needs to believe that he or she is a person of moral worth. The Puritan could partially meet this requirement simply by temperance—the control of excessive desire—and prudence. But note that inhibiting a desire requires no assistance from other people or chance. Each person holds the power to reassure self of its goodness. One is, to use Emerson's term, self-reliant.

The contemporary Western adult finds it much more difficult to praise self for not giving into temptations. Indeed, an American is likely to be teased by friends for excessive self-denial. But the modern adult is not free of the burden of supplying self with knowledge of its value. A vocation with status, high economic reward, and a gratifying love relation, are among the criteria of a good life. But the average person cannot attain these goals simply by willing them. Each adult is forced to be more dependent than was the typical Puritan on friends, benevolent authority, and chance for the evidence needed to persuade self of its goodness.

The emotion generated when a person resists a temptation to violate a standard—perhaps to gossip maliciously about another—is characterized by tension and conflict. Such feelings are to be contrasted with the emotion associated with desperately needing an A in a course or a promotion, but being uncertain about attainment of these goals. The latter emotion, better described as *anxiety,* occurs when self is not in control of events that can cause discomfort, or is unable to guarantee gratification of desires that reassure the self. I am not suggesting that the Puritan mood of conflict is better or more mature than the modern mood of anxiety; I am only noting that historical circumstances can affect the predominant feeling states surrounding adherence to standards.

Modern Western society has become increasingly tolerant of violations of important standards. This condition, which leads youth and adult to conclude that there is no one who will disapprove of many actions, decreases the likelihood of shame. But our society is also insisting, with increasing frequency, that individuals are not responsible for many of their actions. Social conditions are given causal power. Thus, homicide, vandalism, school failure, and even scientific fraud are occasionally blamed on inadequate institutions, poverty, and the conditions of society, rather than on individual lack of effort, will, or commitment.

A committee appointed by the dean of the Harvard Medical School to investigate a young scientist who admitted to fabricating some of his results, reported the following:

> Dishonesty in scientific research results from interactions between an individual and the environment. . . . One factor which may predispose to dishonest behavior would appear to be an intense desire to succeed. . . . More amenable to modification than personality or self-generated pressures are factors related to the environment. Consequently, the committee believes that the preventive measures most likely to be effective are those directed at the circumstances and practices in the laboratory which stimulate dishonest behavior in some people. (*Harvard University Gazette*, 29 January 1982, p. 12)

As explanations of amoral behavior transfer some of the burden of responsibility from self to a vague set of external conditions, the emotional consequences of transgression are vitiated and, as noted earlier, principled standards are transformed into conventions.

Evaluating the Child's Morality

Philosophers' attempts to define the morality of an act have been accompanied, in this century, by the efforts of psychologists to rank children, adolescents, and adults as more or less moral or to assign their moral judgments to stages in a developmental sequence that moves from less to more mature. The pragmatic spirit that dominates twentieth-century psychology inspired an attempt after the First World War to evaluate the child's morality through his or her actions. Unfortunately, observations of children, especially the famous experiments by Hugh Hartshorne and Mark May (1928), revealed no consistency in the disposition to be faithful to a particular moral standard across varied situations. Because no one could agree on how to rank behavior for moral priority, the movement to measure differences in virtue went underground for a few decades until Lawrence Kohlberg, following Piaget's emphasis on the cognitive bases for morality, suggested that a person's verbally expressed rationale for a moral decision could, and should, be ordered from less to more mature (Kohlberg 1981). The basis for the ranking is the quality of the explanation given to hypothetical moral dilemmas, with the lowest rank assigned to explanations based on fear of punishment or anticipation of reward, and the highest rank reserved for explanations that derive from a coherent set of premises. As for content, justice and respect for human life are awarded greater priority than social harmony, and social harmony is given greater weight than anxiety over punishment, disapproval, or social rejection (even though Javanese regard social anxiety as a mature basis for showing respect to elders). Faith in Kohlberg's ideas was enhanced when it was found that adolescents and adults in Western and developing countries are more likely than younger children to defend an ethical solution with a set of coherent premises that emphasizes life and liberty. But this solution to the desire to grade morality has bothered those who want to know the relation between a child's answers to hypothetical moral dilemmas and the basis for his or her moral intentions and actions, and who prefer to base moral evaluations on the latter qualities. "Will you or won't you have it so," James wrote "is the most probing question we are ever asked. . . . We answer by consents or non-consents and not by words" (1981b [1890], p. 1182). A six-year-old who is asked why a man should not steal is most likely to say that the person will get caught and punished, while a seventeen-year-old explains that the stability of the community would be destroyed if all members of the society were thieves. The difference in verbal response is of interest. But it is not obvious either that fear of discovery is the main constraint against stealing among six-year-olds, or that seventeen-year-olds are indifferent to being caught.

Use of verbal rationales as the preferred evidence for diagnosing a person's level of moral development has other embarrassing problems. For example, American adults who have not attended college and upper-middle-class Indian adolescents, mainly Jains and Hindus, give less mature explanations of moral decisions, on the average, than do middle-class Americans who have attended college. This finding has the counterintuitive implication that college-educated Americans function at a higher level of moral development than do high school graduates (Parikh 1980; Colby et al. 1983). Thomas Jefferson would surely have argued with Kohlberg, for the former wrote that all humans have a keen moral sense: "state a moral case to a ploughman and a professor. The former will decide it as well and often better than the latter because he has not been led astray by artificial rules" (cited in Boyd 1955, p. 15).

A more serious objection to ranking a child's moral maturity is the assumption of a universal sequence of unitary levels of moral judgment that transcend particular temptations. I do not believe either children or adults function at a particular level of morality across all ethical situations (Colby et al. 1983).

As I indicated in chapter 1, all descriptions of qualities must add a statement describing the local situation. Five-year-olds will explain their reluctance to steal as due to fear of punishment, but will rationalize the postponement of personal pleasure in order to help a friend as motivated by their empathy with someone in need. (Eisenberg-Berg and Hand 1979). Human biologists recognize that the notion of physical maturity is of little theoretical value, because growth of teeth, bone, muscle, brain, and genitals are not highly correlated. They can rank children on level of physical maturity for each of these systems separately, but avoid the idea of an average growth quotient.

If ranking children's "moral maturity" is the desired goal, most parents and a great many scientists would insist that the child's intention in a situation of moral conflict is as reasonable a basis as the quality of rationalization given to hypothetical situations. It is likely that one reason verbal justification for an ethical decision was selected as a criterion to evaluate a person's morality is the ease with which investigators could gather verbal explanations to moral dilemmas; and it happened that these explanations showed an interesting and orderly change in content with development. By contrast, it is much more difficult to assess children's intentions and feelings of guilt and shame. The empiricist measures what can be measured.

Conclusion

One of the major changes that accompanied the evolution of our species was the shift from actions released by events to actions generated by ideas—a transformation as significant in its implications as the phylogenetic advance from gills to lungs or from external to internal fertilization of the egg. Standards form one of the two important classes of ideas—the other is motive—that monitor most human behavior. They are continuous in their operation, like the train of impulses from the brain stem that maintains our muscle tone, and have as their target the affirmation of self and its virtue. This discussion of standards engages one of the five issues considered in the first chapter. Although the surface virtues children develop will be relative to the cultural demands they encounter, we can count on the appearance of empathy and an appreciation of right and wrong in all children before the third birthday. Thus, there are both biological as well as cultural influences on the growth of morality.

Morality will always be a critical human concern because humans want to believe there is a more and a less virtuous outcome in a situation of choice, and therefore insist on criteria for action. The fact that two-year-olds are concerned with the correctness or the incorrectness of an action implies the primacy of this theme. Humans are driven to invent moral criteria, as newly hatched turtles move toward water and moths toward light. The conditions for moral virtue in modern society—the state that one seeks to attain in order to reassure oneself of one's goodness—include pleasure, wealth, fame, power, autonomy, mastery, nurturance, kindness, love, honesty, work, sincerity, and belief in one's freedom. Each is a construction built over time, though traceable to universal affects. The relative prominence of each of these values is not an inevitable product of the human genome, but stems rather from the capacity for empathy with another's distress, shame and guilt over violating standards, and preparedness to inhibit actions that provoke disapproval. These are not inconsistent views. The young child is prepared by his biology to become attached to his parents; yet Western culture insists that he eventually develop autonomy and independence from them and be able to cope with distress in their absence—qualities that not only require subjugation of the earlier natural disposition but also ones that are probably not biologically inevitable. The moral sense of children is highly canalized because of a capacity for evaluation and the experience of certain emotions, but the surface ethics of a specific community are built from a web of social facts embedded in folk theory. Although humans do not seem to be specially programmed for a particular profile of moral missions, they are prepared to invent and believe in some ethical mission. Pär Lagerkvist had God reply to a question regarding His intention in creating human beings with, "I only intended that you need never be content with nothing" (1971, p. 65).

5

The Emotions

The belief that words have a meaning of
their own account is a relic of primitive
word magic, and it is still a part of the air
we breathe in nearly every discussion.

CHARLES K. OGDEN,
The Meaning of Meaning

IN MAKING EMOTION THE IMPETUS for a principled moral standard, I assumed a general agreement on the meaning of emotion,
and temporarily saved the reader from worrying about the serious
problems of definition and measurement that make this domain of
human experience so controversial. This chapter confronts those
difficulties directly. Although my central interest continues to be
on developmental issues, it is necessary, as it was in the preceding
chapter on morality, to begin with a general discussion of how to
conceptualize human emotions.

Most essays on human emotion written by Western philosophers or psychologists begin by assuming a limited set of distinctive feelings, each associated with a broad but still bounded set of
events, and each named by Platonic concepts—like *fear, joy,* or
anger—that contain no reference to either the source or the target
of the experience (A. O. Rorty 1980). Although scientists do not
agree on all of the events that participate in an emotion (some
scientists place the origin of emotion in the brain, while others
locate it in changes in the facial muscles) all agree that some
change in internal state is a necessary feature of the phenomena

154

called *emotional.* For William James, a change in internal state is the central event and the immediate cause of an emotion (James 1983 [1904]).

I have suggested elsewhere (Kagan 1978) that the term *emotion* refers to relations among external incentives, thoughts, and changes in internal feelings, as *weather* is a superordinate term for the changing relations among wind velocity, humidity, temperature, barometric pressure, and form of precipitation. Occasionally, a unique combination of these meteorological qualities creates a storm, a tornado, a blizzard, or a hurricane—events that are analogous to the temporary but intense emotions of fear, joy, excitement, disgust, or anger. But wind, temperature, and humidity vary continually without producing such extreme combinations. Thus, meteorologists do not ask what weather means, but determine the relations among the measurable qualities and later name whatever coherences they discover. For similar reasons, it is probably not useful for psychologists to spend much time debating the meaning of emotion. The initial task is to detect the many coherences among incentives, thoughts, and feelings, and then to name them.

We should, for example, agree on a name for the combination of seeing a dangerous animal in an unfamiliar place, expecting physical harm, and perceiving a sudden difficulty breathing. But the name for that coherence should be different from the one applied to seeing a frown on the face of a loved one, expecting a sign of rejection, and noticing a similar difficulty in breathing, because the complete profile of physiological reactions to the two incentives is different, and because the behavioral consequences are rarely similar.

The utility of differentiating among the states of an emotional category is seen clearly in the fears of young children. There are at least three different histories for these states, and I suspect that their emotional qualities are different. Conditioned fears are the simplest to understand. A child who has a painful experience will establish a specific fear in response to events that were the original cause of the distress (see the discussion in chapter 2). The classic example involves a dog jumping on a child and the child's subsequent fear of dogs. Somewhat less familiar is the fear some two- and three-year-olds develop over defecating in the toilet because of an unusually painful bowel movement.

A second source of childhood fear is generated by anticipated loss of the love relation to a parent, perhaps because of the birth of a new sibling or chronic marital quarrels. A third kind of fear is triggered by the unfamiliar—a stranger, a clown's costume, or unusual or very loud music on television.

Each of these childhood fears has a different history and accompanying profile of behavior, and clarity is lost when one word is used to describe all three states. Indeed, adults who continually worry about an impending calamity have a different childhood history and physiology than adults who experience a sudden, unexpected feeling of terror or panic, implying that these two emotional states are seriously different (Klein, Zitrin, and Woerner 1978).

Adults from different cultures experience different types of anxiety. Among the Mayan Indians of Guatemala, for example, the possibility of displeasing both local witches and one's ancestors, each of whom can bring serious misfortune, is a major source of worry. Among the Japanese, angering another person is a major source of concern. Among medieval European peasants, imperiling one's salvation because of impious thoughts was a continuing source of uncertainty. In modern America, while none of these sources of anxiety has high priority, uneasiness over disloyalty to one's principled standards is a frequent occasion for dysphoria. Each of these anxieties is a different emotion. It is true that each of the four anxieties is more similar to the other than to joy or anger, but that fact is not sufficient to treat the states as identical. I believe it is useful to regard them as a family of feeling states, as we regard four-footed mammals as a family of animals.

Three Issues

A better understanding of emotions requires resolution of three problems: the importance of distinguishing between bodily changes that are detected and those that are not; selecting the best names for emotional states; and, finally, measuring emotional states.

The Emotions

DETECTION OF INTERNAL CHANGE

Everyone agrees that conscious awareness of a change in breathing, heart rate, or muscle tension can be the occasion for an emotion. But how shall we regard equivalent changes in heart rate or muscle tone that are not detected and are, therefore, not part of a person's consciousness? This problem, which engages the subjective-objective frames discussed in the first chapter, must be addressed because conscious awareness of internal changes is, at the least, seriously muted in the infant and may even be absent.

To an unexpected event they are prepared to evaluate, most adults react with a change in the electrical discharge of the brain (called *event-related potential*) which occurs about three hundred milliseconds after the event and—less regularly—with a decrease in heart rate which reaches its trough about three seconds after the onset of the unexpected stimulus. I doubt that anyone in such a situation is aware of a distinct feeling, either at three hundred milliseconds or at three seconds after the presentation of the event. Similarly, reflex eye blinks and dilation of the pupil accompany attempts to solve a difficult problem, but most persons would not report a change in feeling during these brief reactions.

I believe that whether internal changes are detected is of extreme importance for the person's subsequent emotional state, as detection of volleys from the small pain fibers is necessary if a person is to perceive an injury. I do not suggest that unrecognized changes are unimportant, but that the psychological evaluation following detection usually alters the emotional experience. Many years ago I experienced after each meal a headache that lasted from five to fifteen minutes. I evaluated the throbbing feeling as a possible sign of a serious organic illness and named my affect *anxiety* whenever the headache occurred. After a doctor reassured me that it was due to psychological factors, I began to analyze its relation to my mood and decided, whether validly or not, that it was most likely to occur when I felt sad. From that time forward, whenever the symptom appeared, or I anticipated its appearance, my subjective experience was sadness, not anxiety. My headache had not changed, but my subjective emotion had, solely because of the change in evaluation.

Because every event is part of a larger frame, its consequences are dependent on the frame in which the event occurs. This principle holds even for the individual cells of the motor cortex. Depending upon an animal's set to act, the neurons of the motor cortex respond in dramatically different ways to the same stimulus—namely, an imposed flexion of the paw. In one experiment, a monkey was trained to make a pulling action at the appearance of a red light, but a pushing reaction at a green light. When the monkey was set to issue a pull response, because it had just seen a red light, the motor neurons displayed one pattern of discharge to the flexing of the paw. When the animal was set to push because it had seen a green light, the identical neurons displayed a different pattern of discharge to the same imposed flexion of the paw (Tanji and Evarts 1976). Thus, the emotional consequences of a change in the dilation of the blood vessels of the head and neck, which accompany a headache, depend on the larger psychological frame in which they occur.

I prefer to call the undetected physiological changes *internal tone* and the detected ones, *feeling states.* The perceptual qualities of a feeling state include rise time, perceived origin, intensity, and hedonic quality. The perceived change that defines a feeling state, unlike the change in internal tone, is a discrepant event that invites an interpretation of cause, a name, and, on occasion, a behavioral plan. Hence, such changes might be regarded as motivational and predictive of changes in thought and action. These consequences are missing when bodily changes go undetected.

It might be helpful to treat the physician's distinction between disease and illness as analogous to the differences between the undetected changes in internal tone and the evaluated feeling state. Human biologists posit a set of lawful relations between specific pathogens and subsequent changes in tissue and metabolic function. These coherences are given disease names, like cancer or tuberculosis, whether or not the patient has any conscious recognition of the change in internal function. Indeed, prophylactic medical examinations are intended to find these undetected physiological changes.

However, on occasion, the diseased individual does become aware of the biological changes created by the disease; and if one evaluates them as due to a pathogenic process, one regards the self as having an illness. The recognition typically has significant consequences, for it creates a novel psychological state that can either exacerbate or reduce the symptoms of the disease, depending upon the coping mechanisms implemented. In some cases, the realization that one is ill leads both to new symptoms, because of disturbances in eating and sleeping, and to special reactions from those persons to whom the patient communicates his or her state of illness.

Likewise, an impending responsibility can produce a bodily change that goes undetected. If one eventually detects the change in tone, evaluates one's thoughts, and decides that one is worried, a new feeling state is created that alters the original and often has consequences for interaction with others. The differences between the states preceding and subsequent to appraisal pose a serious quandary with respect to their classification. Should the scientist regard the evaluated feeling state simply as a gloss on the original, undetected one created by the impending responsibility, or treat it as a different emotion? Human biologists prefer the former strategy. If a woman who, after learning she has a malignant tumor, develops insomnia and, as a result, becomes seriously fatigued and develops symptoms, her new physiological state would be diagnosed as an addition to, and not a replacement of, the original cancerous state.

Although many investigators are partial to the medical model, it is not obvious that it is appropriate for the classification of acute emotional states, in part, because many of these states are transient. When the immune system recognizes a few pathogens, it destroys them before the biologist would say that the person has a disease. Both positions are defensible; the choice depends upon the theoretical interests of the investigator. If the scientist wishes to understand the intentional behavior that follows evaluation of a prior change in feeling tone, it is more useful to assume that the evaluation has produced a different emotional state. If, however, the investigator is more interested in understanding the relation between the incentive and subsequent automatic changes in facial musculature or in breathing, it would not be an error to treat the state subsequent to evaluation as a gloss on the original change in feeling tone.

A thought experiment illustrates the usefulness of distinguishing the feeling state that follows evaluation of a change in tone from the state that accompanies an undetected change in tone. Imagine three women, each of whom has just realized that in a month her last child will leave home to go to college and the house will be empty. Over the next few days, the first woman detects a loss of appetite and energy, thinks about these internal changes, and decides they are due to the imminent loss: she must be worried about losing her last child. The second woman detects the very same changes but decides she has been working too hard and is fatigued. Similar bodily changes occur in the third mother, but they are not detected; however, she appears to her husband to be less affectionate and a bit more likely to quarrel, and he tells her so.

In all three cases, the potential loss of the child has generated a bodily change in feeling tone. Thus, the basic ingredients of an emotion are present for all three women. But we need three different terms to distinguish the emotional states of the three mothers. It is a mistake to regard all three as being "sad" because both the conscious state and the behavior of each are qualitatively different. At the least, let us call these states *sadness 1, sadness 2,* and *sadness 3.* All three "sadnesses" are, of course, in the objective frame of the theorist. The emotional state experienced subjectively by the mothers might have been appraised as anxiety, fatigue, or mild irritability.

It will be useful, I believe, to have complementary emotional terms for a given situation, one in the subjective and one in the objective frame. I make this suggestion because the emotional term is intended to explain a relation between events, not internal tone. However, the experiencing person and the theorist often choose to explain different pairs of events that are part of the same coherent phenomenon. Consider, for example, a male patient and his female psychiatrist. During a period when the patient has been talking about his conflictful childhood relationship with his father, which the psychiatrist believes contains repressed hostility, she notices the patient becoming restless and twisting his mustache. The psychiatrist, who is loyal to psychoanalytic theory, notes privately that the patient is experiencing "unconscious anxiety" because of activation of the repressed hostile thoughts toward the father. The emotional term *unconscious anxiety* is intended to explain, in an objective frame, the relation between the content being discussed by the patient and his sudden restlessness.

Simultaneously, the patient feels his face is getting hot and flushed. In an attempt to understand these sensations, he decides, in the subjective frame, that he is too warm because he is wearing a sweater and a jacket; or he may decide that he is ashamed at being annoyed with the therapist for not helping him deal with the repressed ideas. The emotional words emanating from the subjective and the objective frames are different because patient and therapist are trying to interpret different phenomena. The objective frame is not necessarily more valid, but it is not to be treated as equivalent to the subjective one.

The Complementarity of Subjective and Objective Frames   I recently listened to recordings of lengthy interviews conducted with thirty mothers of three-year-olds who came from a broad range of social and economic backgrounds in the Boston metropolitan area. Although the female interviewer asked the same set of questions in a specified order, the questions were open-ended and permitted the mothers to report their feelings, attitudes, and intuitions to queries like, What is your child like now? or, What would you like her to be at age ten? The replies of over three fourths of the mothers suggested to me that these parents wanted their children to be empathic to the distress states of others and able to inhibit overt signs of fear or anxiety to unfamiliar people. However, the actual sentences the mothers used to express these two concerns were varied.

I inferred the mothers' concern with empathy from sentences like "I don't want my child to be mean"; "I want her to be a caring person"; "I'm pleased with his sensitivity to others' feelings"; "I hope he's considerate of other people"; "I'm happy he likes to be so loving"; "I want her to be careful of how people feel"; "I'm proud of her affectionate ways with other people." The mothers expressed their concern with the control of anxiety in phrases reflecting the hope that the child would be "bold," "not intimidated by other children," "not scared to speak her mind," and "confident enough to do what she thought was right."

Because each of these expressions is likely to have a unique, personal connotation for the speaker, am I justified in assuming a single concern shared by the different statements—that is, a concern with empathy or control of anxiety? These two phrases are in the objective frame. No mother ever used those words. Many mothers who had described their children as not bold enough or as shy with others, denied that the child was fearful when the interviewer asked directly, "Is your child fearful?" Even if the interviewer softened the question and wondered if the mother were worried that her child might be fearful, some mothers replied negatively because the term *fearful* did not have the same meaning to them that it did for the interrogator.

The use of self-report data to make inferences about a person's emotional state, or the state a mother feels best describes her child, poses a profound problem. The popular solution permits the investigator to invent a concept, like *empathic* or *anxious,* to decide on the spoken phrases that belong to the concept, and to quantify the subject's statements for instances of the category. If that procedure leads to reliable prediction of theoretically reasonable phenomena, its validity is affirmed. If not, we know nothing. But in no case can the investigator assume that he or she knows the subject's private emotional state. Indeed, when college students were asked to imagine and express nonverbally, during exercise, one of six different emotional states while their heart rate and blood pressure were being monitored, observers' judgments of the subjects' emotional states were in better theoretical accord with the students' physiological changes than were the students' reports of their emotions.

"The findings suggested that the observers were seeing relationships that the subjects themselves did not" (Schwartz 1982, p. 85). This observer added that clinically depressed patients report experiencing more pleasure than observers judge them to be experiencing, while schizophrenic patients report experiencing less pleasure than observers judge them to have. It is not the case that the patients are correct and the observer is wrong; but, rather, the two descriptions have different functions.

However, investigators indifferent to this problem ask their subjects what emotion they are feeling and give the reply special priority. I suggest that the replies are of interest and invite accommodation, but have only slightly greater significance than an eye blink. The words people use to name their feeling states are only a little less disguised as a fact to be used in an objective proposition than a furrowing of the brow. It is common for a three-year-old who has just committed a mischievous act to run to the mother and say, "I love you, Mummy." It is not obvious that the child is experiencing the emotion we believe *love* refers to when an adult uses the same word. Further, it is likely that most psychologists would conclude that this child was experiencing fear of punishment or guilt, not love. Psychologists should use self-reports of feeling states, but must treat them as they do all other evidence. They always require interpretation (Polivy 1981). This issue provides a bridge to the second problem—namely, the best names for emotional states.

THE NAMING OF FEELING STATES

The differences among acting, thinking, and feeling are so compelling phenomenologically that most scholars have assumed they must represent fundamentally different psychological functions. But classifications based on intuition are often misleading. Our intuitions also insist that ice, snow, fog, and water are different substances, and that the sun moves around the earth. Humans invented emotional terms to describe the fact that, on occasion, an action, an external event, or a thought produces a perceptible change in internal feeling state. Even though children and adults in a particular culture agree on the meaning of some emotional terms, the names should not be regarded as referring to fixed material entities that can be defined intrinsically, as they do for trees and robins. Rather, most often these are names for the less than perfect co-variation that exists among the many classes of external incentives, thoughts, and detected changes in feeling states. Thus the variety in potential emotional states is enormous. James suggested that the number of emotions is limitless.

This conclusion has never appealed to most scientists who have elected to study a small proportion of the possible total of internal states and to treat them as biologically more fundamental than the rest. The list of primary emotions studied by Western psychologists—most often fear, anger, contempt, joy, sadness, disgust, excitement, surprise, guilt, and shame—omits reference to many emotions that other cultures would regard as equally fundamental to human nature. Thirteenth-century Japanese Buddhists claimed that the state of enlightenment is the most significant affective mood to attain; modern Japanese regard the emotion of *amae* (a feeling of mutual interdependence with another) as primary (Doi

1973). The Utku Eskimo of Hudson Bay believe *naklik* (the feeling that accompanies wanting to nurture and protect another) to be a primary emotion (Briggs 1970); the Ifalukians of Micronesia treat *song* (the feeling that accompanies the recognition that another person has violated a community norm) as a basic human feeling (Lutz 1982).

Most of the emotions that Western psychologists designate as primary have significant practical consequences. They are perceptually salient events that interfere with sustained thought, accompany successful coping with a challenge, communicate information to another person, or lead to symptoms that interfere with the capacity for love and work. These are persuasive reasons for studying these particular states, but not for regarding these emotions as more fundamental than others. The feeling that accompanies a persimmon-colored sunset, or the mood that follows strenuous physical exercise, although perceptually distinct and temporary, are rarely named as primary emotions—perhaps because neither seems to have important consequences for successful problem solving, communication, or mental health.

Studies of infants, for whom evaluation is less likely, reveal that they often show a rise and stabilization of heart rate when trying to assimilate discrepant information. One way to interpret this association is to assume that infants become physiologically aroused when they attempt to understand information that is not immediately comprehensible. Psychologists may name this state with phrases like *sustained mental effort, cognitively aroused, confused, puzzled, or uncertain.* Whatever name is chosen, there is no reason to assume that this state is a less basic emotion than *interest* or *surprise.* It has not been recognized as a primary emotion simply because the relevant experiments have not been performed. I suspect that many more coherences remain to be discovered. I do not urge complete abandonment of the popular emotional terms, but there should be greater readiness to accommodate to new relations and to inhibit the impulse to assimilate them to the currently popular categories. I believe, with Newton, that occasionally investigators should argue from phenomena, rather than from *a priori* assumptions.

The controversies surrounding the most basic emotional states resemble earlier disagreements among naturalists regarding the basic kinds of animal. Hence, a brief consideration of those debates may clarify comparable problems in the study of emotions. First, it is so easy to find a quality that is shared by diverse events an observer has no trouble placing a particular event in many different categories. The first biologist to study the duck-billed platypus must have wondered whether it should be called a bird because of its bill, a reptile because of its egg, or a mammal because it nurses its young. Similar problems confronted the first psychologist who noted that a person's heart rate increases when he is trying to solve a difficult arithmetic problem: the rise in heart rate might be part of the emotional state of anxiety, arousal, concentrated thought, or frustration.

In deciding which emotional category is the most appropriate, the observer must select a criterion that will indicate which components of a particular emotion should be awarded special significance. Evolutionary biologists agreed that phylogenetic descent was to be the central criterion for categorizing animals; exclusive application of that criterion eliminates many characteristics of animals, like economic value, habitat, or social relationship to man. Unfortunately, psychologists have not yet achieved equivalent consensus on the most useful criterion for classifying emotions, even though most prefer a functional criterion that awards a purpose to the emotion. Those who make communicative potential the central function of emotion concentrate on feeling states accompanied by perceptible gestures, facial expressions, or voice qualities. Hence, when the face of a crying infant assumes the same form as that of a husband yelling at his wife (square mouth, narrowed eyes, and eyebrows drawn together), it is assumed that both infant and husband are experiencing anger. Investigators who make the subjective feelings of pleasure-displeasure the major basis for classification are tempted to group the feeling of justified revenge with the smiling that occurs after a victory because both states make a person "feel better." Scientists who choose similarities in physiology as the basis for classification assume that when heart rate increases and skin resistance decreases, a common emotional state (often called *arousal*) is present (Mandler 1975). Finally, investigators interested in the relation of emotions to motives focus on the subjective intensity of feeling, because strong feelings are most likely to alter motive hierarchies and to maintain in an ascendant position those desires that are associated with intense feelings.

165

None of these schemes is wrong or muddle-headed given the criterion selected, just as it is not incorrect to place deer, partridge, oysters, and frogs in the common category of expensive cuisine.

A major advance in biological taxonomy occurred in the early part of the nineteenth century when observers stopped positing abstract categories, like birds, fish, and mammals. Instead, they first studied the actual similarities among different kinds of animals and waited to invent the more abstract categories only after having discovered sets of shared features. Thus, whale and porpoise are classified together, apart from seal and walrus, because the former pair share many important biological characteristics. I suspect this inductive strategy will be useful in the study of emotions.

Cultural Variation   Because each emotional name is a classification category, the extraordinary diversity among cultures in presuppositions and values should be accompanied by differences in how feeling states are categorized (we cannot know how they are subjectively experienced). Hence, there should not always be consensus across societies on the coherences to which particular emotional words are applied. Indeed, the variation across societies in the classification of emotions may be greater than the variety of categories used to name plants and animals. (B. Berlin, D. E. Breedlove, and P. H. Raven have reported that the names for plants and animals used by certain tribes in New Guinea are close to Linnaean groupings [1973].) The influence of culture on the choice of emotional terms is nicely illustrated in C. Lutz's study of the emotional words used by the approximately five hundred people living on the small isolated atoll of Ifaluk, located in the Western Caroline Islands of Micronesia (Lutz 1982).

Fago, one of the most frequently used emotional words on Ifaluk, has no clear synonym in English. *Fago* is applied to that feeling provoked by individuals who need help, have suffered illness, death, or misfortune, or have subordinate status and, surprisingly, have qualities that are in accord with the ego ideal of the society, which includes a state of calm and generosity. "Sympathy" or "compassion" comes close to capturing the meaning of *fago* for the first three examples, but no English-speaking adult would use the word *sympathy* to name the feeling aroused by a person who is respected and admired. The fact that the Ifalukians do implies a symbolic parsing of emotional experience different from our own.

The Emotions

The Ifalukians believe that a child under age seven is not cognitively mature enough to experience *fago*. It is likely that the ability to appreciate a state of misfortune in another across a variety of situations is one basis for the Ifalukian belief. A Piagetian would be pleased by this hypothesis, for the child under seven is assumed to be too egocentric to appreciate subtle states of need in other persons.

Song, another frequently used term, is best translated as "justified anger." The primary incentive for applying *song* to experience is improper behavior by another person, often a violation of the community norm regarding false gossip or the sharing of resources with another. But *song* is also used when misfortune befalls a person toward whom one feels *fago*. No comparable word in English covers both situations. The Ifalukians use a different term, *nguch*, for states of frustration or annoyance that are less justifiable. Thus, the Ifalukians make a linguistic distinction between two forms of anger which is less clear in English, for we use *angry, irritated,* or *mad* to name either class of incentive.

The importance of context in the application of Ifalukian affect terms is also apparent in the use of *rus* and *metagu*. *Rus* names the feeling that arises when an agent is in a situation of potential physical harm—a typhoon, a violent fight—and experiences a salient internal reaction. *Rus* seems close in meaning to the English *fear,* but not quite, for the sudden death of a person also elicits *rus*. Thus, a mother will say she feels *rus* if her child has died, while English speakers are less likely to declare they feel fear at that event. *Metagu* refers to situations that have the potential to cause *rus*—a future interaction with a stranger, possible encounter with a ghost, or anticipation of the anger of or rejection by another person. *Metagu* comes close to what we might call *social anxiety,* but this is not a perfect translation.

Ifalukians are likely to group emotions together on the basis of similarities in incentive. For example, *song* ("justified anger"), *tang* ("grief"), and *fago* ("compassion"), which are grouped together, are typically generated by the properties or actions of other people. By contrast, the incentive conditions for *metagu* ("anxiety"), *kamayaya* ("indecision"), and *fileng* ("incapability"), which are grouped in a cluster distant from the first set, more often require prolonged reflective thought.

A comparable analysis of the groupings of English emotional words by Americans reveals that similarity in intensity and evaluation of feeling states is more significant than similarity in incentive. English terms typically focus on the quality of the person's felt experience and, unlike the language of the Ifalukians, do not contain a sharp differentiation with respect to the psychological origin of the feeling. Thus, anxiety and anger, which are intense, unpleasant feelings, are closer for Americans than *song* and *metagu* are for Ifalukians. This suggestion is supported by the fact that when American college students rated 717 concepts for their emotionality, the resulting factor analysis revealed that evaluation was the first factor and degree of arousal was the second. None of the factors implied classifications based on context or situation; all involved the quality of the agent's feelings, evaluations, and sense of control (Averill 1980; see also Daly, Lancee, and Polivy 1983).*

The affect terms of the Utku Eskimo (Briggs 1970) are also differentiated by context. For example, different terms are used to name the desire to be with another, to kiss or touch another, or to be under the covers with another. The Gururumba, a New Guinea group, ascribe an emotional term meaning "wild pig" only to men between about twenty-five and thirty-five years of age who lose control of socialized behavior, because during this age interval men assume marital and social responsibilities that arouse anxiety. Similar behavior in a fifteen-year-old or a sixty-year-old would not be awarded the same affect label (Newman 1960).

For the Ifalukians, the Utku, and the Gururumba, other people are significant incentives for emotional states, and motives and emotions associated with people are awarded a special status they do not have in English. We might speculate that individual acts of mastery and achievement in Western society have the same degree of salience that relations with other people do in non-Western

---

*The indifference to context is also apparent in the fixed word order of English sentences, which is typically subject—verb—object, regardless of the situation. Whether a wife asks her bruised husband who has just slipped on the icy street outside, "How did that happen?" or "Where did that happen?" the reply in English is, "I slipped on the ice." However, in some languages the husband's reply can be either, "I slipped on the ice" or "The ice was the place where I slipped," so that the answer places the salient element early in the sentence. It is of interest that the number system of the proto-Elamites, who lived in what is now Iran in the fourth century B.C., varied with context. They used one number system to count people and another to count animals (Friberg 1984).

cultures. Like the cognitive competences we call *memory, perception, inference,* or *reasoning ability,* our Platonic words for emotional names are minimally constrained by the specific situation that provokes them. This attitude is not of recent origin. When David Hume (1969 [1739–40]) declared pride and humility to be the basic emotions, he ignored the contexts in which these passions occur.

Although English emotional terms do not correspond exactly to the terms of other cultures, some psychologists might reply that this linguistic relativism is unimportant for the understanding of emotion. The central fact, they would argue, is that beneath the language, there are universal relations among certain incentives, physiological reactions, and experiential outcomes—a position that has not yet been refuted by any empirical evidence.

There is, of course, a way out of the counterintuitive suggestion that my emotional reaction to a coiled rattlesnake is not like that of the Ifalukian. Identity of subjective experience is probably too strong a criterion to impose. Let us borrow again the biologists' distinction between species and variety and suggest that there are classes of emotion defined by the quality of feeling associated with the evaluation of a thought or an incentive event. The feelings elicited by attaining a desired goal, losing hope of attaining a goal, re-establishing an attachment, anticipating danger to one's body, losing status or wealth, violating a principled standard or failing to meet a conventional one, and confronting an interruption of action, seizure of property, or threat from another compose some basic classes. But within each of these classes, individuals from different age and cultural groups will have different emotional experiences because of variations in the evaluation of the union of incentive conditions, feelings, and thought.

Thus, the argument I used for standards can be applied to emotions. I suggested in chapter 4 that each culture's articulated ethical standards vary due to local conditions, but rest on a common set of emotions. I offer the suggestion now that variations in bodily change, incentive, and evaluation lead to a family of feeling states, each of which has a prototypic core. These prototypes include the emotions we call fear, worry, anger, sadness, joy, guilt, shame, empathy, contentment, and interest. I am not certain how many prototypes are needed to account for all the basic human feelings.

The Measurement of Emotions

The problem of measuring particular internal tones or feeling states is yet another instance of the ancient problem of how a single component of a larger unity relates to that unity. The words of ordinary language refer to unitary objects like a cup, unitary events like an opera, or to some coherent part of a larger unity, like the handle of a cup or the first act of an opera. The presence of a single component can never be treated as equivalent to the larger unity. Thus most scholars in the life sciences accept the doctrine that a particular combination of events creates a synthetic phenomenon different from and not amenable to prediction by each of its individual parts. The growth and differentiation of the fertilized egg, which is made possible by the union of sperm and egg, is as good an illustration as any. Perhaps that is why scientists studying emotion have suggested that "No emotional state is ever specified by a single, unambiguous behavioral measure" (Campos et al. 1983). This principle implies that it is impossible to infer an emotional state from any single participant in that state. First, any one reaction can reflect different emotional states; a rise in heart rate, for example, can accompany both a smile and a cry (Emde et al. 1978). Further, the same emotional state—say, fear of punishment—can be linked with different reactions. To the threat of a spanking, one child may react with a rise in heart rate; another, with stomach contractions; another, with a headache. Yet both child and observer may evaluate the feeling state as fear of the parent.

Once again, the history of taxonomic scholarship can be instructive. Two major insights that permitted progress were the realization that the many relevant morphological features that define a species differ in significance; and, second, the significance of a particular feature will vary with the species being classified. These principles are relevant to the classification of emotions. If a one-year-old in a laboratory watches his mother leave the room, the child is likely to display a rise in heart rate, to look wary, and to utter a sharp cry. Although an unexpected tickle or a piece of cake can also produce a rise in heart rate, the facial wariness and crying do not usually occur to tickling or a sweet. Although the rise in heart rate following separation from the mother should not be ignored, the observer should award it less significance than the cry or the wary face.

Recent technical advances have it made it possible to measure extremely subtle changes in facial expression (Ekman 1980; Izard 1977), and in the pitch and quality of the voice (Scherer 1981). Because many of these changes are lawfully related to specific emotional states, a better understanding of the incentives for various internal tones and feeling states is probable during the next decade. But some scientists who rely on the patterned reactions of voice and face want more. They wish to use the single sign as a valid index of the total emotional state. For example, those who measure facial expression would like to conclude that the changes in the muscles that define a certain form of smile always produce or accompany a particular emotion (Ekman 1980). (They do not make the distinction between internal tone and feeling state as sharply as I do). Although this assumption remains a possibility, it is flawed by the error of inferring a coherent whole from the presence of only a part. Pneumonia is a state doctors ascribe to patients who show the combination of pneumococcus bacteria, a fever, and inflammation of the lungs. No physician would diagnose pneumonia on the basis of any one of the three components. Some call a two-year-old child *happy* when she smiles to a picture of an unusual butterfly. But the smile to the butterfly also invites a descriptive term like *comprehending* or *understanding,* not happy (Reznick 1982). It is unlikely that the smile that follows the receipt of a cookie or a new toy reflects the same state that accompanies successful recognition of a butterfly. The error of mistaking a part for the whole occurs more often with infants than with adults, for when an adult smiles we usually demand more information before we are willing to ascribe the emotion of joy or happiness to the person. We must be equally careful with infants and children. We cannot assume a pony every time we smell hay near a barn.

The Development of Emotion

THE FIRST FIVE YEARS

The popular belief that a child's emotions do not change with growth requires the improbable assumption that maturational changes in the brain that produce new cognitive evaluations and special feeling tones have no influence on the older person's emotional experiences. However, because one often uses the same language to name emotions in two- and twenty-two-year-olds, it is easy to believe that the emotional experiences are the same. American mothers also assume, incorrectly I believe, that three-month-olds can experience the emotions of interest, anger, joy, or fear that are attributed to adults (Johnson et al. 1982).

During the first three or four months the infant displays many reactions that are suggestive of emotional states, but it is probable that most are unevaluated changes in internal tone. As I noted, it is useful to name these emotions in accordance with their origin and associated reactions. One set of reactions, composed of attentiveness and motor and vocal quieting to a physically salient event, might be called "interest to salience." Widening of the eyes, an open mouth, and a sharp decrease in heart rate to an unexpected event might be called "surprise to novelty." Increased motor activity, closing of the eyes, heart rate acceleration, and crying to pain, cold, and hunger might be named "distress to physical privation," but the first three reactions, without crying, to a clap of thunder might be called "startle to the unexpected." Decreased muscle tension and closing of the eyes following feeding might be named "relaxation to gratification," while increased motor tension, smiling, and babbling to a familiar event could be called "excitement to comprehension of the unexpected." I can add many more examples, but in all cases the name for each emotional state will always contain a reference to its supposed origin.

New emotional reactions appear between four and twelve months because of the maturation of cognitive functions, especially retrieval memory and evaluation of the relation of the event to knowledge. For example, eight-month-olds react to some unexpected events with a special facial expression of wariness, cessation of play, and, on occasion, crying. Because this behavior to the unfamiliar does not occur earlier, we are justified in declaring a new emotion—"fear to the unfamiliar." It is not necessary to treat this fear as a derivative of the earlier distress to privation, or to assume that the earlier distress is a necessary prerequisite for this fear. Recall from chapter 3 that the feeding behavior of a three-month-old rat is not a derivative of the suckling of the newborn.

Another set of reactions appearing during the latter part of the first year involves resistance, protest, and, on occasion, crying at the interruption of a continuing response or at the loss of an object of interest, which we might call "anger to frustration." In his seminal essay on emotion, George Mandler (1975) awards interruption of a response a central place, suggesting that it increases internal arousal. The principal difference between this emotion and those displayed during the first few months is that in order to experience "anger" one must evaluate events. That is, in order to become angry to the loss of a toy, a child must both recognize its absence and attribute the loss to the action of another person. The one-month-old whose toy is taken by an adult usually does not become upset because the younger infant is not mature enough to relate the loss to the action of another.

It is not possible to list all the new coherences that emerge during the second year. Two prominent reactions include an initial protest, followed by inhibition and apathy, to the prolonged absence of a primary caregiver—emotions that are popularly called *depression* or *sadness* and require retrieval of schemata of the past. The two-year-old must be able to recall the caregiver's former presence, relate that idea to his current situation, and additionally, hold that information in consciousness so that it is not lost after a few seconds. These phenomena cannot occur without maturational advances in cognitive function, as well as an attachment to a caregiver.

During the second year, children also show emotional reactions that might be called "anxiety to possible task failure". Recall from chapter 4 the children who became distressed after a woman modeled some acts that were difficult to imitate. The children fretted, cried, ran to their mother, stopped playing, protested, or insisted they wanted to go home. These reactions occur in children in Cambridge, Massachusetts, in children growing up in huts on islands in the Fiji chain, as well as in children who have recently arrived in northern California from their homes in Vietnam (Kagan 1981).

Two-year-olds also show emotional concern at the sight of a broken cup or dirt on a blouse, and empathy with the distress of another. Both emotions require the child to make an inference. In the first case, the child must infer that someone broke the cup; in the second he must infer the feelings of the victim. The smile that follows successful completion of a task in which one has invested effort, which also appears during the second year, requires recognition that a self-generated goal has been met. Thus, during the second and third years, the causes of emotions involve cognitive evaluations that are not possible earlier. The painful injection that produces the emotion of distress in a six-month-old produces a different emotion in the six-year-old, even though pain is felt on both occasions. The older child might feel pride because he has met a prior standard to be stoic, or feel the anger that arises when one is threatened by another person.

Because the emotions of the first two to three years appear to be universal, it is of interest to ask about their psychological advantages. One possible function of the reaction to discrepant events is to protect the child from physical harm. Restraint as a reaction to the unfamiliar keeps the child from approaching less familiar objects, and the child's crying is likely to bring a protective adult.

The causes of anger toward another person include interruption of purposeful activity, frustration of a motive, or seizure of an object the child regards as her own. Because it is not obvious that anger protects the child from harm, why does she react with vigor of voice and body to the interruption of a goal-directed action or to loss of property? One possibility is that this reaction and its accompanying responses serve to establish a resistant, rather than an acquiescent, response to the intrusion of others. Anger that successfully produces retreat on the part of an intruder will become part of the child's repertoire. In time, the child will react to interruptions and seizures with angry protests. Consider a two-year-old who never reacts with anger to any intrusion. The child will lose the object he is holding, and always cease goal-directed actions when interrupted. If interventions are frequent, the child will eventually become passive to domination and intrusion.

The excitement provoked by interaction with an adult (surprise, physical contact, and talking) prolongs the contact with the adult. One possible function of this affect is to facilitate mutual interaction and bonding of child and adult.

The function of sadness to loss of a caregiver object is less obvious. Why should a two-year-old child react to the prolonged loss of an object of attachment with signs of depression or apathy? One possible purpose is to keep the child close to familiar people. As the child approaches the third to fourth birthday, she is physically and psychologically able to leave the family group, at least temporarily. She can wander from the home, although not still without some danger. The extreme fear of the unusual, which keeps the one-year-old close to her parents, is less potent, and the new sadness at loss may function similarly, provoking the older child to return to family members. The child chooses to stay close to them in order to avoid the unpleasant feeling she has learned occurs when she is apart from them for a long time.

The function of an emotional reaction to the violation of an adult standard seems obvious. The child who is to remain accepted by the social group must inhibit behaviors that are disapproved by the group—typically destruction, aggression, and lack of cleanliness. The affects called anxiety, shame, and guilt are unpleasant (in part, because the accompanying ideas are linked to evaluations that the child is bad), and the child will avoid initiating these prohibited behaviors. As I noted in chapter 4, it may have been necessary in human evolution for inhibition of aggression to emerge early in development in order that behavior dangerous to others would be curbed. The importance of controlling aggression is seen in a rare event in which a thirty-month-old killed his twenty-two-month-old regular playmate by pounding the victim's head on the floor and striking his skull with a heavy glass vase. The fact that this is a freak phenomenon indicates that, by the third birthday, most children appreciate that such violence should be inhibited.

The appearance of guilt is delayed because its cognitive base takes time to mature. The cognitive talent in question is the ability to recognize that one has a choice. A two-year-old is not capable of recognizing that he could have behaved in a way different from the one he has chosen. But the four-year-old has this ability and so experiences the emotion we call *guilt*.

There seems to be a complementary relation between the emotions of the first year and those of the second and third years. The earlier emotional states and their accompanying behavior offset the child's impotence and protect him against harm and victimization. The emotions of the next two years, especially those following violation of standards, restrain the child. The protest to intrusion characteristic of the first year is balanced by the shame of the second, allowing the child to avoid both the Scylla of impotence and the Charybdis of destructive arrogance. Nature intended the child to be neither too humble nor too aggressive, just civilized.

THE MIDDLE YEARS: THE OTHER AS REFERENT

The emotions that appear during the fifth and sixth years have as their immediate cause an evaluation of self's properties in comparison with others—a process that is less prominent during the first three years of life. The products of that evaluation lead to emotional reactions to which we give names like *insecurity, inferiority, humility, pride,* and *confidence.*

We are so accustomed to assuming that all reactions must be the result of an external force imposed on the self that we are reluctant to consider the psychological potency of the simple fact that another individual is present in the psychological consciousness of a person, even though the other may direct no actions toward the person. In dominance hierarchies among animals, the presence of a more dominant animal will influence the behavior of the less dominant one, even if the two never have a dispute.

In order to evaluate their own qualities, humans select particular others as referents, typically siblings or peers of similar age, sex, and background. The comparison of self's qualities with another's, which may be unique to humans, is an important basis for mood and behavior. Animals respond to physical signals from another; humans react to imagined qualities, and that process creates incentives for both emotion and action.

The American six- or seven-year-old possesses standards for abilities, attractiveness, honesty, bravery, dominance, popularity, and a host of other qualities and is able to rank himself and his friends on these qualities with remarkable consensus. As a result, the child's concept of self is influenced by the private evaluation of the degree to which ego possesses those characteristics in comparison with others. The crucial new cognitive competence is the ability to make this evaluation. The incentive is not a specific action of self that deviates from an internal standard, but is rather a property of the self that deviates from that same property in another person. But what determines the referent chosen? Children automatically detect similarities among objects and people; hence, as the child's concept of self becomes articulated, he naturally compares qualities of self with those of other people he knows. The qualities are physical and functional as well as membership in a common category like sex, ethnic group, and family. In this mental comparison, the presence of distinctive properties shared by self and other, but not shared with everyone, is an important determinant of who is chosen as referent. The child is especially disposed to compare herself with those who share with self properties that are unusual or infrequent. When people are asked to describe themselves, they usually name distinctive dimensions first (McGuire and Padawer-Singer 1976). For example, when sixth-graders were asked, "Tell me about yourself," few named their gender, while many listed the activities and possessions that would differentiate them from members of their family (like recreations or daily routines) and from their peers (like siblings or pets). More important, only 7 percent of the children who were born in the United States spontaneously mentioned their birthplace as a distinctive attribute; while 44 percent of the foreign-born children mentioned their place of birth.

Because the child is disposed to select properties that are infrequent, and to regard those who possess those properties as belonging to a common category, physical qualities like red hair, skin color, freckles, or a handicap are potent. Gender is always a salient dimension; and as early as two years of age, children are aware of some of the psychological dimensions that define the sexes, including modal actions, control of fear, and adult vocation (Kuhn, Nash, and Brucken 1978).

Family will be a dimension of importance because the child learns that she and her family share biological properties, the family's last name is typically uncommon, and certain behavior typically occurs only within the home. Crying, boisterousness, yelling, aggression, and extreme hilarity occur in the home, rarely outside.

The child recognizes that she, too, behaves in this manner and, as a result, regards herself as more similar to family members than to most people outside the family. Hence, the child comes to believe that all family members belong to a common category, and she begins to share vicariously in their emotional life (see chapter 4).

Outside the family, attendance at the same school or residence in a common neighborhood can be a basis for similarity. A seven-year-old boy is more likely to compare self with the boys in his classroom than with all the boys he knows or has heard about. One corollary of this assumption is that the smaller the effective peer group available for comparison, the more likely a particular child will evaluate the self positively on a given psychological property, simply because there will be fewer children with more outstanding qualities. The child with a large peer group compares himself with many more children who possess more outstanding attributes. As a result, he will regard self as farther from a desirable standard and will experience the unpleasant feeling state of a sense of "inferiority."

The advantages of some of the emotions that characterize the older child are not obvious because the child will develop feelings of confidence (or lack of confidence) depending upon the peer group to which he is exposed. Perhaps these emotions, like the human chin which was a consequence of the development of the jaw and teeth, were unintended consequences of the cognitive ability to compare the self with others. On the other hand, it is possible that when all human groups were small in number, there were rarely more than a half-dozen peers of similar age. A typical seven-year-old in a hunter-gatherer group probably had only three or four other children five to nine years old with whom to compare himself. Under these conditions, the child would be likely to evaluate the self as coming close to meeting the standard for desirable properties, and to generate more positive feelings about the self. In large cities, civilized man has created conditions in which many children are exposed to hundreds of youngsters of similar sex and age, leading many to conclude that they seriously deviate from a desirable standard. The resultant feeling of inadequacy does not seem to be very adaptive.

The Emotions

As adolescence approaches, new conditions with both cognitive and physiological components appear. Although the physical changes that accompany puberty are interpreted as signs of a change in role. the changes in sexual feelings, due partly to hormonal secretions, play an influential role in the emotion we call *sexual excitement*. But even for this feeling state, the detection of deviation from standards is relevant. The adolescent is aware of her ability to meet the local standards of sexual attraction and romantic success. In most species, the males are in a dominance hierarchy based on their ability to dominate others; the less dominant males defer to the more dominant ones in gaining access to females. One human analogue is the contemporary adolescent's evaluation of his or her ability to attract a partner and to maintain a romantic relationship, a principle that holds for both sexes. Males and females evaluate their sexual competence and initiate or withdraw from participation in accord with their private evaluation of the degree to which they deviate from the standard of appropriate sexual characteristics.

A final pair of affects that usually occurs during adolescence waits upon cognitive advances. Piaget's (1950) description of the stage of formal operations implies that the adolescent becomes capable of examining her beliefs, in sets, for logical consistency. If she detects inconsistency, she automatically tries to rearrange or alter them to attain coherence among her beliefs, and between her beliefs and behavior. Failure to do so results in a special feeling state we might call *cognitive dissonance,* which is not identical with guilt (which follows recognition that one's voluntary actions deviate from a standard).

The twelve-year-old's ability to examine the logic and consistency of existing beliefs—an ability that may be dependent upon biological changes in the central nervous system—is actualized by experiences that confront the adolescent with phenomena and attitudes that are not easily interpreted with existing ideology. These intrusions nudge the pre-adolescent to begin an analytic re-examination of his knowledge, searching for inconsistencies in it and between his beliefs and related actions.

For example, the fourteen-year-old broods about the inconsistency among the following three propositions:

1. God loves man.
2. The world contains many unhappy people.
3. If God loved man, He would not make so many people unhappy.

The adolescent is troubled by the incompatibility that he immediately senses when he examines these statements together. He notes the contradiction and has at least four choices. He can deny the second premise that man is ever unhappy; this is unlikely, for its factual basis is overwhelming. He can deny that God loves man; but love of man is one of the qualities of God by definition. The adolescent can assume that the unhappiness serves an ulterior purpose God has for man; this possibility is sometimes chosen. Finally, he can deny the hypothesis of God.

The last alternative, which has become a popular form of resolution for many people in Western society, has profound consequences. In denying a belief that has been regarded as true for many years, the child is tempted to conclude that if there is no God, then all other equally strong beliefs held at the moment are also in jeopardy. Suddenly, what one has always regarded as permanently valid has become tentative. A fourteen-year-old girl, asked how her present beliefs differed from those she had held several years before, replied,

I had a whole philosophy of how the world worked. I was very religious, and I believed that there was unity and harmony, and everything had its proper place. I used to imagine rocks in the right places on the right beaches. It was all very neat, and God ordained it all, and I made up my own religion, but now it seems absolutely ridiculous.

Consider another inconsistency many adolescents discover and try to resolve.

1. Parents are omnipotent and omniscient.
2. My parent has lost a job, or failed to understand me, or behaved irrationally [or any other liability the reader cares to select].
3. If my parents were omniscient, they would not be tainted with failure and vulnerability.

The statements are examined together, and the inconsistency is noted. As with the first example, the adolescent can deny the truth of the second premise, but it demands too severe a straining of objectivity and is not usually implemented. The adolescent can invent a statement about parental motivation and excuse the show of incompetence as being due to lack of will, rather than of capacity. This alternative is rarely chosen because its acceptance elicits another troubling notion: it implies that the parent does not care about the emotional life of the family. Hence, the child is tempted to deny the original hypothesis of parental omniscience. As with the denial of God, the fall of this belief weakens all the others.

A third set of propositions placed under analytic scrutiny involves sexuality:

1. Sexual activity—self-administered or interpersonally experienced—is bad.
2. Sexuality provides pleasure.
3. If sex is pleasant, it should not be bad.

I shall forgo the obvious analysis of these propositions and simply note that again the most likely conclusion is that the first assumption is not tenable. The increased masturbation at puberty forces the child to deal with the fact that he is violating, in private, a strong social prohibition. However, the consistent sensory pleasure cannot be denied, and this silent violation has to be rationalized. As that rationalization is accomplished, the child is tempted to question a great many other standards and begins to examine all prohibitions with the same skepticism.

Each culture presents its children with a different set of beliefs to examine. In our society, standards surrounding family, religion, sexuality, drugs, and school are among the major ideological dragons to be tamed. Partial support for these ideas comes from interviews I conducted with American adolescents which suggested that fourteen- and fifteen-year-olds begin, for the first time, to wonder about the legitimacy of their belief systems. Sometimes this analysis leaves the adolescent temporarily without a commitment to any belief. I asked a fifteen-year-old about the beliefs she was most certain of: "None really. I just take in things and analyze them. Maybe it will change my opinion and maybe it won't. It depends, but I'm not really stuck to anything."

Cultures that are in transition from rural, isolated villages with traditional values to urban centers with Western values—a condition common to many parts of the developing world— produce many adolescents who are less committed to the traditional standards. There is, however, a price to be paid for this dissonance. The adoption of a standard that is inconsistent with one to which loyalty has been given for many years creates emotional uncertainty, for there is still pressure from friends and family to maintain traditional beliefs. Adolescents in Japan and India, for example, who are socialized for loyalty, obedience, and dependence on the family, find the Western value of autonomy attractive because it frees them of the tension generated by anxiety over violating parental wishes. These young adults have higher rates of psychiatric symptoms than do comparable adolescents in previous generations who were protected from this discord.

A second emotion characteristic of adolescence requires a second cognitive competence that is a part of formal operations. This emotion is based on the ability to know that one has exhausted all the possible solutions to a problem. When the sixteen-year-old is faced with a problem, like rejection by a romantic partner or failure in school, she assesses her potential coping reactions to the problem and believes she knows when she has exhausted every reasonable solution. This state is accompanied by an affect some psychologists might call *helplessness* (Seligman 1975); others call it *depression*. This state can be simulated in animals: if a dog is allowed to behave in a way that permits it to avoid electric shock and subsequently is prevented from using that response, the animal struggles initially, eventually stops struggling, and becomes passive. If the opportunity to escape occurs later, the animal does not avail itself of the opportunity, but remains inactive.

Adults who believe there is nothing they can do to avoid future tragedy (death from cancer or sorcery) often become inactive and stop eating; some die in hopelessness. This emotional state requires, as a prior condition, recognition that all possible coping solutions have been considered and the conviction that no effective response is available. Five-year-olds are not capable of this affect state because they are not cognitively mature enough to review all solutions and conclude there is nothing they can do. Although it is difficult to see why this emotion would be adaptive, one can argue that when older persons became fatally ill, it would be adaptive for their family if the person would die quickly and not burden a kin group obliged to provide support. The support drains effort and energy from the younger members of the group who are still engaged in reproduction and care of children.

The Emotions

CONCLUSION

In this brief review of the affects that appear from infancy through adolescence, I have emphasized four ideas. The most important is that one class of emotions—feeling states—is the consequence of detected and evaluated changes in internal tone; that is, cognitive processes acting on a perception of altered bodily sensations in specific contexts. Developmental changes in these feeling states are due, in part, to the maturation of new cognitive functions and to new knowledge. (The phenomena composing internal tone, which are not evaluated, may be less dependent upon these cognitive developments and may require different names.) The psychological state that follows evaluation of both the setting and feeling tone forms a unity that cannot be decomposed without losing the phenomenon. If a single critical atom in a molecule of insulin is removed, the entire molecule loses its biological potency. We can talk or write about the cognitive and biological elements separately; the phenomenon is the coherence of these events.

Second, although some emotions and their display have psychological advantages, it is not obvious that changes in feeling state had to accompany the cognitive functions that evolved phylogenetically. One can imagine our species evolving so that concrete and formal operations matured without accompanying changes in feeling state, and facial displays of fear, anger, and sadness were unconnected to distinctive feelings. The fact that the affects did evolve implies, but does not prove, that they were useful. Because feelings can dominate consciousness in a way that thoughts do not, one can argue, after the fact, that the perceptual dominance of feelings keeps one's mind focused on the desires and events of the moment and directs one to find ways to maintain pleasant feelings and eliminate unpleasant ones. Most important, as I suggested in chapter 4, emotions form the basis for a principled morality.

A third theme is that emotional states can be altered through information. If an infant with a wary face avoiding the deep side of the visual cliff sees his mother smile, his face changes, and he crosses the deep side (Klinnert et al. in press). If a child is angry at a peer because of an insult, but learns that the other child does not intend to insult her, the affect of anger is likely to vanish. Similarily, if an adolescent is anxious over a supposed illness but learns that he is healthy, the anxiety vanishes. Some emotions are difficult to alter because no information is alleviating. Guilt due to the belief that one has caused the death of a parent is one example. Affects vary, therefore, with respect to their vulnerability to new information. Some resist new evidence and remain potent. With growth, fear and anxiety become easier to alter because the child can gain information more readily; guilt is more difficult to alleviate because the child cannot change the fact that he or she has acted in a particular way.

The fact that emotions can be altered by knowledge is in accord with the argument that many emotions are dependent upon thought. During the first years of life, emotions are generated most often by external events; by seven years of age, ideas have become critical. As a result, emotional states are easier to alter in younger than in older children. Younger children's emotions are labile because of their responsiveness to changes in external situations, not because young children have a labile physiology. We distinguish, therefore, between acute emotions provoked by specific events, and chronic moods based on persistent beliefs. The adult is characterized by fewer changes in acute emotions and by more stable moods because feeling states have become more dependent on long-standing belief systems and less responsive to minor perturbations in the environment.

Finally, I have urged that psychologists should question the theoretical utility of the popular emotional terms used by poets and parents, and search for coherences among related events. This suggestion resembles Cuvier's plea to his fellow taxonomists, at the end of the eighteenth century, to search for the relations among observable features in defining a species.

I have not presented this essay on division that it may serve as the beginnings of the determination of the name of species; an artificial system would be easier for this, and this is only proper. My aim has been to make known more exactly the nature and true relationships of the *animaux à sang blanc* [invertebrates], by reducing to general principles what is known of their structure and general properties. (Quoted in Mayr 1982, p. 184)

6

The Generation
of Thought

Don't let me catch anyone talking about the
universe in my department.

ERNEST RUTHERFORD,
radio broadcast

A FOUR-YEAR-OLD GIRL, pointing at a large, dark cloud, asks her father, "Why is the sky mad?" If this question were rare, it could be attributed to some idiosyncratic association. But because such questions are common among all young children, we must explain why most four-year-olds assume that the sky's dark cast must be caused by some force and why dark colors imply anger rather than joy, shame, or excitement. An interpretation of this tiny slice of thought confronts the central problems of cognitive development.

Two Issues in Cognitive Development

Before I begin a discussion of the generation of thought, it is useful to point out that this domain of study is rent with controversy over two seminal issues—both were themes considered in chapter 1: the balance between maturation of the brain and experience in promoting change in mental functions; and the best descriptive categories for cognitive functions, given the present state of knowledge.

THE COMPLEMENTARY RELATION BETWEEN MATURATION AND EXPERIENCE

The abilities to remember the past, to impose a symbolic meaning on an object, and to be aware of what the self is doing appear in all children at remarkably similar ages. Is this concordance due to the fact that all children have similar experiences, or is it partly a consequence of the growth of specific parts of the central nervous system? Until recently most American psychologists have preferred to award most of the power to experience and have resisted the fixity implied by the elaboration of a genetic script. For example, the majority of psychologists have assumed that prior conditioning is the reason highly aroused adult rats bring their forepaws up to their whiskers. But if the forepaws of infant rat pups are surgically removed, the aroused adult animal moves the remaining stumps in ways that are consonant with the muscular actions that would lead a normal rat to rub its whiskers. Similarly, if a white crowned sparrow is raised from hatching to adulthood in complete isolation, without exposure to the singing of other birds, it will still sing a song. Although the song is not the same as the one that normally reared sparrows sing, it is a form of the normal adult song (Marler 1970). These surprising facts suggest that the rats' whisker rubbing and the sparrows' singing originate in structures in the central nervous system whose appearance requires neither prior practice nor support from sensory input.

Many developmental psychologists writing between the two world wars believed that the child learns the language of her community by first imitating what she hears and then slowly perfecting a correct grammar and appropriate vocabulary through trial and error. This tedious argument has now been replaced by one that assumes each child is born with the potential competences to understand and to speak a language, each of which will be actualized when the brain reaches a certain level of maturity, as long as the child has been exposed to the speech of others (Brown 1973).

Experience can either hasten or retard the time of emergence of the basic human competences: children living in extremely isolated areas of the world with minimal variety and cognitive challenges can be four, five, or even six years behind American children in the development of some of the basic strategies of thought. But these abilities will appear eventually in any environment containing people and objects, even if the people know little of what a child requires and there are no books, pencils, radios, television sets, or manufactured toys. The basic cognitive competences are best viewed as processes that are prepared to be actualized given proper experience, as a sparrow is prepared to learn the song of its species when it reaches a certain stage of growth—at about ten days of age—and is exposed to its song during the next forty days. Consider just a few fundamental members of the class of prepared competences.

The conviction that the world contains discrete objects that exist over time is an obvious candidate. The five-month-old becomes visibly upset if he continues to reach for what appears to him—due to an arrangement of mirrors—to be an object, but feels nothing.* If the child did not expect to feel an object, he would not become surprised and subsequently distressed. By eighteen months, children will, after lifting a cloth and finding no object, search persistently for the toy they have watched being hidden under that cloth moments earlier for they know the object must be somewhere.

Second, by their fourth birthday, children appreciate that the appearance of an object may not reveal its true identity. They know that most of the time an object can be recognized at a distance by a few salient, frequently occurring qualities, but that, on occasion, a salient feature can be misleading. If a four-year-old sees a smoothly polished white stone that resembles an egg, he will say it is an egg. But after being allowed to feel the object and bang it on a table, he will acknowledge that the object really is a stone (Flavell, Flavell, and Green 1983).

The idea that a change in the position or the appearance of an object must have been produced by a preceding event is a third idea the mind is prepared to invent. Two-year-olds who see a broken cup or a distorted mask of a face will ask, "Who broke it?" or, "Who hit him?" They would pose these questions only if they

*D. Starkey, personal communication, 1983.

believed that the distortion had been caused by a prior event. Children learn quickly which of the many events prior to an outcome is its likely cause. In one experiment, four-year-olds were shown a box containing two inclines. Each child saw a ball roll down one of the inclines and a light "roll" down the other; both the ball and the light traversed their inclines and passed out of sight simultaneously. A second or two later, a jack-in-the box popped up from a box to the right of both inclines, and the child was asked what made the jack-in-the-box appear. The children's answers indicated that they regarded the ball, and not the light, as the cause of the appearance of the jack-in-the-box (Bullock, Gelman, and Baillargeon 1982).

Fourth, the child's mind finds it easy to treat one event as representative of another—that is, to have a symbolic attitude toward events. A three-year-old assumes that a schematic outline of a house can stand for the real object, and that a vocal utterance can refer to a real event in the world. When a father who is feeding a child says, "Milk," the one-year-old assumes that the pattern of sound refers to the cup and/or its liquid contents and is not a random event having no relation to the real world. This talent may be especially elaborated in humans, for, despite great patience, David and Anne Premack had difficulty teaching a chimpanzee to treat a picture of an apple as equivalent to a real apple or to recognize an eye as part of a face (Premack and Premack 1983).

A category is a fifth idea the child is prepared to create. The three-year-old is addicted to treating all objects that share dimensions as if they were related to each other. He will spontaneously pick out four small red blocks from a large array of objects with varied shapes and colors and, after placing them on a separate part of the carpet, will smile. Children will treat the larger of two square pieces of plain wood as representative of an adult and the smaller as representative of a child, simply because of the shared dimension of relative size. And, despite the fact that very few parents point out the similarity in form between a crescent moon and a thin sliver of lemon peel, a majority of children insist on calling the latter a moon. Children quickly learn to distinguish among the basic categories of physical objects (like people and balls) and among dynamic events (like running and eating) and, within physical objects, among animals, plants, and nonliving objects. Children also create categories for qualities, features, or dimensions of both objects and events. They appreciate that dirtiness is a likely quality of a blouse, size a quality of cars, and sweetness a quality of food. Five-year-old children know, therefore, that the qualities *heavy, shiny,* and *upside-down* are used only to describe objects like chairs or cars, not events, and will tell an adult that "it's silly" to use those words to describe a party, a game, or a motor trip (Keil 1983; Clark 1983). The fact that the words for objects (usually nouns), events (usually verbs), and dimensions (usually adjectives and adverbs) appear in the child's speech in the second and third years is taken as evidence for their primacy in the child's conceptualization of experience (Clark 1983).

As the child creates categories, she is disposed to invent their complement. Soon after learning the meaning of *up,* the child learns the meaning of *down;* after learning the meaning of *high,* she learns the meaning of *low;* after *good,* she develops the meaning of *bad.* The appreciation of opposites is comprehended too early and too easily to be the product of painstaking instruction.

Finally, the idea that a current state of affairs can be reversed in thought or action and a prior state reconstructed seems to be an intrinsic quality of human mental life. One four-year-old asked his mother if a person who dies can get another person's bones and become alive again. As we shall see, Piaget nominated this competence as the most essential in his theory of cognitive development.

Although intuition suggests that a three-year-old who has been locked in a dark, objectless room for three years would not display these competences after only a few months of recovery in a natural environment, it is important to note that monkeys raised under such deprived conditions from the opening months of life have, after their initial fearfulness subsided, shown many of the abilities displayed by normally reared monkeys (Sackett 1972; Kenney, Mason, and Hill 1979).

The function of experience is to provide the conditions that actualize the universal competences and to supply information for new structures. Many cognitive processes, like the life functions, are inherent and not learned in any simple sense. By providing targets for the child to act upon, experience creates opportunities to form new structures, as the seed needs soil, water, and sunshine to initiate the photosynthetic events that will produce flowers.

The Paradox of Piaget One would expect a theorist who believed that the development of cognitive processes follows a universal sequence to award the balance of power to maturation rather than to the child's active experience. But Piaget, who remains a central figure in cognitive development, argued for half a century that, because all children act in and on the world in similar ways, their experiences should produce a sequence of cognitive victories that are the same in all children (Piaget 1953 and 1970; Piaget and Inhelder 1969).

It is helpful in understanding Piaget to appreciate, first, that he regarded himself as a philosopher, and not as a child psychologist, for he was concerned more with the grounds for holding a belief than with the belief itself. That is, children and adults regard many of their ideas as true, but they are usually not aware of why they treat a particular belief as correct. People base their beliefs on four different foundations: actual direct experience (a stone falls to the ground if thrown); a statement of authority (the earth is round and one of many planets); intuition, which combines experience, emotion, and the statements of authority to create premises (children are basically born good and become corrupted with experience); and logic (a statement cannot be both true and false simultaneously).

Piaget believed that a major change in cognitive development occurs after six or seven years when the child begins to use logic more often and intuition less often as the basis for beliefs about the physical world. Thus, both the eight-year-old and the five-year-old may intuitively sense that there is more water in a tall, thin cylinder than in a flat dish in which the water rested moments earlier. But the older child subdues the intuition with a recently acquired rule that states that the amount of water in a vessel must remain the same if the only change is in the shape of the container holding it.

Second, Piaget was a pragmatist. He believed that knowledge has a purpose, which is to aid adaptation to the puzzles encountered in the world. Thought is to serve action. Hence, Piaget concentrated on the cognitive processes activated when the child is solving problems, and he was relatively indifferent to perception, fantasy, and dreaming because these functions seem to have little to do with problem solving.

190

The Generation of Thought

Third, Piaget assumed that the child is cognitively active and inventive, acquiring knowledge initially through manipulation of objects and later of ideas. The child is always trying to construct a more coherent understanding of events. Although people and objects provoke the child to do mental work, even in the absence of these external pressures the child is continually integrating what he knows and making sense of discrepant experience. As a result, children arrive at insights without the help of adult tutoring. The seven-year-old appreciates that a set of sticks of different lengths can be arranged in a series according to their length, even if he never has witnessed that particular arrangement or has been told about it by friend or parent. The realization that objects can be placed in a series in accord with their magnitude on a physical dimension is one of many private discoveries that accompanies intellectual growth.

The next two assumptions are related. Cognitive growth is supposed to be both gradual and connected. New structures grow slowly over a period of years, and the structural products of the earlier stages are contained in those of the latter. Thus, the fourteen-month-old's ability to open and close his hands in imitation of an adult performing the same act is part of a continuous growth sequence that begins with the grasp reflex of the newborn.

The central cognitive process in Piagetian theory is the *operation*, whose essential quality is reversibility. An operation, created from actions with objects, permits the child to reverse a state of affairs in action or thought. The ability mentally to divide six stones into subgroups of various sizes (3 and 3, 4 and 2, 5 and 1) and to recombine them into a single set of six is an operation. So is the ability to plan mentally a sequence of actions that takes one from home to school and then back to the beginning of the sequence.

Margaret Donaldson (1982) provides a nice example of the ability to reverse an action in mind. Suppose someone were careless enough to let an expensive Ming vase fall and shatter. What has happened is irreversible, for the vase will never be the same again. However, it is possible to reverse the series of events in one's mind, return to the moment before the vase fell, and to restore the vase to its prior state of integrity.

Unlike many American investigators who are concerned with the accumulation of static knowledge contained in categories and rules, Piaget was concerned with *process*—that is, with the acquisition of ways to transform knowledge. Caricature exaggerates but conveys the contrast. Many American theorists have regarded cognitive growth as the acquisition and elaboration of schemata, words, concepts, and rules. These knowledge elements, added one by one to the repertoire, permit increasingly accurate and efficient mental work. By contrast, Piaget went to the other extreme, awarding centrality to processes and implying that use of these processes would generate the basic knowledge. If an evolutionist were Piagetian, he would talk primarily about the changes in breathing, eating, and reproduction, rather than the changes in the anatomical parts that participate in these functions.

The use of cognitive structures is monitored by two complementary processes Piaget calls *assimilation* and *accommodation*. The child who, in balancing the two, attains a successful solution to a problem is in a state of equilibrium. The process by which equilibrium is reached is called *equilibration*. The key tension in every problem is the initial preference for using knowledge and abilities that have worked in the past, pitted against the recognition that old habits are not adequate and must be altered. Imagine an experienced surfer on an unusually windy day who finds himself riding a wave whose force and speed are greater than any he has experienced. While retaining the posture he has always used, the surfer makes subtle and novel muscle adjustments in order to maintain his balance. When the balance between his usual posture and the new one permits him to ride out the wave successfully, our surfer is in a state of equilibrium. Piaget insists that equilibration is not merely descriptive, but an idea that is necessary to explain cognitive change, for inherent in the state is a change in structure.

Although Piaget's writings have had a major impact on our study of the child and put cognitive processes at the center of psychological inquiry, there are some critical vulnerabilities in the system. First, Piaget failed to provide strong principles to explain the transition from one stage of development to the next. The stages he called *sensory-motor, concrete operational,* and *formal operational* are essentially descriptive, akin to saying that tadpoles become frogs but unable to state the processes that permit the metamorphosis. The mechanisms of assimilation, accommodation, and equilibration are simply too general to explain why a seven-year-old, but not a five-year-old, realizes that changing the shape of a clay ball does not alter the quantity of clay.

Second, Piagetian ideas are not relevant to many important aspects of cognitive functioning. Language provides an example. Some two-year-old children use and understand terms such as *you*, *is*, *like*, and *why*—words that have little relation to overt actions. But Piaget argued that action schemes form the basis of the knowledge possessed by the two-year-old who has just emerged from the sensory-motor stage of development, and thus implied that the intellectual growth of a normally endowed infant who cannot use his arms or legs will be slower than normal. However, the cognitive growth of children born without limbs or with paralyzed arms and legs is normal in most ways.

Third, many children possess some competences long before Piaget said they should. For example, Piaget suggested that preschool children cannot solve problems involving relative dimensions such as *larger* or *darker*. However, two-year-old children can think relationally about the relative dimension of size when it refers to a familiar comparison such as adults and children. In one study children between eighteen and twenty-three months were shown a small and a large piece of wood. The examiner said, "I have a baby and a daddy. Which one is the baby [or the daddy]?" Over half of the children correctly pointed to the smaller piece of wood for the baby and to the larger one for the daddy. The examiner then showed each child a new pair of wooden forms of different sizes. Now the smaller piece of wood was larger than the original large piece that had been assigned to the adult. Again, over half of the two-year-old children consistently treated the larger of the two pieces of wood, regardless of its absolute size, as the adult and the smaller of the two as the child (Kagan 1981).

Perhaps one of the most basic criticisms of Piaget's ideas is that he assumed that many of the principles of Western logic and mathematics are demanded by each person's everyday experience in the world. Such a claim demands a universal logic that is not always realized. In Western logic, the affirmative statement, "The sky is blue," is equivalent to a double negative, "It is not true that the sky is not blue." Yet, in a logical system used in one form of Indian philosophy, these two statements do not have the same meaning.

Piaget, like Immanuel Kant, believed that the combination of the structure of the human mind applied to experience will yield the basic operations. Scholars who favor this view often use the discovery of number as an example, noting that it is easy for the child to discover that when one adds one stone to a second stone there are two stones, and that the number is independent of the specific stones being combined and of whether one counts them from left to right or from right to left. But it is also common for a child to see one drop of water fall on a second drop and yield one drop rather than two. In this case the addition of objects does not yield an increase in their number. Now it is less obvious that the basic principles of arithmetic are given by experience. The logical principle of transitivity states that if A is greater than B on some dimension and B is greater than C, then A must be greater than C. But experience teaches that if school A beats school B in football and B beats C, it is still possible for C to beat A. Past experience is again a poor guide to a logical rule. Piaget claimed that the past experiences of all seven-year-olds should lead them to conclude that if a ball of clay is flattened, it should still have the same amount of clay. Yet, experience teaches that a little bit of material is always left on the examiner's hand when she changes its shape; and a few children insist, rightly, that the new piece of clay must have less substance because of these tiny losses. Thus, it is not obvious that the logic we learn to apply to information originates in and is totally dependent upon active encounters with the world.

Further, not all scholars have shared Piaget's premise that the function of knowledge is action. In John Locke's famous seventeenth-century essay (1690), understanding and a sense of knowing are the primary purposes of knowledge. Correspondingly, Locke made perception and reasoning, rather than action, the mode by which knowledge is gained. Indeed, Piaget regarded as unreliable and immature the very knowledge that Locke viewed as most certain.*

Finally, it remains a puzzle why Piaget minimized the role of maturation in early intellectual growth. Even though he acknowledged that the child is born with important sensory-motor actions and processes, making a purely environmental interpretation of in-

---

*The revival of hermeneutics in philosophy, psychiatry, and sociology represents a return to understanding, and a partial rejection of the emphasis on action which has dominated Western thought for a little over a century.

tellectual development impossible, he wanted to award to biology as little fixed influence as possible. "Hereditary transmission," he wrote late in life, "seems to play only a limited role in the development of cognitive functions" (1972, p. 58). A similar assumption is present in a debate the twenty-year-old Piaget had with a Polish taxonomist regarding the bases for variation among species of freshwater snail. In sharp disagreement with his older colleague, Piaget minimized mutation and maximized the influence of the environment by proposing that the structures of the snail are transformed gradually through their interaction with the environment (Piaget 1913). Such a theoretical position may rest on an idealistic premise regarding the way evolution ought to proceed, for the twenty-one-year-old Piaget wrote to Romain Rolland that morality was to be based on science (Vidal 1981). In this sense, Piaget shares with contemporary social scientists who hold an egalitarian ethos the desire to make encounter with the environment—rather than biological events which are less controllable—the most influential sculptor of growth.

THE SELECTION OF TERMS

As I noted in chapter 1, the selection of constructs is one of the most important tasks of any science. Major progress in physiology, for example, followed the realization in the early nineteenth century that the cell and not the organ was the more fundamental biological unit. What are the basic units in thought? What level of construct will be theoretically most useful to describe uniformities and variation in cognitive function? Is it best to use general constructs, like *intelligence;* moderately general ones, like *spatial ability;* or highly specific ones, like the *ability to remember faces?*

For a long time, most Western psychologists and philosophers have favored positing a single term or a few terms to summarize a person's ability to process experience, recall knowledge, and solve problems accurately and quickly, regardless of the domain or the way a problem is posed. There are obvious differences between older and younger children, as well as among children of the same age, in depth of knowledge and in speed and quality of problem solution. These impressive differences, some of which are stable over time, lead Western theorists to prefer a single term to summarize a person's quality of cognitive functioning. The most popular English word for this characteristic is *intelligence.* This term may seem helpful in everyday conversation, for it seems to save us from listing all the processes and structures involved in a correct, efficient performance in a specific context; but *intelligence* is not theoretically useful for two reasons. First, rather than being defined by its constituent processes or the individual's history, the term is usually defined in terms of the final outcome of a host of independent processes. The error is clarified by an analogy from evolutionary biology.

Because the clam has survived for a longer time than the dinosaur, it might be regarded as biologically more fit, even though the latter has a more complex central nervous system. But the dinosaur vanished not because of any inherent flaw in its constitution, but rather because chance produced changes in ecology that the clam managed to escape. Thus, to claim that clams are more fit than dinosaurs only restates the fact of differential survival due to chance events; it does not explain much about the qualities of clams *qua* clams. Similarly, to state that differences among children in school test scores are due to different levels of intelligence does not explain the reasons for those differences.

A better reason to be skeptical about the utility of the idea of intelligence is that children and adults are not uniform in their quality of thought across different problems. There is so much specificity in cognitive functioning that it is a serious distortion to average a set of uneven performances on a variety of problems and to regard the average as theoretically useful. Several years ago, my colleagues and I studied a group of twelve-year-old boys who were reading at third-grade level, and a second group of boys of the same age who were reading at sixth- or seventh-grade level. The group who read well had slightly higher I.Q. scores than those who were reading so poorly. But when the reading-disabled group had to decide, as quickly as possible, whether a particular oral statement was true or false (for example, "Plumbers print maps"), many responded as quickly as the boys with good reading skills. If *intelligence* were a useful term, the better readers should have shown faster decision times than all the poor readers on most of the items.

Similarly, quality of memory for a series of unrelated photographs of objects is not related to the quality of memory for orally delivered sentences. It is not even possible to generate a principle for recognition memory that is valid for children growing up in two different cultural settings (Newcombe, Rogoff, and Kagan 1977). An original black-and-white photograph of a realistic scene which had been inspected earlier was paired with a slight transformation that involved addition of an element to the scene, rearrangement of the elements, or a change in perspective. American children were much better at detecting the transformations that added an element to the scene or changed the perspective of the photograph, but they made many errors if the objects in the scene were rearranged. By contrast, Mayan Indian children living in isolated villages in northwest Guatemala were equally competent at detecting all three classes of change in the photographs and performed as well as the Americans on the scenes that either added an element or changed the perspective.

These illustrations—many more are possible—imply that the concept of general intelligence is not faithful to the extraordinary differences in quality of cognitive functioning among children or within any one child across a period of months. The usual reply to this argument is that factor analysis* of the scores obtained in a variety of intellectual performances typically produces a first factor that involves linguistic knowledge. Because language is intimately involved in most of the problems presented to children in clinics, laboratories, or schools, scientists friendly to the notion of a unitary ability claim this fact as support for the theoretical utility of "general intelligence."

But suppose a visiting Martian who wants to learn the most important facts about the objects Americans use in their homes brings a ruler as his only measuring instrument. Our visitor measures every object he finds in a sample of one thousand homes, factor-analyzes the resulting data, finds that the first factor contains objects less than two hundred square inches in area and less than one thousand cubic inches in volume, and calls this factor "small objects." It included forks, books, oranges, bars of soap, shoes, watches, pencils, combs, ashtrays, cigarettes, and matches. These objects share no important common function—not potential for harm, origin, fragility, or price, each of which is a theoretically

*Factor anaylsis is a special mathematical treatment of the correlations among scores on different tests.

important quality of objects. All they share is a common size, but a common size is of minimal utility in a theory of object use. The fact that language ability emerges as the first factor in an analysis of children's performances on popular intellectual tests says more about the typical selection of questions for the tests than it does about the basic nature of human talent.

It is useful to regard different classes of cognitive ability as having long developmental histories. Each emerges in a narrow context early in development; with growth, each is applied to an increasing number of contexts until it is reliably activated in most, but rarely all, relevant problem situations. The development of cognitive functions might be viewed as a series of growth functions, one for each competence, in which the proportion of relevant contexts in which a competence is activated grows with age.

The phrase "contexts in which a competence is activated" hides an important distinction that I have glossed over up to now—the distinction between cognitive competence and public performance. Although these ideas seem reasonable, close analysis reveals a fuzziness to the concept of competence which deserves to be explored. One must distinguish first between the ability to use knowledge or a talent a person already possesses, and the ability to acquire a new skill or segment of knowledge. There may be no relation between these two meanings of competence. I call the former an *actual competence* and the latter a *potential competence.* A simple example of an actual competence is a person's ability to remember the name of a close friend. The competence in this case is specific—"knowledge of the name of a person." This competence does not include the ability to recall the names of people in general and certainly is not as broad as the competence to remember all classes of verbal information.

Similarly, a three-year-old who cannot count six objects—that is, say aloud, "one, two, three, four, five, six"—nonetheless will indicate that an error has been committed if the examiner makes a puppet omit a number or reports the same number twice while counting the same six objects (Gelman and Meck 1983). A three-year-old has the competence to recognize the number sequence one through six but apparently does not have the competence to execute it. Although some psychologists are likely to say that this child has the actual competence to count to six but simply did not display it, other scientists will use the failure in performance to infer an incomplete or absent competence. But it is not always clear which actual or potential competence is to blame for a performance failure. When a child or an adult fails a problem—let us say that a child cannot recall a list of six unrelated words—we do not know whether the poor performance is due to failure to use an actual competence (the child knows and registers the names but is not motivated to recall them) or to a flaw in the potential competence to register lists of unrelated words. The latter could be due to not knowing the meanings of some of the words, to not knowing how to rehearse them, to not being able to focus attention, or to a host of other cognitive deficits that could produce the same flawed performance.

But suppose, through careful experimentation, we are able to locate the exact nature of the fragile competence. How general a name should we give it? Let us assume that we determine that the inferior performance is due to an imperfection in the potential competence to focus attention on the words as they were being read. It is unlikely that this person would be unable to pay attention to all verbal information on all occasions, and just as unlikely that the impaired competence is limited to this particular set of words. Elimination of these two admittedly extreme alternatives leaves an enormous space in which to find the best description of the person's "lack of competence."

This hypothetical example contains the essence of the controversy surrounding the word *competence.* Some psychologists prefer to move toward enlarging the domain of the competence; others wish to narrow it. Because the data are ambiguous, it is a matter of taste which level is preferred. I favor a restricted conception because, as I noted earlier, nature is usually very particular. Mayan Indian eight-year-olds living in the northwest highlands of Guatemala have great difficulty remembering a series of words or pictures. Despite many trials and a patient tester, the children cannot recall more than three or four words when, after each series is mastered, an additional word is added to the series just memorized. American children of the same age can remember a series of twelve words under the same testing procedure. Thus Mayan children seem to lack the potential competence to register and retrieve verbal information across half a dozen different memory tasks. The consistency of this performance would tempt most psychologists to regard the competence failure as being broad in scope. Yet when these same children were required to learn to associate a series of different geometric designs with different meaningful words, they learned them quickly and efficiently. Apparently there was something about this particular task that was friendly to their abilities (Kagan et al. 1979).

The importance of the context is revealed in studies of discrimination in animals. Most scientists study discrimination by placing the animal in an ecologically unnatural setting. The animal is restrained in a small cage sitting in front of two geometric forms. The experimenter baits one of the forms with food; and if the animal uncovers the correct object, it gets the food. Under these conditions, monkeys learn to discriminate the form that covers the food from the one that does not—but they only do so after many, many trials, implying that the discrimination is difficult. But if the testing situation is altered to resemble more closely the natural setting in which the animals live, the discrimination can be learned in one trial. Groups of marmosets tested in a situation in which they were not constrained learned, in a single trial, to discriminate the object that contained the food from objects that did not (Menzel and Juno 1982).

Each structural unit in nature has a specific set of potential competences. The ovary secretes estrogen, not a variety of steroid hormones; finch have a potential competence to learn the song of their species, not the song of the cuckoo. Children do differ in their potential competence to acquire many specific skills and domains of knowledge. But given the meager evidence, it is probably wise at this stage of psychological understanding to conceive of that competence as applying to limited, rather than broad, domains, whether the competence is adding *ed* to a verb to indicate past tense or being able to add numbers.

A great deal of scientific advance turns out to be discovery of the limits of a process that had been overextended. Pasteur and Jenner found that specific forms of life spoil wine and produce human illness—effects that had been attributed to broad forces. Rejection of transplanted organs by a host has been attributed, until recently, to properties inherent in the entire organ that is placed in the host. It now appears that the rejection of the organ is due specifically to white blood cells and not to the entire organ. It is likely that currently popular potential competences—like intelligence or even spatial, verbal, musical, and mathematical ability (Gardner 1983)—are much too broad, and that future research will reveal their proper, limited sphere of operation.

A serious, and as yet unresolved, problem that makes it difficult to infer an actual or a potential competence from a child's performance arises from the child's occasional misunderstanding of a problem posed by an adult. Most of the facts about cognitive development are based on the child's answers to problems posed by an examiner. Often the child interprets a question in a way that differs from the intention of the interrogator, and the answer that is correct from the child's subjective perspective is judged incorrect by the examiner. Consider the following example.

A four-year-old child is shown an array containing four toy garages and three toy cars. Each of the cars is in a garage, leaving one garage empty. The examiner asks the child, "Are all the cars in a garage?" The young child typically says, "No," and the examiner concludes that the child does not know the meaning of *all*. But if the examiner first asks a systematic series of questions about only three cars and then repeats the test question, the child will answer correctly. In the first instance, the child assumes that if there are four garages, there must be four cars. Why would someone build a garage if there is no car for it? The child infers that there is a missing car somewhere, and therefore it cannot be true that all the cars are in the garages. The child understands the meaning of *all* perfectly well but brings to the problem an assumption the examiner did not expect.

Each question—indeed, every communication from one person to another—contains hidden understandings between speaker and listener who share a common culture. Because children must learn the assumptions held by adults who ask questions, the improved cognitive performance with age is due, in part, to a change in a special competence—namely, the child's learning the adult's hidden intentions. But unfortunately, psychologists often conclude, incorrectly, that the child does not possess the knowledge or ability to solve the problem posed.

It is useful, therefore, to distinguish between the publicly observed solution, on the one hand, and, on the other, an actual competence that may not be realized, or a potential competence to acquire the skill requisite for a problem. But how shall we describe the competences that change over development, if we reject broad terms like *intelligence* or *spatial ability*? Because mental processes are poorly understood, it is helpful to compare the mind to a more familiar object and thought to a better-known process. Before William Harvey's discoveries of the relation of the heart to the circulatory system, the heart was compared to a furnace, and breathing to the familiar relation between the bellows and the flames in a fireplace. Indeed, seventeenth-century naturalists believed that the primary reason for breathing was to prevent the heart from overheating. Modern psychology holds two different conceptions of thought: one takes the computer as the model; the other uses the most recent findings of neurochemistry and neurophysiology. Each conception provides some helpful insight; each is limiting.

The computer model currently assumes that symbolic propositions are among the most basic units of thought, because it is relatively easy to program computers to accept and manipulate propositions.* The scholar feeds the computer sets of sentences, together with rules for manipulating them and for judging the acceptability of new propositions. The computer is so talented with propositions that it can beat a chess master and hold a meaningful conversation with an adult. However, there are two serious limitations on its utility for modeling and eventually elucidating human cognitive processes: first, it does not make certain errors that most adults make; and second, it does not handle well nonsymbolic information that cannot be represented as a spatial image. The second flaw is serious, for all the infant's knowledge is nonsymbolic, and a great deal of adult knowledge is composed of remnants of scenes, melodies, tastes, smells, and feelings. It is not yet possible to program a computer to recall the unpleasant feeling that leads a person to avoid offering an answer to a difficult question because of yesterday's humiliation.

The biological model originates in the small points of connection between neurons called synapses. Modern neurophysiologists tell us that all information that will be stored as knowledge must

---

*John Anderson (1983), who is friendly to a computer model, suggests that propositions, spatial images, and their temporal order are the three basic units in thought.

squeeze through many millions of the narrow, moist synaptic clefts lying between individual neurons. In this tiny world, it is difficult to think of entities as large as propositions being transferred from nerve cell to nerve cell. The synapse forces the theorist to think in terms of much smaller units, especially dimensions like the frequency of black/white gratings or the changes in sound energy and frequency that differentiate the end of the last word of a sentence from the first syllable of the next. Thus, psychologists must choose between a behemoth that gobbles up propositions and a minuscule hydra that digests tiny bits of energy. Since neither picture seems to fit one's everyday experience of hearing a voice and recognizing at once that it belongs to a friend, we lack an intuitively attractive model that might serve as a heuristic guide for a description of human thought. Further, unlike the earlier chapters on connectedness, morality, and emotions, for which sound evidence is sparse, the greater accumulation of facts on the growth of thought permits a richer commentary on the current state of scholarship. As an initial framework, I have decided to adopt the useful and popular division between structures and their functions and shall describe the varied cognitive processes as acting upon relevant units of knowledge, as the processes of mutation, reproductive isolation, and natural selection act upon generations of individual organisms to create new species.

The basic units of cognition are still undetermined.* The present consensus is that they are schemata, images, concepts, and propositions. The analogy to varied classes of cells in biology and to electrons, protons, and neutrons in physics is obvious. An alternative strategy is to posit patterns of associations as the basic units, with schemata, images, concepts, and propositions linked to each other with different probabilities of association, depending upon the incentive event that elicited the pattern. The many shapes of a set of charged iron filings that are altered depending upon where an iron magnet is placed can be used as a metaphor. In this conception, the pattern is basic. The smaller units do not exist alone, but are always part of a larger pattern.

Meaning is defined by the pattern elicited by an incentive event.

---

*Cognitive units are not synonymous with classes of problem-solving skills, which Howard Gardner has described in his persuasive book *Frames of Mind* (1983).

Thus, the meaning of the "smell of coffee" is contained in a pattern of schemata, categories, and propositions elicited by the fragrance. The sight of coffee elicits a different pattern, and reading the word *coffee* in a book elicits yet a third pattern. Each of the different signs of coffee has a different meaning because it generates a different pattern. This idea clarifies the definition of meaning, makes the basic cognitive units dynamic, emphasizes the links among schemata, concepts, and propositions, and, finally, distinguishes between objective and subjective meanings.

Because all the available evidence treats the smaller units as basic, I shall accommodate to that historical fact and treat them as primary in the discussion that follows. However, in evaluating the evidence, the reader should bear in mind the suggestion in chapter 1 that the meaning of a construct depends on the source of its evidence. For the distinction between what one believes and the bases for the belief is especially relevant to all of the scholarship on cognition. The majority of scientific studies on perception, memory, and reasoning in adults involve American college students. American eighteen-year-olds are as representative of humans as laboratory-reared white rats are representative of vertebrates or mammals. Indeed, a major theoretical advance occurred when psychologists recognized that many of the principles based on studies of white rats did not apply to other animal species.

Of equal significance is the fact that investigations of cognition in children or college students typically involve relatively unique conditions that do not occur outside the laboratory. For example, in many investigations of verbal memory, the psychologist presents the subject with a set of unrelated words—say twenty to thirty—of equal familiarity, and usually finds that subjects more often remember the first and last words than words in the middle of the list. But rarely, if ever, does a person encounter a list of totally unrelated, but equally familiar ideas. Most of the time experiences and ideas are symbolically connected to each other, and some are always more familiar or emotionally more salient than others. Under these more natural conditions, the person typically remembers the more salient information, even if it is in the middle of a long but unitary episode. I recently asked a large group of mothers to listen to a four-hundred-word essay on the advantages and disadvantages of a restrictive or a permissive regimen in raising children.

The Generation of Thought

The first sentence of the essay said that experts do not agree on the best way to train children; the last sentence said that parents should try to be relaxed and consistent. A minority of mothers remembered these ideas. But a sentence in the middle of the essay said that if parents do not punish disobedience, children may get into trouble as adolescents. Over three fourths of the mothers remembered that idea, presumably because it mattered emotionally to them.

Perhaps the most significant application of the warning to reflect upon the source of a presumed fact is found in studies that use, as the basis for inference, a child's verbal answers to questions. A child's verbal replies to questions engage a special domain of cognition. Even though a five-year-old cannot tell an examiner the meaning of the "equality of two numbers," the same child is able to match five buttons in one row with an equal number of buttons in another row, suggesting that, at one level, she knows the meaning of equality. This is not a trivial issue or a semantic quibble. An observer who watched me drive my car to work would infer correctly that I behave as if I believe the earth is flat. But an observer who asked me why the hours of daylight decrease in autumn would infer correctly from my verbal reply that I believe the earth is round. The two inferences are not inconsistent. Thus, as I survey what is known about the development of human thought, the reader should take into account the exact conditions that generated the scientific knowledge.

Cognitive Processes

PERCEPTION AND SCHEMATA

A child looks out the window and sees variations in shapes of trees, colors of houses, heights of people, and speeds of cars and from this mosaic extracts information in the form of schemata. The child's ability, after turning away from the scene, to know what was and was not outside is mediated by his schemata for the scene.

As I indicated in chapter 2 (pages 35–36), the schema is the infant's first cognitive unit and contributes to cognitive units that develop later. The schema is an abstract representation of the distinctive features or dimensions* of an event. Like a cartoonist's caricature, it preserves in a unique pattern the defining and distinguishing aspects of the event.

Schemata exist in all modalities—auditory, olfactory, tactile, taste, and visual. The ability to recognize a melody, the fragrance of a rose, the feel of velvet, or the taste of an apple is possible because one has created a schema for each of these experiences. In all these examples, however, the schema represents the pattern of physical qualities in the original event; the schema is not a symbolic or linguistic representation. Further, the schema is to be contrasted with an image, which is a consciously elaborated representation created from the schema. Because conscious mental effort is required to generate an image from the more abstract schemata, the young infant probably has no images, only schemata. Although subjective experience provides commanding support for the existence of images, laboratory data, too, require the invention of this idea. If a person, asked to decide whether "a cat has claws," tries to evoke a mental image of the cat, it will take longer to make the decision than if the person were deciding according to conceptual knowledge (Kosslyn 1980).

The fact that schemata are constructed from events does not validate Locke's suggestion that all knowledge originates in sense experience (1690). For the mind invents schemata that have never been witnessed, like the place where the sun goes in the evening. Although many cognitive inventions wind their way back to some event, implying that the schematic representation is an elemental unit, the mind also contains structures—like infinity, quark, and spirit—that have minimal reference to experienced events.

A major controversy surrounding the schema is whether the mind creates an idealized "average" from all prior exposures to a particular class of events—called a *schematic prototype;* or whether the mind holds in separate schemata all the exemplars ever experienced, even while it extracts features common to all. The former process is more likely for several reasons. First, a three-year-old

---

*Technically, a feature is a discrete quality, like the beak of a bird, and a dimension is a graded one, like size. I shall use the terms *feature* or *quality* to stand for both.

who has seen fish, but never a picture of one, will correctly name a schematic illustration, even though the child has never before encountered the few lines that suggest a fish.

More convincing support for the existence of a prototype is found in a five-year-old's ability to know the style in which he draws. In one study, five-year-old children were asked to draw four objects on separate pieces of paper—a man, a flower, a tree, and a bird. An artist then examined the four drawings made by each child, attending to four stylistic qualities that children consistently apply across their drawings: the amount of space the child covers on the paper, the pressure of the penciled strokes, the use of straight or curved lines, and the amount of detail. The artist then drew two objects that the child had not drawn before—a dog and a house—but each drawing was in that particular child's style. Each child was then shown four drawings, three in the drawing style of other children and one in the child's own style. A significant proportion of these five-year-olds were able to select the drawing that was done in their style. Because it is unlikely that these children had ever drawn the particular dog or house that they identified as their own, it appears that they had unself-consciously abstracted from all of their prior artistic products a prototypic schema that represented their unique style (Nolan and Kagan 1980).

Creation of the Schema. The features of a schema are determined, in part, by their physical salience, by the probability of their being a part of a particular event, and always by their uniqueness relative to related events. For example, children and adults from different cultures, even those that have no word for the color red, remember best the crimson typically printed on Christmas cards and regard that shade as the best representation of the category red. Eyes, mouth, and nose are always part of a person, while a hat and a jacket occur far less often: thus, the former qualities will be more definitive components of the schema for a human being than will the latter. But eyes, nose, and mouth, despite equal frequency of occurrence, are not of equal significance. The eyes are more essential for an infant's schema of a person—in part, because of the physical contrast of the darker iris against the white sclera (note that in trying to disguise a person's face, newspapers block out the eyes and not the mouth).

Each prototypic schema shares some qualities with selected other schemata. The qualities that most effectively differentiate two schemata that share many features will be salient. Birds have both eyes and beaks, but the beak is the more distinctive feature because it differentiates birds from other animals that have eyes, not because the beak is physically more salient than the eyes. The mind simultaneously assesses (1) the frequency of correlated features, (2) their physical salience, and (3) their relative uniqueness with respect to "related" qualities in other events. The features that meet all three criteria are likely to be most distinctive for the prototype. Thus, the perceptual quality of "hardness" is distinctive for stones because there are so many objects in the world that are soft. If all objects were of equal hardness this quality would not be perceived and would not be included in the schematic representation for stones. Hardness is not an inherent characteristic of stones; it derives its distinctiveness because the mind implicitly compares the feel of the surface of stones to the feel of other surfaces.

The salience of the features of an event also varies with the person's intention, especially whether the purpose is to identify an event or to discriminate it from another. We use size to differentiate a blueberry from a huckleberry, but color and shape to identify the fruit. A boy in a forest trying to determine whether a moving object is a bear or a man searches for a critical feature, like clothing or fur. But the same boy on a dark street in a large city hearing footsteps behind him would want to know if the source of the sound was a man, a woman, or a child—it is unlikely to be a bear. Now the presence of clothes would not be critical in identifying the figure, and the child would probably search for characteristics in the footsteps. More benignly, if a child wonders whether a stranger is going to hug or kiss her, she will attend to the position of the stranger's hands and arms. If she wonders whether the stranger likes her, she will attend to his face and voice. Thus, identification of an event and discrimination of one event from another often rely on different qualities. What is it? and Is it X or Y? are questions requiring different evidence for their answers.

These two queries are also applied to private experience. If I feel a rapid beating of my heart, I ask, "Am I afraid?" and use the increased cardiac rate as the distinctive feature to identify my state. However, if I ask, "Am I afraid or angry?" the increased heart rate is insufficient, and I must consult other qualities. The increase in heart rate is a distinctive identifying feature of the schema for fear, but not informative if I must decide whether my state is fear or anger. Less frequently we address a conjunctive question to experience. If, upon seeing an object lying on the ground, I ask, "Is it a dead bird?" I look for features that define both birdness and loss of life. Finally, people occasionally wonder about other qualities, like the consequences of an event. They ask of an object, "Is it about to move away or to attack?" The signs of the future action require attention to yet another set of features. Thus, each private question—identity, disjunction, conjunction, and "if . . . then"—often require attention to different features of an event. The schematic prototypes hold in potential readiness a variety of features that may be consulted for specific questions.

The specific problem a child is trying to solve creates a mental set that determines the features selected for attention. A nice example of the role of mental set on perception involves a procedure, often used by neurologists, called the *face-hands test.* The child, whose eyes are closed, is touched simultaneously on one cheek and on the opposite hand and asked to indicate where he has been touched. Typically, children under six years of age report that they were touched on the face, but fail to acknowledge that their hand was also stimulated. Some neurologists believe that the failure to report the latter touch indicates an immaturity of the central nervous system. But the younger child's failure to mention the hand is due simply to a mental set that leads her to expect that she will be touched only in one place. If before the test question the examiner says, "Sometimes I'm going to touch you only on the cheek, sometimes I'm going to touch you only on the hand, and sometimes I'm going to try to fool you and touch you in two places," the young child reports accurately being touched on both hand and cheek. Simply preparing the young child for the possibility of two loci of stimulation changes the pattern of performance completely (Nolan and Kagan 1978).

Permanence of Schemata   Do schemata vanish? This question is part of a larger issue regarding the materialistic bases of schemata and the permanence of knowledge. Even though biologists tell us that, after fulfilling their function, some material features in the developing embryo disappear, and that proteins are continually being replaced, psychologists have been reluctant to acknowledge that schemata might disappear (Anderson 1983). They have wanted to believe that any knowledge, once registered in the brain, is stored permanently, even if it cannot be recalled or recognized and despite the recent discovery that synapses, which are likely to be the structural lattice providing form to particular experience, are continually being eliminated or replaced.

In one investigation, two-and-a-half-year-olds were shown a series of slides, some of which illustrated unusual scenes (a woman with no head, a man with four arms). When these children were ten years old, they were shown some pairs of pictures, one of which was the scene they had seen seven and one-half years earlier, the other a new one; and they were asked to guess which picture they might have seen when younger. No child did better than chance. Although some psychologists might contend that the original schemata were present but not activated in this situation (a reasonable reply), these results imply that the original schemata might have vanished because they were not renewed (Kagan, Lapidus, and Moore 1978).

The attractiveness of assuming the permanent stability of schemata may rest on presuppositions similar to those considered in chapter 3 and contained in Plato's argument for hidden, indestructible structures that form the foundation of experience and permit individuals to know the good and to act upon it. Knowledge is an ethical good in the West, the foundation of morality and of scientific advance. It may be uncomfortable to acknowledge that such sacredness might quietly disappear simply with the passage of time.

INFERENCE AND CATEGORIES

As the child enters the second year, *inference,* the amplifier of knowledge, takes information extracted from experience and "blows it up" into concepts and principles, permitting children and adults to categorize the present, anticipate the future, and interpret the past. In inference, the mind makes a leap, and, by classifying an event as belonging to a category or a related sequence of events, adds information to the original experience. A three-year-old asks his mother, "Where does the sun go when it goes into the ground at night?" The child's experience has taught him that all objects that move have a resting place, permanent or temporary. Because the sun appears to be an object that moves, the child infers that it, too, must have a place to rest. Categories and propositions are two units often involved in inference; I shall consider categories first.

Categories Children's representations of events do not contain every detail of an original experience. Hence, a serious theoretical problem arises when the second encounter with an event is a discriminated transformation of the original. What does the mind do with the related, but different, experience? It might create a representation of the second event which has the same status as the first, even though the mind detects a relation between the two. This suggestion may seem counterintuitive, but adults can recognize correctly many unfamiliar faces, scenes, or words seen only once (Nickerson 1968; Shepard 1967; Standing, Conezio, and Haber 1970). Despite a high degree of similarity among events, the mind is able to keep representations sufficiently separate to permit remarkably accurate recognition.

A second possibility is that the mind creates an additional representation that combines parts of the multiple experiences in an emergent cognitive structure reflecting the features shared across similar events. This product, which many psychologists and philosophers call a *concept* or a *category,* is a representation both of the features and of the relations among the features that are common to a set of discriminably different events. My colleague, Sheldon White, prefers the term *idea.*

The spontaneous sorting behavior of two-year-olds requires us to attribute to the young child the ability to represent qualities common to a set of different objects. When a child playing with twenty physically different toys confidently removes an oblong yellow banana and a spherical cluster of purple grapes, we have to explain why those two objects were selected from the larger array of equally attractive toys. One reasonable hypothesis is that the child knows that the two objects share the qualities that define the category "edible things." Because the meaning of a construct often depends upon the procedures that generated the motivating data, it is reassuring that a second procedure also provides information indicating that the child stores representations of common qualities. For the child will show an increase in attention, more vigorous sucking of a nipple, or a decrease in heart rate to an example from a category that is different from the one that has been experienced over the last few minutes. (Milewski 1979).

The classes of shared features that constitute a category include:

1. Perceptually available qualities like form, hue, pattern, movement, pitch, loudness, and taste. It is likely that perceptually based features dominate the categories of young infants.

2. Functional qualities that include the potential actions of objects, the actions imposed on them by others, and their potential uses by people or animals. The essential quality of chairs is that "people can sit on them."

3. Mental states evoked by events. The features of a concept need not be public but can refer to internal feeling states or ideas. The exemplars that belong to the concept *hobby* or *game* do not share any external qualities. But even though stamp collecting and tennis have no obvious common characteristic to which one can "point," they do share a private attitude toward the activity. (Wittgenstein's famous paragraph asserting that games are not a category because they share no property, ignored all characteristics that were not publicly perceptual, especially the fact that games share an attitude or emotional mood [Wittgenstein 1953].)

4. Names shared by events. The fact that flies and roses are called "alive," and Zeus and Athena are called "gods," can be a sufficient basis for a child to treat both pairs as members of separate categories, even if the child does not know the biological qualities of life or the functions of gods.

5. Relations between schemata, words, or ideas—such as complementarity, opposition, inclusiveness, and relative magnitude or spatial location—can be the basis for categories that are typically part of similes and metaphors. A four-year-old who told her mother that cough medicine and cookies were like night and day was using the quality of opposites to group day and a sweet taste, on the one hand, and night and a sour taste, on the other.

Categories and Language   Although many concepts have an accompanying word to name some, but never all, of the shared features, and a few concepts are based only on a common name, a concept need not have a word attached to it. One-year-olds possess the concept *household furniture,* even though it is highly unlikely that infants so young know any word that captures this idea (Ross 1980). And adults possess concepts for the silence of a forest, the tension of a city, or the special feeling of fatigue that follows an hour of strenuous exercise, each category being based on the qualities shared across similar experiences. Eve Clark (1983) notes wisely that

The Generation of Thought

words evoke concepts, they do not represent them. Karl Gauss said of complex numbers, "The true sense of the square root of minus one is always pressingly present in my mind but it would be difficult to grasp it in words."

Many concepts that are nonlinguistic symbols need not have words attached to them. The child of six or seven years treats dark colors as sharing a quality of unpleasantness and light colors as sharing a quality of pleasant feeling tone (Demos 1974). Similarly, six-year-olds group together graphic illustrations that are relatively straight and unchanging:

and contrast them with illustrations that are curved and more dynamic.

They regard the former as more symbolic of unpleasant feelings and the latter as symbolic of pleasant emotions (Demos 1974). Yet few six-year-olds possess a single linguistic term that effectively summarizes these symbolic categories.

Thus, some kinds of meaning do not reside only in language but are present whenever there is a relation between two psychological units, be they schemata, feeling states, categories, or words. If an infant who is frightened by a large hairy dog develops a conditioned fear reaction to all large animals with four legs, the schematic representation of this class of events has meaning for the child, even though that meaning is not linguistic in form.

The exact relation between a representation of a category and a linguistic term that attempts to capture the category remains a puzzle. As I indicated earlier, there are good reasons for doubting a faithful relation between a word or a phrase and the schematic representation it attempts to summarize. Most psychologists now acknowledge that the young child usually has a schematic category for a class of events before he learns to name it with terms like *ball, milk,* or *go.* But it is also likely that the child can learn a new word for a specific event and subsequently create a category. Recall from chapter 2 the eighteen-month-olds who learned in one trial to call a novel Styrofoam form a "zoob." When one child returned to the laboratory a month later, she asked the examiner where the "zoob" was and applied that novel word to another unfamiliar object. But it is easier for the child to learn a new word if he or she already has some representation of the relevant idea—in this case, the notion that a certain class of events has names. Two-year-olds who know one or two color terms, and thus appreciate that color is a namable category, more easily learn a totally new color term than do children who know no color words at all (Carey 1982). An adult, unfamiliar with physics, learns a new category when the meaning of "black holes" is explained. But words have three properties that most schemata lack. First, words for categories can be nested hierarchically. The concepts *kitten, mammal, animal,* and *living thing* form such a hierarchy and permit manipulations that involve a logic unavailable to schematic categories. Second, words participate in communication and, within a language community, gain a consensual meaning that is denied to schemata which are not amenable to communication. Finally, a linguistic category may elicit more predictable associations with other linguistic terms than do nonlinguistic categories.

Dan Slobin (1982) suggests a "waiting room" as a fruitful metaphor for the idea that a schema or category is acquired first, and then waits until the child can figure out what features of this new knowledge are expressible in his or her language and how they are expressed. When that detective work is completed, the idea leaves the waiting room to join the conversing public outside. But the room is always full of impatient ideas eagerly seeking passage on a linguistic vehicle.

A second basis for a skeptical attitude toward a close relation between thought and language is apparent in English, where the preferred word order in a sentence is subject, verb, object, regardless of the salient element in the idea that is to be expressed. If a large boulder fell on a small, sleeping dog or a small pebble hit a raging dog, the description in an English sentence would be the same, "The stone hit the dog," even though the boulder is the more salient element in the first event and the dog more salient in the second. There are some languages, Turkish for example, where the speaker can change the word order so that the salient element appears early, or even first, in the sentence.

The Generation of Thought

Some scientists believe that linguistic categories can affect the adult's ability to reason. For example, the Chinese language does not have an easy way to express the idea of the negation of a hypothetical event—what logicians call the *contrary-to-fact,* or *counterfactual conditional.* In Chinese, it is difficult to express such a sentence as, "If John had not arrived on time, he would never have met Mary." And Chinese students have much more difficulty than Americans in drawing conclusions from texts that contain such propositions (Bloom 1981). Similarly, the Chinese language has no easy way to make an abstract noun of an adjective or a verb, while English permits easy construction and understanding of sentences like, "Whiteness is a lovely quality," or, "Racing through life is harmful to health." Chinese adults claim such ideas are "un-Chinese," affirming the stereotyped supposition held by some commentators that the Chinese are not attracted to the hypothetical and the abstract.

But do speakers of English find it easy to think counterfactually or in the abstract because English contains syntactic strategies for creating new abstract nouns and counterfactuals? Or, is it that all humans are capable of dealing with both, but the language of a community either enhances or suppresses these talents. I suspect that the latter is true, and that all children probably are able to deal with many hypothetical and abstract issues, albeit in limited ways. Children from many different cultures will adopt, early in life, a pretend set and answer questions like, "Suppose you were a bear, what would you do?" or, "What would happen if all the water in the ocean dried up?" The ease with which adolescents answer these questions implies that they are able to assume a hypothetical set, although the local language can interfere with the ability to display that talent.

Why Create Categories?   Two additional puzzling aspects of categories continue to provoke debate. Why do infants and children have an addictive tendency to create categories? What features are salient for particular classes of events? The first question does not permit an easy answer in the way that "Why do infants breathe?" provokes the reply, "To supply the body with oxygen." First, we do not know whether the creation of categories is exaggerated in humans or is as common in animals as it is in young children, for pigeons seem to possess a remarkable categorization ability (Herrnstein 1979; Herrnstein and De Villiers 1980).

Young children are prepared to detect physical and functional qualities shared by events, but it is not obvious why the child sorts objects into a group after noting their similarities. Even if we posit an innate tendency to recognize similarity among events, it is not clear why the child acts after that private cognitive process. In most cases, the child is not trying to communicate any information to another person. The categorization expends energy yet has no obvious instrumental value, gains no external prize, and is accompanied by no obvious sensory pleasure. Eighteenth-century observers thought that it represents surplus energy that is not needed for survival. The most popular view a century later was that such forms of play are practice for the future and necessary for adaptation. G. Stanley Hall (1906) suggested that such behavior is a harmless sublimation of phylogenetically simpler instincts. But all of these explanations of "playful behavior" rest on the premise that a self-initiated action that expends energy and involves thought must have some purpose in the future and an immediate cause in the child's energy economy.

Although it is possible that the detection of similarities is accompanied by the generation of a special state of excitement, which, in turn, provokes the child to do something appropriate, this assumption is attractive only because it satisfies the desire to postulate some cause for the behavior. It is just as reasonable to assume that the act of grouping similar objects occurs just because it can be performed, not unlike a well-fed sea gull swooping down over a sandy spit just because the spit is there and gulls are capable of swooping.

The Weighting of Features   The different salience of the qualities defining a category remains an unsolved issue. There are heuristic, but few empirically grounded, principles to guide inquiry. Infants seem to regard similarity in relative motion, size, shape, and spatial pattern as sources of similarity in the visual mode; loudness, continuity, and frequency, in the auditory mode; pleasure and pain as sources of similarity for private feelings. These qualities guarantee that all children will draw a small set of universal inferences. But with development, the conditions that are local to a particular environment persuade older children to award salience to qualities that are ignored by children growing up in other communities.

One way to determine the differential salience of events is to see if the varied languages of the world typically attend to certain qualities while ignoring others. Although some languages indicate whether an object is singular or plural, close or far away from the agent, or capable of activity simply by adding a linguistic feature, called an inflection, to the relevant term (like a plural *s*), it is rare for languages to add an inflection that signifies an object's color or usefulness. Similarly, it is common for languages to add inflections to verbs that designate whether the action is in the present or the past, whether one or many agents are acting, or whether the action is causal. But inflections that indicate the time of day or the emotional salience of an action are rare (Maratsos 1983). These interesting facts suggest that the color or usefulness of objects is not as salient as their location or capacity for movement, and that the number of people acting is more salient than the time of day in which the action occurs.

However, each culture also emphasizes unique qualities, and with development, the conditions that are local to a particular environment persuade older children to award salience to qualities that are ignored by children growing up in other communities. For example, children growing up in subsistence farming villages, with domesticated animals in the village and predators outside, treat the quality of being "domesticated" as a more important feature of similarity among animals than do children growing up in urban environments in the same country; the latter treat dogs, cows, foxes, and wolves as more similar than do rural youngsters.

The features of a category that are shared most often will become salient. But even among the features that always occur together, one is typically more salient than the others. The category *animal,* for example, usually includes face, limbs, and body; but two-year-olds behave as if the limbs and face possess greater salience than the body.

Thus, a concept is not a static element of knowledge but a dynamic and constantly changing one. The mind is continually working on its knowledge and detecting features shared by two events or ideas that were originally separate and unrelated. One source of support for this active view of mind comes from errors in the child's use of a word following a time when the child used the very same word correctly. One way to explain the errors is to assume that the child suddenly detects a quality shared by words that he formerly regarded as unrelated. One psychologist kept a diary of the speech of her two daughters. At two years of age, one of the girls correctly used the words *put* and *give* in her sentences. She would say, "Christy will put on her hat," or "Daddy gave my ladybug to me"; but a year later, she began to make occasional errors in which *put* was used when *give* was proper, and vice versa. She said, "You put me bread and butter," instead of, "You give me bread and butter"; and, "Give some ice in here," instead of, "Put some ice in here." One way to interpret these mistakes is to assume that, after first learning the meanings of *put* and *give,* the child realized that both involved the actions of an agent with an inanimate object. Once that shared quality was recognized, the two words became semantically closer in meaning, and thus the substitution errors occurred. Because it is unlikely that the child was taught the shared quality, it is reasonable to guess that the detection occurred unconsciously. The mind is continually working on its knowledge (Bowerman 1978).

Even common linguistic concepts like *animal* change in definition, in degree of consensus, in availability for thought, and in accessibility to verbal report as the child develops. For first-grade children, the word *animal* refers primarily to mammals; for ten-year-olds, birds and insects have become part of the category (Livingston 1977).

Uniqueness also influences the salience of a quality. The features common to one set of events, but absent in a related class, are candidates for salience. Pointed ears, for example, are more salient than eyes for the category *dog* because humans do not have the former, while both humans and dogs possess the latter. Even though the majority of species of bees are solitary, not social, most texts categorize bees as social animals because the cooperation in a hive is unique in the animal world. Qualities that differentiate classes of events that share many properties often become salient— a principle in accord with E. Rosch's work on prototypes (Rosch 1973, 1978) and A. Tversky's work on similarity (Tversky 1977; Tversky and Gati 1978). The mind has two simultaneous missions: to detect the qualities shared by events, while simultaneously differentiating similar events into classes that differ on a small number of qualities. Indeed, some psycholinguists believe that the acquisition of new words is best understood as an attempt to name correctly a contrast the child has detected and cannot ignore. For example, the child who has been calling all animals *dogs* feels pressed to learn and to use the word *horse* when he realizes that horses contrast with dogs with respect to size, shape, and typical location.

Propositions   When two or more linguistic concepts are related, the unit we call a *proposition* is constructed. The proposition "Autumn is nostalgic" specifies the existence of a relation between two linguistic categories. Propositions can define a category ("An opera is a musical play"), state a function or a relation between categories ("The temperature rises in the summer"), name a feature of a category ("Dogs have legs"), or state a procedural rule that is applied to categories ("The speed of a car is found by dividing the distance covered by the time").

A child faced with a problem, especially in an academic setting, typically generates solution hypotheses in the form of propositions. Two major developmental changes relevant to such propositions are: first, that children become able to perform complex cognitive manipulations on propositions; and, second, they become able to coordinate two or more propositions when solving a problem (Siegler 1983).

The ability to coordinate two or more ideas is an example of a basic principle that explains the mastery of related linguistic categories during the first half-dozen years of life. The intuitively reasonable principle states that, among a set of related linguistic categories, those that have more dimensions will be mastered later than those that have fewer (Brown 1973). For example, three-year-olds appreciate the meaning of *on* before they master the meaning of *under*. Why is this so? The two ideas both involve only the relation of one object to another. *On* refers to the relation of one object to the surface of another; but when a shoe is *under* a table, it is also *on* a rug. Thus, to understand *under*, the child must deal with two ideas, eliminating one and favoring the other. Similarly, children learn the meaning of *big* before *tall* because the former refers to size in any dimension, be it height, width, depth, or volume; while *tall* specifies a particular dimension—namely, height. Thus, the child must suppress information from the other spatial dimensions. Finally, children learning English generally learn to add an "s" to indicate more than one object before they correctly use forms of the verb "to be" (Brown 1973). In the case of plurals, all the child has to master is the distinction between one and many objects. But in order to know whether "am," "are," "is," "was," or "were" is the correct form the child must know at least three other factors—the number of people, the time when the action occurred, and whether the agent is the self or someone else. Cognitive difficulty varies with the number of schemata, categories, or dimensions the mind must detect, accommodate to, or coordinate. This ability seems to grow most rapidly during the years prior to puberty and, judging by the folk belief that mathematicians are most creative during their twenties and thirties, may begin to decline slowly after the third decade.

Children and adults are vulnerable to two habits that obstruct the generation of effective propositional solutions. The first is a resistance to retiring hypotheses that have been effective in the past. The three-year-old who believes that all metal objects sink in water may resist renouncing that belief in favor of the more exact rule that the density of an object relative to water will determine whether that object sinks or floats. When the situation involves personal problems with a strong emotional component, the resistance to casting aside premises about people or self that prevent an insightful solution is more common. Many young children believe that all violations should be punished, regardless of the circumstances. Hence, a five-year-old who violates a standard (steals money or tells a lie), and is undiscovered, is likely to feel uncertainty. The child has a problem because he has broken a rule and has not been punished. Hence, the rule seems invalid. But the child does not want to discard the rule and so may commit another, more obvious misdemeanor which does attract the parents' attention and, as a result, provokes punishment. This sequence allows the child to retain his original rule. Some of the most painful moments during adolescence occur when beliefs held for years regarding the wisdom of parents, the loyalty of friends, or the trustfulness of teachers are invalidated. The adolescent, with considerable regret, is forced to question a proposition that has been a loyal guide to action for a long time.

A second obstacle to the generation of good solutions is failure to detect the less salient qualities of familiar events (Tversky and Kahneman 1981). Children were given the following problem: A man is in a log cabin whose windows have no glass on a cold windy night. The only materials in the cabin are some glass bottles, a pot, and a pile of old newspapers. What might the person do to protect himself against the cold?

The key to the solution is to detect the relation between the most essential quality of a window—that is, an extension across an open space—and one of the noncritical qualities of a newspaper—namely, that it can be used to cover open spaces. Although all children may know that newspapers have that atypical characteristic, most children are unlikely to retrieve this knowledge and to use it in this context. This homely example contains a key characteristic in the generation of fruitful hypotheses. Most of the day, children and adults solve problems that are routine; the problem situation calls for ideas that are normally used in that situation. The door is stuck, so one pulls harder. The room is cold: one turns up the heat. In these and numerous other situations, one activates old rules that have worked in the past and so are readily available. There is minimal thought, and the reaction is almost automatic.

But in problems where the solution is not immediately obvious and thought is required, the ideas generated are typically the most reasonable or the ones that come to mind quickly. For example, if a finger is cut, and there is no Band-Aid available, one looks for a small piece of cloth and Scotch tape. The ability "to protect and absorb" is a dominant quality of both cloth and Band-Aids, and adhesion to skin is a salient quality of both Scotch tape and the adhesive normally on the Band-Aid.

Many problems require the generation of qualities that are not very representative of the event central to the solution. Children are much less likely than adults to search for these uncharacteristic features. In one study, children of different ages were shown a tall cylinder holding a few centimeters of water with a small bead floating on the surface. They were then shown a tray containing scissors, string, gum, tongs, a block, and a glass of water, and were asked to figure out how to get the bead out of the cylinder without turning the cylinder upside-down. The string and the tongs were purposely made too short to reach the bead because most children would automatically think of solving the problem that way. The problem was rigged so that the only way to solve it was to fill the cylinder with the water in the glass so that the bead would float to the top. Although all children must have seen objects float to the top of containers with liquid many times in their past experience, very few first-grade children generated that solution in this particular situation because more reasonable ideas were available, like using the string and gum or the tongs. They did not think of using the glass of water to fill the container because a glass of water is normally used for drinking. The idea of rising water levels is more characteristic of faucets on sinks or of rising rivers. The few children who regularly generate uncharacteristic qualities of events that lead to original and instructive solutions to problems are typically called *creative*.

While most intelligent children are not necessarily creative, most creative children are intelligent. But their creativity is based on three other characteristics: they have a mental set to search for the unusual; they take delight in generating novel ideas; and they are not unduly apprehensive about making mistakes. A major hallmark of the creative person is some indifference to the humiliation that can follow a mistake. This attitude gives the child freedom to attempt mental experiments that may fail and to consider high-risk solutions without worrying too much about their potential failure.

Scientists have tried to determine the personal characteristics of creative adults. One investigator asked experts in architecture to nominate the most creative architects in the country (Mackinnon 1965). Forty of these creative architects were compared with others who were judged very successful but not exceptionally creative. The three most important differences between the two groups were that the creative architects placed a premium on imagination and originality, enjoyed being alone and doing solitary work, and were less concerned with what others thought of their work. Creative people search for original solutions, however unpopular or unconventional.

A child's birth order is associated with his or her receptivity to original ideas. Frank Sulloway (1972), a historian, has found that, among eminent scientists, later-born men are likely to be ideologically rebellious, while first-born men are a little more reluctant to disagree with the dominant theoretical position. The development of evolutionary theory required a willingness to oppose the strong and pervading nineteenth-century belief in the biblical story of creation. Both Darwin and his fellow discoverer of evolution, Alfred Russell Wallace, were later-borns; and only thirty-five of the ninety-eight scientists who publicly opposed Darwin or the earlier pre-Darwinian evolutionists, from 1750 to 1870, were later-borns. By contrast, only two of thirty pre-Darwinian scholars favoring evolution were first-borns. Sulloway has also examined the different revolutionary ideas promoted by Copernicus, Bacon, and Freud. Of twenty major opponents to one of these three ideas, 80 percent were either first-borns or eldest sons; 20 percent were later-born. Of the forty-three early proponents of one of the ideas, 84 percent were younger sons, and only 16 percent first-borns or eldest sons. Even though first-borns attain higher I.Q. scores than later-borns (Zajonc 1976), they are less likely to invent or promote a controversial theory that places them in opposition to the ideas of the respected majority.

MEMORY

When psychologists say that the knowledge stored in schemata, categories, and propositions is remembered, the term *memory* is being used broadly to embrace a variety of separate processes. A three-month-old watches an orange ball move up and down on a pulley mounted against a black background, and creates a schema for this complex experience. When this infant returns a day later to see the same event, he becomes bored more quickly than an infant who is watching this event for the first time because the former child recognizes the original event (Super 1972). A ten-year-old is shown a series of twelve pictures of familiar objects in a particular order. The pictures are then turned over, and she is given a matching set of twelve pictures and asked to duplicate the original order. After the child performs that task successfully, the examiner takes the child's pictures away, leaving only the original twelve pictures, which are still turned over, interchanges the positions of pictures 2 and 7, gives the child's pictures back to her, and asks her to duplicate the new order. The successful performance requires a recall of information that was stored, in part, as categories (Kagan et al. 1979).

In *recognition*, the child simply has to decide whether an event in the perceptual field was experienced in the past. In *recall*, the child must retrieve all the necessary information without the help of reminders. Most of the time, recognition memory is better than recall memory, with the difference between recall and recognition being more dramatic in younger than in older children. The ten-year-old who has been shown a group of twelve pictures is usually able to recall spontaneously about eight of them but is able to recognize all twelve even if they are included in a much larger set of photographs. A four-year-old will also recognize all twelve but is able to recall only two or three of the pictures.

There are three major aspects to the development of memorial competences. The first is the firmness of the registration of information. Because familiarity aids registration, and adults have more knowledge than children, adults generally register more information. Familiarity can be roughly equated with the richness of the associations, especially symbolic ones, generated by an event. There is evidence for the interesting suggestion that, after the third birthday, when growth of language is accelerating, the firmness of registration is enhanced. When adults were asked if they remembered where they were and what they were doing when they first heard the news of John F. Kennedy's assassination, those who were between four years and seven years of age at the time of the tragedy had a very good memory of that moment. However, those who were less than three years of age did not (Winograd and Killinger 1983).

Registration is also facilitated if the child actively rehearses, elaborates, or recodes information. If a child and an adult are shown a circular array of eight designs for a brief period (say, a tenth of a second), and are then asked to recognize the position of any one of the designs, children do as well as adults if there is a very short delay (less than a half-second) between the original display of the designs and when they have to answer. This finding suggests that children and adults are similar in the ability to register an equally familiar event. But if the delay between seeing the circular array and being asked to respond is as long as two seconds, adults perform better than children; hence, it may be that the adults are doing something with the information during the delay that aids their later memory. They may be rehearsing, elaborating, or recoding the original information (Haith 1971). Young children do not automatically utilize these cognitive processes that aid registration.

The Generation of Thought

Children were asked, "If you wanted to phone your friend and someone told you the phone number, would it make any difference if you called right away, after you heard the number, or if you got a drink of water first?" Since kindergarten children were just as likely to say they would phone first as to reply they would get a drink of water, we infer that they did not realize that the numbers might fade from memory if they did not rehearse them. By contrast, most fifth-graders said they would make the call at once (Kreutzer, Leonard, and Flavell 1975).

Just before adolescence, the typical American child seems to have consolidated many of the essential competences that facilitate recall of new information that has been presented in the immediate past. Children six to thirteen years of age were shown two pictures and asked to remember their order. A third picture was then added to the first two, a fourth to the first three, and so on until each child had to remember the order of twelve pictures. American children were able to remember all twelve by ten years of age, and some could master this task as early as age six. By contrast, most Indian children growing up in a small farming town in rural Guatemala were not able to remember all twelve pictures until they were fourteen years old, because, unlike the American children, they did not use strategies for rehearsing and organizing the information (Kagan et al. 1979).

Strong motivation to remember can provoke use of these strategies. In one study, rural Costa-Rican nine-year-olds were first tested on six different memory tasks to evaluate the quality of their recall memory, and then trios of children with similar memory scores were assigned to one of three experimental groups—a motivation group, a strategy group, and a group that had no special experience. The children in the motivation group were given memory tasks on five occasions during which they were encouraged to try as hard as they could in order to get a prize. The children assigned to the strategy group were taught a set of strategies to aid memory: to rehearse the information, to try to make up associations, to detect patterns of organization in the information, to count, and to cluster information that belonged to the same category. The children who were neither motivated nor taught a strategy were simply given memory tasks identical to the ones given to the other children. One year after the first testing, all children were retested on the same six memory tasks that had been administered a year earlier. The children who had been taught the strategies showed a significant memory gain on all tasks. But, surprisingly, the children who were motivated improved on five of the six tasks because they spontaneously invented some of the effective strategies. The advantage of being taught the strategies was greatest for a very difficult task in which the child had to remember the changes in the spatial position of some pictures. The children who were neither motivated nor taught strategies showed the least amount of improvement over the year (Sellers 1979).

Personal preoccupations also influence what is registered; hence, children of differing motivations, despite similar ability and age, will preferentially register and remember different information. For example, highly aggressive preschool girls remembered pictures illustrating aggressive scenes better than minimally aggressive girls (Gouze, Gordon, and Rayias 1983).

A second aspect of the growth of memory involves the processes that are activated when the child tries to recall information registered in the past. The older child uses rules more systematically, including the search for a category, a time, or a place marker that acts as a clue to retrieve appropriate information. The older child seems to know something of how his or her knowledge is packaged and so gains access to it more efficiently (Brown 1983).

A third aspect involves the psychologists' measurement of what has been registered. Progress in the study of human memory is frustrated by the fact that experiences can be registered in different structures, including schemata, categories, and propositions; but the psychologist usually probes a person's memory of an event in only one way. Adults who were asked to recall a specific personal event evoked either by an olfactory stimulus (the smell of coffee, of baby powder, or of moth balls), or by a printed word that represents each of the odors, remembered different events. The memories evoked by the actual odors were less often discussed with others and had more pleasant associations (Rubin, Groth, and Goldsmith 1983). The child who is shown a picture of three people playing on a beach may represent their clothing in schemata, but their actions in a linguistic category. If the psychologist asks the child to report verbally what is in the picture, the child may not say what the people are wearing, even though that information is represented in schemata.

The Generation of Thought

Years ago I showed school-age children a series of scenes with brief exposures, initially for less than a second. They saw each scene six times at increasing durations until the last, which was visible for over one second. Each time they saw the scene, they described it; and, on the last exposure, when the picture was clear, they were asked to describe it in detail. Immediately after this verbal description, the lights in the room were put on, and each child was asked to draw the picture they had just described. It was common for some children to omit important elements in the drawing that they had mentioned moments ago in their verbal description. If I used the child's drawing to decide what he or she saw I would conclude the child did not see a particular feature of the scene. If I used the verbal recall, I would conclude that he or she had seen it.

Additionally, each method used to probe what a child registers has its own internal logic. A verbal description is monitored by a desire to use correct grammar and retain a logical relation between sentences. A drawing is constrained by the motor ability to represent the objects and their proper relation to each other. Although recognition of an experience seems to be more sensitive than recall in assessing what is in memory, this method can exaggerate what is registered, for the child might represent only part of the event, yet he is presented with the entire event. Thus, as I have noted many times, the truth value of a statement about a child's memory is limited by the method used to evaluate what has been stored.

EVALUATION OF AN IDEA

As the child grows, she more regularly evaluates the accuracy of her perceptions, the quality of her solution hypotheses, the appropriateness of a category, and the correctness of a conclusion. *Thoughtfulness* is a good term for this quality, and children differ in degree of thoughtfulness. Some children accept and report the first idea they generate, and act on it after only the briefest consideration: we call these children *impulsive*. Other children, of equal talent, devote a much longer time to evaluating the accuracy of their ideas; hence, they reject incorrect conclusions and offer a correct answer on the very first attempt; we call these children *reflective*.

This property—called *reflection-impulsivity*—is applicable only to those problem situations where the child believes an aspect of his intellectual competence is being evaluated; he holds a standard for quality of performance on the task, understands the problem, and believes he knows how to achieve its solution. Several equally attractive response alternatives must be available, but the correct answer should not be immediately obvious. Under these conditions, the child who does not want to make an error must evaluate each solution hypothesis. These children who are concerned with minimizing error take a great deal of time to search for the best solution. Those who are less concerned with error devote too little time to evaluating their ideas (Kagan et al. 1964).

One test that measures this quality is called the Matching Familiar Figures Test. The child is shown an outline drawing of an object (say, an airplane) and six other drawings of planes. One is identical to the original; the other five are similar but have minor variations. The child is told to look at the six variations and to pick the one that is exactly like the original. Reflective children study all the pictures carefully, perhaps for ten or twenty seconds, before selecting the correct one. Impulsive children make their choices before they have scanned all the pictures carefully, usually respond in less than ten seconds, and, as a result, make more errors.

On some intelligence tests, the form in which the question is asked produces a great deal of response uncertainty, while the question form on other tests generates minimal uncertainty. If a test of vocabulary, for example, requires the child to select from a set of six pictures the one picture that matches the word spoken by the examiner (as in the Peabody Picture Vocabulary Test), the impulsive child obtains a lower score. But if the test of vocabulary requires the child only to respond verbally to a question like "What is a potato?", there is little difference in vocabulary score between reflective and impulsive children (Margolis et al. 1980).

Socialization experiences during the preschool years are an important determinant of whether a child will be reflective or impulsive. Japanese children show a reflective attitude earlier than American or Israeli children (Salkind, Kojima, and Zelniker 1978), and Japanese parents communicate to their children a concern with proper behavior earlier and more consistently than American or Israeli parents. However, temperamental factors might make a small contribution to this style. Japanese infants show a greater vulnerability to inhibition and fearfulness than do Caucasian children (Kagan, Kearsley, and Zelazo 1978), and Caucasian infants who show a tendency toward inhibition in unfamiliar situations are more likely to be reflective as older children than are less inhibited infants. When the extremely inhibited twenty-month-olds described in chapter 2 were tested at four or five years of age, they were much more reluctant than the uninhibited children to offer guesses to different problems, presumably because they felt unsure about their answers and did not want to be wrong.

Because most societies socialize their children to avoid error, most children become more reflective as they grow older. Lower-class children, however, tend to be slightly more impulsive on intellectual tasks than middle-class children, due, in part, to less concern with error on these tasks. As might be expected, children with academic problems in school tend to be a little more impulsive than a comparable group without academic difficulty. Being pessimistic about their ability to solve different problems, the former adopt a "devil-may-care" attitude. Since they do not believe they will be able to solve a problem correctly—or do not care—they do not find it useful to take the time to weigh carefully each possibility. Academically more successful children have higher standards for avoiding error on cognitive problems and believe it is worthwhile to evaluate the potential validity of each solution.

The Executive Processes

The number of problem situations in which an actual competence will be actualized increases dramatically during the interval from two to twelve years. Consider the actual competence, reflective evaluation of alternative solutions. Although two-year-olds will inhibit a potentially incorrect response when recalling the location of a toy hidden under one of five cups, and three-year-olds will evaluate the accuracy of their answers on a test in which a picture of an animal is disguised in a set of distracting lines, four-year-olds will not behave reflectively on the Matching Familiar Figures Test. Why is this so?

One reason is that four-year-olds do not yet understand that ten seconds of reflective study of the different pictures will make an initially correct answer more probable. The application of an actual competence to a broad array of problems is accompanied and perhaps explained by the growth of a set of executive processes. I call these processes *executive* in order to imply that each is superordinate to the processes of perceiving patterns of features, inferring categories, generating solution hypotheses, and remembering information. John Flavell might call some of these processes *metacognitive functions* (1977). I now discuss some of these functions.

1. *Articulation of a problem and its solution.* The first step in any problem is to generate an idea of the solution. Although six-month-old infants will reach for a nearby toy, and newly hatched turtles will crawl to the sea, most scholars are reluctant to award to infant or turtle any awareness of the terminal state toward which each is moving. But a two-year-old playing with a doll will ask the mother where a doll's dress is or initiate a systematic search for the dress, even though she is not mature enough to generate an idea of what actions another child might expect of her if they were playing together. The seven-year-old, by contrast, automatically seeks to determine what a friend might mean by an unusual gesture. With growth, the child becomes increasingly familiar with a broader array of problems and, as a result, is able to specify the solution sought in a large variety of situations.

2. *Awareness of the cognitive processes necessary to solve a problem.* A second executive process is awareness of the factual knowledge and abilities necessary to solve a problem, and the ability to adjust cognitive effort to match the difficulty of the problem. Although middle-class six-year-olds appreciate that recognizing a past event is easier than recalling it (Speer and Flavell 1979), young children do not appreciate all of the processes that might facilitate recall memory (Wellman 1978; Flavell and Wellman 1977). Children in kindergarten and third- and sixth-graders were asked specifically to pick words that they believed would be easy to remember. The older, but not the younger, children suggested words that are easy to recall, like rhymes, antonyms, or words belonging to the same conceptual category (Kreutzer, Leonard, and Flavell 1975).

Young children also fail to appreciate that an investment of attention will aid memory. Four-year-olds who were told that they had to remember a series of photographs for a week did not prolong their inspection times; eight-year-olds did because they understood that looking at the pictures longer was necessary to hold the information in memory for a period as long as a week (Rogoff, Newcombe, and Kagan 1974).

3. *Activation of cognitive rules and strategies.* The third executive process follows naturally from the first two. If the child is aware of the cognitive units and processes necessary to solve a problem, he should activate them. And older children do spontaneously generate strategies and rules that aid solution. For example, adults cannot hold more than seven unrelated items of information (for example, numbers) in working memory if they do not have the opportunity to rehearse that information or to organize it. Consider this string of numbers:

$$1 \quad 2 \quad 4 \quad 8 \quad 1 \quad 6 \quad 3 \quad 2 \quad 6 \quad 4 \quad 1 \quad 2 \quad 8 \quad 2 \quad 5 \quad 6$$

If one notices that the string is organized so that each number after the first is twice that of the preceding number, one can remember an infinite string, for all one has to do is recall the first number and the rule of doubling. Six-year-olds who know certain rules often fail to use them when they are appropriate for a problem. For example, many six-year-olds know the rule of alternation—right, left, right, left, or up, down, up, down—but do not activate that knowledge in a memory problem where such knowledge would help them. In one experiment, children had to remember whether each of a series of identical dolls was right side up or upside-down when the dolls were laid out in a horizontal row. When the orientation of the dolls was random, six-year-olds remembered a series of four or five, and eight-year-olds could remember six or seven dolls. But if the series of dolls had an organized pattern (say, alternating up and down), older children detected that pattern and remembered a longer string. Most of the six-year-olds possessed the rule "alternate" but were unlikely to impose that rule in this particular situation (Kagan et al. 1979).

4. *Increased flexibility.* The ability to discard inefficient solutions that are not working and to search systemically for better alternatives also grows with age. This quality is often seen when the young child is working on a puzzle. A three-year-old who is trying unsuccessfully to fit two pieces that do not belong together will persist and eventually withdraw from the task. The eight-

year-old is able to recognize the flawed hypothesis sooner and will begin to search for a better solution.

5. *Control of distraction and anxiety.* A fifth quality of the executive is to keep attention focused on a problem, to resist being distracted by extraneous stimulation (outside noises, the behavior of other people), and to control the anxiety that mounts when a problem is difficult. Older children seem better able to prevent fear from overwhelming the system and interfering with productive thought.

6. *Monitoring the solution process.* As the child matures, he more consistently relates his ongoing performance to his idea of the correct solution and makes appropriate changes if he decides that his performance is too slow or unlikely to reach a successful solution. This function is similar to the cognitive process we called evaluation.

7. *Faith in thought.* A seventh characteristic of the executive is the belief that when one is having difficulty solving a problem, thought may help one to generate the correct solution. If an initial solution does not work, young children stop trying—in part, because they do not appreciate that mental work may be useful. I recall an unusual five-year-old boy who was shown two identical pieces of clay that he acknowledged to be equal in quantity. I then rolled one piece of clay into a thick sausage and asked him if one piece had more clay or if the two pieces were equal. The child looked at the two pieces of clay, put his head down on the table, and remained quiet for almost two minutes. When I repeated the question a bit impatiently, the boy looked up and said, "I'm thinking."

8. *Desire for the best solution.* The young child seems to lack a generalized standard for the best solution to a variety of problems. Although the two-year-old will, on occasion, want to imitate the mother exactly and become upset if he cannot, he is not usually concerned with finding the most elegant, error-free solution to most problems. Indeed, that is one reason the young child is impulsive on tests like Matching Familiar Figures. The five-year-old offers a hypothesis quickly because he does not regard an error as a serious violation of a standard of performance. By contrast, ten-year-olds have a general desire to perform with the greatest possible elegance on many tasks.

The Generation of Thought

Although many of these executive processes eventually develop in all children, conditions of rearing have a profound influence on their rate of growth. Generally, children growing up in modern societies with good schools and continual exposure to events that challenge existing beliefs show faster development of these executive processes. Performance on memory tests is one index of the appearance of some of these processes. In one study, recall memory for a series of ten to twelve pictures, words, and orientations of dolls was better in American than in rural Indian children. The American children reached maximal performance around nine to ten years of age, with the greatest improvement between seven and nine years of age. The children living in an isolated village with inadequate schools, minimal variety in everyday life, and parents who felt impotent to change their lives, did not begin to approach maximal performance until late adolescence. The children growing up in a more modern Indian village a few kilometers away reached maximum performance on the test by thirteen years of age (Kagan et al. 1979).

PIAGET'S THEORY AND THE EXECUTIVE PROCESSES

Although the executive processes are important accompaniments of the changes in cognitive performance during the half-dozen years prior to puberty, they seem, on the surface, to be unrelated to the operations that, according to Piaget, bear the burden of explaining the improvement in thought over the same interval. Consider the operation of the conservation of quantity: knowing that the quantity of clay in a ball remains the same even though the examiner changes the shape of the clay. As I noted in the earlier discussion of Piaget's ideas, children who interpret the examiner's question literally would give answers regarded as nonconserving because tiny pieces of clay were left behind on the examiner's hand. But that is not what Piaget had in mind. The question the child is actually being asked is: "Ignoring very tiny pieces of clay, is it or is it not true that, generally, changing the shape of the piece of clay does not, theoretically, affect its mass?"

It is possible that the eight-year-old answers correctly because she has acquired an appreciation of the intention behind the examiner's question. Recognizing the problem is one of the executive processes. The child is always interpreting an examiner's question in a specific social context and trying to make sense of what the examiner asks in light of what has happened in the immediate past. In the conservation procedures, the examiner shows the child two balls of clay, two containers of liquid, or two linear arrays of beads, asks a question about their equality, and receives an answer. Then the examiner changes a feature of the array in a deliberate manner and asks the same question. The child is trying to understand the entire context, not just the words, and may regard the fact that the examiner changed the clay, the liquid, or the beads as a condition requiring a different answer. Although the isolated string of words that forms a question may seem to have a constant meaning, the meaning of any sentence that is part of a continuing conversation does not.

Similar problems surround Piaget's claim that the five-year-old cannot regard two complementary categories simultaneously. When shown three black cows and only one white cow lying on their sides and asked, "Are there more black cows or more cows?", most six-year-olds, but no ten-year-olds, say there are more black cows. According to Piaget the child cannot mentally compute the equation "All cows equal three black cows plus one white one." But when the question is changed to, "Are there more black cows or more sleeping cows?", many more of the six-year-olds answer correctly and reply, "More sleeping cows" (Donaldson 1978). That simple change in the question makes a dramatic difference because the six-year-old is likely to think that the original question was, "Are there more black or white cows?" The child does not expect the examiner to ask him to compare a part (the black cows) with the whole. By adding the adjective *sleeping* to the question, the examiner calls the child's attention to the property belonging to all the cows, and so the child answers correctly.

This suggestion gains force through a different demonstration in which children were shown ten blue and five red building blocks and were asked, "Who would have more toys to play with, someone who owned the blue blocks or someone who owned the blocks?" Many six-year-olds replied that it would be the child who owned the blue blocks. But when the question was changed to, "Who would have more toys to play with, someone who owned the blue blocks or someone who owned the pile?", many more children answered correctly and said, "The pile." The use of the word *pile* called the children's attention to the whole collection of blocks (Markman and Siebert 1976). The set to consider more than one dimension in a statement or problem is a major characteristic of development (recall the "face-hands" test where young children had to be reminded that they might be touched in two places).

Piaget made the error of not taking into account the young child's subjective frame of understanding. He treated the five-year-old's understanding of a question about quantity as if it were the same as that of an older child, and assumed that the different answers offered by younger and older children were due to differences in how the same understandings were manipulated—that is, operated upon. The young child's frame is so special he will often agree with propositions he knows are not possible. For example, children between three and five years of age were read a story, an extract of which follows:

> She would like to work in the big Post Office, but she works in a branch. . . . As they were driving along, they saw a hare run across a field. . . . Then they got back into the car and drove to the seaside. When they got there, they went for a walk along the quay. . . . "Look at this castle," said Jane's Daddy. "The oldest wing is over 500 years old." . . . They got held up behind a lot of other cars all going very slowly. "I hope we get out of this jam soon," said Jane's Daddy.

When the children were asked to draw the branch, the hare, the quay, the wing, and so on, many drew a branch of a tree, a head of hair, a key, and a bird's wing. When questioned, "What does a hare look like?", a child touched his hair. "Do you think it would be running across a field?" "Yes." When asked, "What sort of thing is a quay?" or "What's a quay for?", a child would answer, "For opening doors." But to "Do you think they could walk along a key?", a child would nod Yes. About one third of the responses had this curious quality. "We have repeatedly seen that young children's interpretations of language may be powerfully influenced by contexts so that they fail to show adequate respect for the words themselves" (Donaldson 1978, p. 70).

Although three-year-olds are able to infer some mental states of adults—like sadness, anger, or joy—it is not until the years before adolescence that children are able to understand the specific intent of many adult questions and to offer appropriate answers. From the subjective frame of the respondent, a child's replies to intelligence test questions or a schizophrenic's answers to a psychiatrist are rarely wrong or irrational, although they may be treated as such by an interrogator who does not know how a question is being interpreted. One essential characteristic of cognitive growth is an increasing ability to appreciate the mind of the other, so that one knows at once the unspoken assumptions that surround a question.

Conclusion

In order to understand the ways children and adults react to problems, psychologists have invented units like *schema* and *concept*, and processes like *retrieval, inference,* and *evaluation.* These theoretical inventions seem reasonable because psychologists conceive of the human mind as composed of entities that represent experience and functions that manipulate these entities. An analogy from early twentieth-century physics illustrates how powerful *a priori* conceptions can be.

The idea of an atomic nucleus was posited by Ernest Rutherford to explain why a sheet of zinc sulfide, after being struck by energy originating in a sample of radium and passing through a thin piece of gold foil, emitted brief flashes of light that were occasionally deflected by more than 90 degrees, when the angle of deflection of most of the light flashes was usually much smaller. Rutherford assumed that particles coming from the radium must have first struck something in the gold foil which had a mass as heavy as their own and, like a car hitting a truck, bounced far from the target they encountered. Rutherford suggested that this mass was the nucleus of the gold atom. If one considers only the observed facts—a piece of radium, gold foil, and brief light flashes on a sheet of zinc sulfide—the inference that atomic nuclei in the foil are the reason for the deflected light flashes is likely only if the concept of an atomic nucleus is a deeply held premise.

In a typical psychological experiment on cognitive development, the investigator presents information to a child, and the child displays some public reaction. A one-year-old, for example, is shown eighteen different pictures containing a pair of dogs of different shapes, sizes, and colors, and looks equally long at each of the dogs. On the nineteenth trial, the infant is shown a new dog, but one paired with a bird, and looks much longer at the bird than at the dog. Unless the scientist assumes that the infant possesses a concept "dog," to which he relates each of the eighteen pairs of different dogs, and is eager to look at a member of a new concept, the infant's looking behavior will seem mysterious. The notion of a *concept* generated from experience is as reasonable to psychologists as the idea of an atom with a dense nucleus was to Rutherford.

Ideas like schema, concept, and proposition are deeply held premises psychologists use to explain how humans react to information. Let us hope that these ideas are as valid for psychology as the notion of an atomic nucleus has turned out to be in the physical sciences.

The ideas and evidence presented in this chapter have implications for those concerned with the intellectual development of children. Teachers, parents, and psychologists should conceptualize the child's cognitive competences as intimately yoked to narrow rather than to broad classes of problems. The five-year-old who knows that a mosquito remains small in size, even though it appears large under a magnifying glass, does not know that the amount of water in a large, flat dish remains unchanged after all of it has been poured into a tall, thin cylinder. On the one hand, the psychologist can attribute to the five-year-old the general competence Piaget calls *conservation of quantity,* and rationalize the child's failure with the containers of water as being due to his inability to extend the principle to this specific problem. On the other hand, the psychologist can deny the general competence and treat the conservation of size or quantity as a set of highly specific competences tied to highly specific situations.

I believe it is more useful, at this stage in the development of psychology, to choose the narrower view. The ancient Greeks thought the world was made of only fire, water, air, and earth and treated the extraordinary variety of objects in the world as derivative of these four abstract substances. Oil was simply a derivative of water; pebbles, of earth. Although physicists eventually may derive all matter from a few basic particles, chemistry still finds it valuable to assume the existence of over one hundred different basic chemical elements whose properties and functions can change with alterations in temperature, pressure, electromagnetic field, and the presence of other elements. Human thought cannot be less complex, and I have summarized the evidence demonstrating how specific a child's competences seem to be.

This chapter has been concerned with the lawful changes in the many cognitive capacities that accompany development, and not with a child's relative mastery of an academic skill, like reading or mathematics, based on a comparison with other children in an age cohort (see chapter 3). These two meanings of cognitive competence are very different, and it is the second that has the more important pragmatic consequences. Technically advanced societies need less than a third of their youth to assume adult vocational roles that require mastery of difficult technical skills and a standard that dictates continued commitment to others' safety, health, wealth, or legal protection. Because these vocations are generously rewarded with status and economic security, there are many more youths available than there are positions to be filled. America wishes to be a meritocratic society and tries to select candidates to fill these positions from those adolescents whose profile of academic skill places them in the top third of their age cohort. Each adolescent's absolute level of intellectual ability does not matter as much as his or her position relative to the position of peers. Middle-class seventeen-year-olds in 1983 are less competent at spelling, composition, and mathematics than comparable seventeen-year-olds were in 1963. But professional positions are still filled by eager candidates, and there is no evidence to suggest that the quality of engineering, medical care, legal protection, or architectural design has declined. An exclusive concern with filling the technically demanding positions with the most talented youths and too little concern with the total range of talent in a generation have troublesome implications for the larger society. As I suggested in chapter 4, ethical decisions require one to rank the primacy of one beneficiary over another. When Americans decide about the allocation of educational resources, they prefer to award priority to the individual at risk, rather than to the welfare of the larger community, except in rare instances like war when it is obvious that the society is seriously threatened. I believe that the gap in academic competence between economically disadvantaged and advantaged children has become so large that it poses potential hazards to the larger community. For when the range of skill is too great, youths in the bottom third of the distribution become excessively discouraged over the possibility of gaining a technically challenging vocation. Such a mood can be the occasion for an epidemic of apathy or asocial behavior that damages the community and destroys both the esthetic pleasure and the pragmatic benefits enjoyed by those in the top third. It is imperative, therefore, that American teachers work as hard at closing the gap of accomplishment, as they do at actualizing the talents of those fortunate children who enter school with an initial facility in written words and numbers, higher standards, and more sustained motivation for academic mastery.

Finally, teachers might begin to tutor some of the executive processes I have described, especially teaching children how to specify a problem, to control anxiety over failure, to search for and use appropriate rules and strategies, to reflect on alternative solutions, and to know why the solution chosen was best. We want the child not only to acquire knowledge that correctly represents experience, but also to know why he believes what he does.

7

The Role of
the Family

Science is the great antidote to the poison of
enthusiasm and superstition.

ADAM SMITH,
Wealth of Nations

I HAVE SAID LITTLE about the influence of experience on the child,
especially the consequences of parental behavior. The most important reason for this omission is that the effects of most experiences
are not fixed but depend upon the child's interpretation. And the
interpretation will vary with the child's cognitive maturity, expectations, beliefs, and momentary feeling state. Seven-year-old boys
who are part of a small isolated culture in the highlands of New
Guinea perform fellatio regularly on older adolescent males for
about a half-dozen years; but this behavior is interpreted as part of a
secret, sacred ritual that is necessary if the boy is to assume the
adult male role and successfully impregnate a wife (Herdt 1981). If
an American boy performed fellatio on several older boys for a
half-dozen years, he would regard himself as homosexual and possess a fragile, rather than a substantial, sense of his maleness.

Children growing up in Brahmin families in the temple town of
Bhubaneswar in India hear their mothers exclaim each month,
"Don't touch me, don't touch me, I'm polluted." These children

do not feel rejected or unloved, because they know this command is a regular event that occurs during the mother's menstrual period (Shweder in press). And a small proportion of American children, whose affluent parents shower them with affection and gifts out of a desire to create in them feelings of confidence and self-worth, become apathetic, depressed adolescents because they do not believe they deserve such continuous privilege.

As these examples make clear, the child's personal interpretation of experience, not the event recorded by camera or observer, is the essential basis for the formation of and change in beliefs, wishes, and actions. However, the psychologist can only guess at these interpretations, and the preoccupations and values of the culture in which the scholar works influence these guesses in a major way. For example, Erasmus (1530), who believed the child's appearance reflected his character, told parents to train the child to hold his body in a controlled composure—no furrowing of brows, sagging of cheek, or biting of the lip, and especially no laughter without a very good cause.

Educated citizens in early sixteenth-century London, who were disturbed by the high rate of crime, begging, and vagrancy among children of the poor, blamed the loss of a parent, living with lazy parents, being one of many children, or a mental or physical handicap. These diagnoses ignored the possible influence of genetics, parental love, or social conditions existing outside the home. Two centuries later, a comparable group of English citizens concerned with identical social problems, but still without any sound facts, emphasized the influence of the love relation between mother and child (Pinchbeck and Hewitt 1969 and 1973).

Many contemporary essays on the influence of family experience also originate in hunches, few of which are firmly supported by evidence. This is not surprising; the first empirical study to appear in a major American journal that attempted to relate family factors to a characteristic in the child was published less than sixty years ago in *The Pedagogical Seminary* (Sutherland 1930). The fact that a hunch about the role of family originates in a society's folk premises about human nature does not mean that it is incorrect. Eighteenth-century French physicians believed that a nursing mother should bathe the baby regularly and not drink too much wine—suggestions that have been validated by modern medicine. But those same doctors also believed—mistakenly, I suppose—that cold baths will ensure a tough character in the older child. The absence of conclusive evidence means that each theorist must be continually sensitive to the danger of trusting his or her hunches too completely, for at different times during the last few centuries of European and American history, the child has been seen as inherently evil, or as a blank tablet with no special predispositions, or, currently, as a reservoir of genetically determined psychological qualities. Modern Western society follows Rousseau in assuming that the infant is prepared to attach herself to her caregiver and to prefer love to hate, mastery to cooperation, autonomy to interdependence, personal freedom to bonds of obligation, and trust to suspicion. It is assumed that if the child develops the qualities implied by the undesirable members of those pairs, the practices of the family during the early years—especially parental neglect, indifference, restriction, and absence of joyful and playful interaction—are the major culprits.

I cannot escape these beliefs which are so thoroughly threaded through the culture in which I was raised and trained. But having made that declaration, I believe it is useful to rely on selected elements in popular theory, on the few trustworthy facts, and on intuition in considering the family experiences that create different types of children, even if my suggestions are more valid for American youngsters than for those growing up in other cultures.

The Child in the American Family

Among the nomadic Hebrews who herded sheep in the Sinai desert three thousand years ago, and for many contemporary African and Latin American communities, the basic social unit is composed of genetically related adults and children living together in a group to which loyalty is given and from which identity is derived. The fate of each person rests with the vitality, reputation, and success of the kinship group. Hence, the conception of self is dependent on the resources, status, and socially perceived qualities of the family group. Although the nuclear family existed in some early societies, it has replaced the larger kin group in many places and is, at the moment, the most common social unit for most of the world's communities. The future of the children in these societies is determined almost completely by each family's status, wealth, resources, and practices.

But in the modern Western world, the individual, not the family, is slowly becoming the basic unit. The high divorce rate, the large number of single-parent families, and the public's willingness to work toward a more egalitarian society through interventions that abrogate the family's power make the person the central entity in the eyes of the law, the school, and the self. Additionally, early socialization practices that promote autonomy, and individual, rather than group, effort and responsibility, lead many adolescents to conclude that their future mood and material success depend upon their personal abilities and motivation. A divorced woman with only a high school education who was living with her three-year-old, said, "I must develop myself, I can't be dependent on anyone but me." This attitude may be historically unique. Although historians argue about the form of the earliest families and when the nuclear structure emerged, no anthropologist or historian has ever suggested that the majority of adults living in older societies believed that their survival, personal reputation, and material success did not depend primarily on their family of rearing. Thus, each American adult must acquire a special state of mind which most families, consciously or unconsciously, train for from the earliest months of life. Few citizens of ancient Athens, Babylon, or Jerusalem, or of modern Tokyo, Jakarta, or Beijing (Peking) would understand this attitude. Thus, some of the qualities of the modern Western family are specific to this historical era.

A second significant characteristic of contemporary Western society is the dignity and respect awarded to women. Although women had high status in a few Polynesian societies and in polyandrous groups, for most cultures about which we have knowledge women had far less power than men, achieved status through marriage rather than through their own efforts, and were punished more severely than men for illicit sexuality. In some communities of Indians in Northwest Guatemala, for example, the most insulting accusation one man can level at another is to call him a woman.

The rise of women's status in Europe and North America over the past four centuries has been associated with an increasingly benevolent evaluation of romantic love. Carl Degler writes, "The growing acceptance of affection as the primary ground for family formation was an important stage in the evolution of women's place within the family and in our understanding of how the family has altered over time" (1980, p. 18). Although sexuality has never been unimportant in any culture, and is central to the romantic literature of the Middle East, romantic love is today regarded not just as a source of pleasure, but as an experience of great beauty and a major basis for feelings of vitality and self-enhancement.

Love is an intimate, spiritual experience in a world perceived to be impersonal and amoral. The deep anger toward pornography held by many Americans is based, in part, on the threat pornography poses to the idea of faithful romantic love, as distinct from sexual gratification. A love relation is regarded as such a vital part of adult life that families try to prepare their children for that function in ways that some cultures would not understand. Parents arrange parties for young children with boys and girls present, begin explanations of reproduction by noting how much the mother and father love each other, and accept romantic attraction as the most reasonable basis for marital choice, despite differences in status, ethnicity, wealth, and religion.

A third relatively distinct quality of our society is its celebration of the freedom and selfhood of children. Although this attitude was enhanced in seventeenth-century Europe, it has become more pervasive with time. All societies, ancient and modern, love and value children, even though eleventh-century European fathers were not severely criticized for killing their newborn infant if he or she failed the test of fearfulness and cried after being put on a high branch of a tree (Queen, Haberstein, and Adams 1961). The relation of child to parent in most societies is one of loyalty and obligation. In Chinese families, filial love defines the primary bond. The special ingredient in the American form of child-centeredness is its one-sidedness. Parents are supposed to sacrifice for their children, while the children are expected to grow increasingly independent of their parents. For many middle-class families, the child is a beautiful young bird to be cared for until it is ready to fly free in the forest.

Finally, as I noted in chapter 4, in contrast to many, but not all, contemporary societies, Americans place greater value on sincerity and personal honesty than on social harmony. But in many cultures—Java, Japan, and China, for example—the importance of maintaining harmonious social relationships, and of adopting a posture of respect for the feelings of elders and of authority, demands that each person not only suppress anger but, in addition, be ready to withhold complete honesty about personal feelings in order to avoid hurting another. This pragmatic view of honesty is regarded as a quality characteristic of the most mature adult and is not given the derogatory labels of insincerity or hypocrisy. The West derides the person who does not say what she thinks, who does not "call a spade a spade." People who are polite to someone whom they dislike, offer tea and cakes to a gossipy neighbor, and tell an incompetent employer how skilled he is are less admirable than those who "speak their mind." These "white lies" are supposed to reflect fear, timidity, and obsequiousness. But what American parents regard as obsequiousness, citizens of Java and Japan regard as appropriate respect.

With the exception of the celebration of romantic love, these qualities of modern American life award exaggerated value to the individual and less significance to the social groups in which each person acts.

In American families, the primary loyalty is to self—its values, autonomy, pleasure, virtue, and actualization. Most parents accept this criterion for maturity and try to arrange experiences that will make it easier for their children to attain this ideal. Some societies tip the other way. In a popular book for parents written about twenty years before China became the People's Republic, the psychologist Chen Heqin listed the seven inborn qualities of children that parents should promote: active play, imitation of others, curiosity, mastery, mutually binding social relationships, pleasure in the outdoors, and seeking the praise of others (Chen 1925). Three of these ideals stress the social, not the individualistic, urges of children. I suspect that Professor Chen would have had some difficulty understanding John Dewey who wrote, at about the same time, that what men have esteemed and fought for is the "ability to carry out plans, the absence of cramping and thwarting obstacles, . . . the slave is the man who executes the wish of others" (1922, p. 304).

THEORIES OF AMERICAN PARENTS

During each phase of the child's development, different problems become foci for parental concern and subsequent action. During the first year, irritability, illness, sleeplessness, and excessive fear of the strange dominate the consciousness of American parents and guide their regimen of care. During the second year, when the child has become both mobile and self-aware, the possibility that the child will hurt himself or others, destroy property, or be shy with peers replaces the earlier worries. By the third year, disobedience, aggression, incomplete toilet training, an inability to play cooperatively with others, and a delayed growth of verbal skills ascend in the hierarchy of preoccupations. Because each of these sources of uncertainty elicits a different pattern of corrective action, the parents' behavior is controlled in an important way by the inevitable products of the child's growth.

When the child's profile begins to deviate from the parents' idea of what it should be, American parents typically call upon one or more of four kinds of explanation. Some parents believe that the child's behavior results from temperamental characteristics inherent in the child's biology and is, therefore, beyond the control of both child and parent, although destined to vanish with time. The mother of an extremely timid, inhibited three-year-old girl told an interviewer, "She was a difficult baby from the beginning, so fussy, with an ungodly scream. She was born a discontent baby. Now she tests a lot and brings out unkindness in me. She is defiant, so strong-willed that I don't think there is anything I can do to change her." Other mothers see the dominant mood of their children as a phase in the universal script for development. The mother of a three-year-old describes her son's first three years:

> You never saw a better baby . . . he cooed, he never fussed, he was bright, alert—he was terrific and good-natured. . . . Then around a year and a half he started to get a mind of his own—able to talk back. I remember fifteen to eighteen months as being a kind of cut-off period in his behavior. He went from being completely good-natured to being ornery at times. . . . By his third year sometimes I'd want to kill him, he really gets so ornery."

A smaller group of parents assume complete responsibility for their child's profile, believing that they have done something to cause the problem behavior. If the child's behavior does not improve, their initial guilt can turn to anger. Other parents attribute most of the child's behavior to the power of environmental forces over which they have little or no control—the birth of a sibling, a small apartment without a backyard, marital strife, other children in the neighborhood or nursery school, and, always, financial stress. The smallest group of parents ascribe malevolent intention to the child, attributing motives to the child that she is not yet capable of possessing. This imputation is usually accompanied by hostility toward the child. Although well-educated mothers are a little less likely to ascribe anger and malevolent intent to their young child, no parent is immune from this temptation. Generally, parents who are secure about their own qualities tend to be accepting of the child's deviations. Parents who are threatened by their own personal failures are likely to interpret extreme disobedience as a reflection of the child's willful hostility.

The choice of techniques to keep the child on course depends on the parents' explanation of the deviation and on the qualities they regard as most important for the child to acquire. Each parent holds a template for a small set of developing characteristics that represents their ideal form, the time each should appear, and what to do if its arrival is delayed. The mother of a timid three-year-old, who was concerned that her son was being victimized by peers, told an interviewer:

I tell him that you don't hit first, but if somebody hits him, I want him to hit back. It's too easy for him to become a victim. He tends to get hit and be upset and cry. I'm trying to back off, because I generally pick him up and hug him. But now I tell him, he ought to hit them back if they hit him. That's the only way he's going to learn. I hate the whole idea of being less cuddly with him, but you can't have your child be a victim, especially when they go to school.

This mother began to inhibit some of the actions that had flowed spontaneously from her immediate feelings, and to substitute behavior that was based on her theory of how to help her child's future adjustment.

A mother who saw her three-year-old girl as extraordinarily sensitive to reprimand and too obedient told the daughter she was not going to punish her any more, in the hope that, by lifting the fear of disapproval, the girl would become a little more rebellious.

Parental socialization practices are under the stewardship of two complementary influences. One is the child's changing surface of behavior, which is controlled partly by maturation, partly by the child's temperament, and partly by earlier experiences with family and peers. The second influence is the tension between the ideal each parent holds for the stage the child is in and the parents' often unarticulated ideal for the future. For an elite Athenian mother of a son in 400 B.C., the ideal was loyalty to family and to *polis* and perfection of specific talents, especially music, athletics, and oratory. A seventeenth-century Puritan parent promoted control of impulse and the development of piety. And for most contemporary American mothers, the distant ideal rests on five abstract qualities: autonomy, intelligence, humaneness, sociability, and control of fear. The child must learn to operate independently of the family, to master school tasks, to be kind to and liked by other children, and to be unafraid of challenge or attack. When the child's behavior violates any of these ideals, parents move into action. If the two-year-old is too timid with other children, the mother may initiate a play group, enroll the child in nursery school three mornings a week, or not insist that the child restrain aggression when attacked unjustly. If the child is too dependent upon the parent for attention, affection, or security, the mother will encourage him to play alone. If he seems slow in learning to speak, she will accelerate his linguistic progress.

Display of aggression, destruction, stealing, and unprovoked assertion of power are threatening to most mothers not only because these acts provoke peer rejection, but equally important, because they are inconsistent with a mood of considerateness toward others. While listening to interviews with both mothers and fathers of three-year-olds, I have been struck by the fact that mothers are more threatened than fathers by signs of meanness in their children. Most mothers value a caring attitude. They want their sons and daughters to be empathic with others and to inhibit urges to intimidate, to frighten, or to hurt other children. This concern, together with the desire to produce an independent youngster, leads many mothers to check their own impulsive, unreflective attempts to punish their children harshly or to frighten them into slavish obedience to parental norms.

Thus, most American parents try to balance promotion of the child's autonomy and separateness from others with encouragement of a desire to be with, rather than apart from, people and a commitment to aiding the welfare of others. The axiom that human beings are basically social is viewed as complementary to, rather than inconsistent with, the celebration of autonomy, even though every interaction contains an implicit set of rules that restricts each person. However, in America at least, these constraints are gentle enough that individuals are supposed to be able to move in and out of psychological contact with each other, always prepared to sever a relationship if it bites too deeply into their freedom of choice.

Carol Gilligan (1982) regards the two ideal qualities as separate voices within each person. In American society, the former speaks louder to men; the latter, more forcefully to women. On each encounter with an unfamiliar person, one of the modes characteristically dominates the other. Do I try to determine who will be dominant and who submissive when I first meet a stranger? Or, do I try to establish an affective bond that minimizes hostility and fear in the other? American men are more likely to ask the former question; American women, like Japanese men and women, the latter. As relations deepen, both modes can become part of a relationship; but it is unusual for these two urges to have equal force in any particular relationship.

The Influence of Social Class   There is considerable variation in a parent's ego ideal and theory of how the child works; and a family's social class is an important basis for such variation (Kaye 1982; Kohn 1977). Parents who have not attended college, who see themselves and their children as part of the working class, and who live with chronic financial insecurity, often attribute their personal *angst* to economic stress, which they view as being not completely under their control. These families award a high priority to job security; and a central goal in socializing their child is to ensure that he or she will develop the qualities that guarantee a secure job. Two key qualities are acceptance by peers and the ability to resist being exploited by those with more power.

College-educated parents, especially those with professional vocations, regard freedom of choice, intellectual challenge, and the status of one's work as more important than job security. They believe that anxiety over peer rejection or disapproval obstructs the attainment of these goals, and they try to inoculate their youngsters against the anxiety that accompanies peer rejection, while emphasizing autonomous choice and competition.

Despite cultural differences across modern societies, middle-class parents are generally more firmly convinced that each child must develop internal controls on temptation, while working-class parents are more likely to believe that some of the control lies with outside referees (Kohn 1977). Further, middle-class parents have a somewhat firmer faith than working-class parents in their own ability to control life events, to mute the malevolence of circumstance, and to guide the child, through their agency, to the ideal they hold. This belief receives occasional confirmation when a mother's telephone call to the school principal produces a change in a teacher's practices or the reassignment of her child to a new classroom. Melvin Kohn notes that an essential feature of middle-class status "is the expectation that one's decisions and actions can be consequential"; the economically less advantaged parent believes "that one is at the mercy of forces and people beyond one's control" (Kohn 1977, p. 189). A child's class membership, unlike the temporary loss of a parent or a brief period of tension in the home, represents a continuing set of experiences. That is the reason it is such a powerful influence on the child.

The Role of Family during Infancy and Childhood

In their attempts to evaluate the influence of the family on the child, psychologists have selected a few child qualities from the large array of potential characteristics. It should not be surprising that the attributes selected are those that are related to adaptation in American society. These include: intellectual skills, as indexed by IQ scores, school grades, and verbal ability; a secure attachment to parents; sociability with peers; reasonable conformity to authority; and autonomy in making decisions. The selection of family qualities is based on the complex assumption that physical affection, interactive play, and a proper balance between restriction and permissiveness have the most significant influence on the establishment of the desirable child qualities.

In order to take advantage of the existing evidence, I have chosen to organize the discussion around these ideas. The best evidence evaluates the influence of the mother. There is insufficient information regarding the role of the father or of siblings, and I shall say little about their influence, even though I believe it to be great (see Dunn 1983). Finally, it is useful to remember that when Copernicus's monograph *On the Revolution of the Heavenly Spheres* was published in 1543, no piece of evidence could be unambiguously interpreted as supporting his claim that the sun is stationary and the earth mobile. This hypothesis was appealing to some scholars only because it made more coherent salient facts that had been difficult to understand. Thus, while the suggestions that follow make some of what is known more easily understood and, therefore, lend coherence to the larger theme of human development, none is demanded by the evidence.

THE INFANT IN THE FAMILY

Most observers have been interested in two processes during infancy: intellectual development, especially language; and the infant's emotional attachments to the parents. As I noted in chapter 2, the infant's cognitive competences include sensory-motor coordinations, schemata, and improvements in memory. The expectation that each of these processes grows optimally when the infant is exposed to comprehensible variety is verified by the fact that infants raised in institutions that fail to provide much variety are usually slower in their attainment of these qualities than are children from homes where mothers play and talk with them often (Clarke-Stewart, Vander Stoep, and Killian 1979; Ramey, Farran, and Campbell 1979; Bradley, Caldwell, and Elardo 1979). Although the relation between variety and cognitive growth is not always robust, and occasionally fails to be realized, rarely is the direction of the relation reversed. The conclusion that variety of experience facilitates cognitive development may be the least impeachable principle in developmental psychology.

The opportunity to use and to practice emerging competences affects the speed with which sensory-motor coordinations grow. The infant who is restricted to a crib or tightly swaddled takes longer to reach, stand, and walk than the one who is allowed to play with objects and to explore the environment freely. But even though opportunities for play and exploration facilitate motor development, these experiences may not be absolutely necessary. Infants who have little or no opportunity for motor activity or exploration, because they are swaddled during the first year of their lives, will—then given freedom to locomote and to explore after their first birthday—walk, run, and manipulate objects as skillfully as infants who have never been restrained. A boy who could not move about in his environment because he had been in a protective plastic bubble since his birth (due to a vulnerability to infection) appeared to be intellectually competent when he died at twelve years of age.

I considered in chapter 2 the history and meaning of the concept of attachment and the controversy surrounding its measurement, but did not discuss in any detail the consequences of variations in the attachment relation produced by experiences within the family. Although the vast majority of children in the world are raised by moderately predictable and reasonably nurturant adults, there is extraordinary variation in the duration, continuity, and affective quality of the interaction between parents and infants. Most American parents and psychologists believe that this variation has significant implications for the child's future adjustment.

Imagine an environment in which an infant is nurtured gently and reliably. The child is fed before he becomes too hungry, diapered before he experiences excessive discomfort, protected from injury and unpredictable events he cannot understand. However, this infant rarely experiences the excited emotional states that accompany reciprocal interaction with an adult. Mayan Indian infants living in northwest Guatemala are raised in this way.

Compare this infant with one who, in addition to receiving nurturant care, experiences frequent, pleasant, playful interaction with caregivers. These children should become emotionally excitable babies who vocalize and smile with the caregiver. American infants are raised in this way; and, as expected, American one-year-olds are more vocal and excitable than Mayan one-year-olds who do not experience much playful interaction with adults.

If a society values emotional spontaneity and worries about children who are subdued, the latter child will be at risk in adolescence and adulthood. Such a child might be ignored or rejected by peers and, as a consequence, become vulnerable to anxiety. However, in a culture that does not celebrate emotional spontaneity—like that of the Mayan Indians—absence of playful interaction during infancy may not be harmful.

The Role of the Family

A second component of a secure attachment rests with the availability of the caregiver when the child is in distress. All infants experience pain and unpleasantness, and the persons who come to soothe a child will become associated with the pleasant feelings that accompany relief of distress. The child learns to expect that these adults will reduce her distress in the future and will seek them when she is hungry, tired, in pain, or frightened. But imagine a child in a group where the caregivers come irregularly and with long delays. This child will be forced to develop other behavior when distress arises. She may twist her hair, bury her head in a blanket, or go to sleep. She will not learn to anticipate the care of adults or to approach adults when uncertain. Such a child is insecurely attached. This quality has a singularly significant consequence.

Restraint of aggression and destruction, as well as acquisition of the standards that define mature behavior in a culture, are major goals of development. An attachment to a caregiver creates in the child a special receptivity to being socialized by that caregiver. Because the child resists adopting some socially desired behavior, as well as the standards underlying it, one must have a psychologically compelling reason to inhibit lying, destruction of property, stealing, and disobedience, and be motivated to attain other qualities promoted by the society. The child who is securely attached to caregivers is prepared to curb asocial behavior because he or she does not want to threaten that relation. As a result, the child accepts the family's standards and is likely to establish harmonious relations with other people.

The insecurely attached child grows with more serious risk because he is less receptive to adopting the standards that his parents are promoting. Because he is likely to develop a deviant behavioral profile, he will be rejected by others and, as a consequence, will become vulnerable to uncertainty. The prediction that an insecurely attached infant will become an anxious adolescent is probably correct. What is controversial, however, is whether the adolescent anxiety is due primarily to irregular nurturance during infancy which has produced a permanent change in the infant's affective mood; or to the poor fit between the personal characteristics of a child who has not accommodated to socialization pressures, and peers and adults who expect everyone to display the normative behavior of the society.

The belief that the emotions experienced repeatedly during infancy are preserved is attractive to parents and social scientists. But this outcome is not inevitable. Older children who have experienced a great deal of uncertainty during the opening two or three years of life do not always become distressed adolescents, especially if their environments become benevolent after the period of infancy. A twenty-seven-year-old woman who had been abused continually as an infant, and had lived in three foster homes before she was three years old, managed to convince herself during adolescence that she was not inherently bad. She became a loving, satisfied mother who was deeply identified with her only son. By contrast, adult Mayan Indian men living in small villages in northwest Guatemala are hostile, suspicious, and aggressive toward their wives, despite a secure attachment to their mothers who nursed them on demand and stayed close to them for most of the day.

I am not suggesting that it is irrelevant how adults care for infants. It does matter! But an insecure attachment during the first year need not always lead to adult pathology, and a secure attachment is no guarantee of future invulnerability to distress. If a secure attachment motivates the child to adopt characteristics that are maladaptive in the larger society, as can happen during periods of transition when old values are changing, the attachment might not be beneficial for the child. Children living in Bombay have a secure attachment to mothers who are playful, caring, and loving. Nonetheless, many contemporary Indian adolescents are anxious because new cultural demands are inconsistent with the values they adopted earlier as a result of their close attachment to their mother. An infant girl in Boston who is closely attached to a mother who promotes passivity, dependence, inhibition of intellectual curiosity, and excessive sexual modesty will grow up possessing qualities that are not adaptive for women in modern America.

Infants need variety of experience and opportunities to explore and to manipulate their environment in order for cognitive development to proceed optimally. To develop a secure attachment, they need a consistently nurturant adult who regularly relieves distress. The consequences of these benevolent experiences, however, will depend on the demands that the social environment will make upon the child in the future. There is no way to inoculate the infant against adult misery, even though parents might be able to make that mood a little less probable.

254

The Role of the Family

Language   The ability to speak words and sentences emerges in most children during the second year. Very few children utter meaningful words before their first birthday, yet some are speaking complex sentences by their second. The current belief, which is well justified, is that the human brain is prepared to detect the subtle differences in spoken phonemes—as between *ba* and *pa,* or *go* and *ko*—as it is able to detect subtle changes in color, density of contour, and movement. The child is biologically prepared not only to perceive an object as a unit but also to hear the bursts of sound that define speech as discrete units and to infer that these bursts of sound have something to do with the objects and actions that he or she perceives in the real world. Although this ability develops in all children, it does require exposure to speech. Hence, one of the central experiences of the second year is hearing people talk, especially being spoken to directly by others. But there is no simple relation between the amount of speech heard and the rate of language development (Maratsos 1983). Even though young children attending day-care centers in Australia hear less speech from adults and speak less often than children of the same social class being reared only at home, the two groups of children are very similar in language development. The author of one study concluded that "the absolute amount of input from adults is not a factor which determines the rate (or course) of language development."*

Learning Prohibitions   As I indicated in chapter 4, all children during the second year begin to develop an appreciation of standards for correct behavior, but they need their parents to inform them which behaviors are proper and which improper. If parents indicate that yelling is wrong on one occasion but imply that it is permissible on another, the child is less likely to adopt a standard against yelling.

I now pose two difficult questions. Are there some actions that adults should always disapprove? Does it make a difference which methods parents use to encourage adoption of their standards? Parents ask these questions more simply: What should I punish? How shall I punish? A complete answer to the first question has to be

---

*A. Cross, personal communication, 1982.

somewhat relative to the culture in which the child lives. Aside from chronic disobedience to adults, physical aggression toward family members, destruction of property, open sexual display, and indifference to all standards of personal cleanliness, there is considerable cultural diversity in the behavior selected for socialization. In villages where there is no running water, parents do not insist that children wash their hands before eating; in homes without valuable objects, children are not warned continually about being careful. Parents unconsciously promote those standards that are likely to be adaptive when the child is older. It is not adaptive for adults in modern America to hold racist ideas, although such attitudes would not have provoked shame or guilt in colonial Virginia. Academic ability is far less central to adaptation in rural villages in Latin America, Africa, or Indonesia than it is in America; and working-class mothers living in Guadalajara, Mexico, encourage hard work, making money, obedience, and emotional expressiveness more forcefully than they promote academic talent.*

I now turn to the more difficult question of mode of socialization. Most parents rely on a combination of five mechanisms to socialize their children, but use these mechanisms with varying frequency. The mechanisms are: observation, punishment, praise, withdrawal of emotional support and signs of value, and, as noted in chapter 4, acting as a model with whom the child can identify. Adults of most societies assume that children will learn what is correct, and practice it, simply by seeing what others do and listening to what adults say. This assumption is valid for a standard on how to eat at the dinner table. But observation, without some sign that certain behavior is disapproved, may not work for qualities like honesty. Observation is most effective when the relevant behavior is public and most of the people the child encounters behave in the same way. The child who is told never to hit another but plays with some peers who yell or strike out when frustrated, while others do not, will be less likely to accept restraint on aggression as being obviously correct. In societies, like ours, where there is so much behavioral diversity, observation will not be an effective mechanism for all standards. Hence, combinations of the other four mechanisms are necessary for socialization. But two of these

* R. H. Magaña, personal communication, 1981.

mechanisms—punishment and withdrawal of love—are direct restraints on the child's freedom to choose which standards to adopt. Although restriction of a child's personal freedom does not bother parents in most communities around the world, it is a tender theme for American parents.

The Consequences of Restriction   Western scholars and parents remain preoccupied, as they have since the Enlightenment, with two relatively independent aspects of parental behavior toward children. The first is defined by the display of love; the second, by restriction. Contemporary theorists assume that a child who is loved and not restricted excessively—that is, given freedom of choice—is most likely to adjust successfully to our society and take joy from life. The child who is unloved and restricted severely has the poorest prognosis. The reasons for awarding prominence to parental love will be considered later. I consider the issue of restriction first.

The balance between a restrictive or a permissive attitude toward children seems to cycle historically, at least in European society. English parents from the mid-sixteenth to the mid-seventeenth century suppressed the indulgent attitudes they had been showing and began to restrict children more seriously and to promote suppression of many of their natural impulses. During the next hundred years, bourgeois English families became permissive; but in the nineteenth century, families locked their children in closets and disciplined them harshly, until the end of the century, when, a lenient, impulse-accepting attitude became popular once again.

During the last years of the nineteenth century, long before there were any scientific data, American and European scholars urged mothers and fathers to let a child disobey them in order to develop the child's independence and necessary emancipation from the family. James Sully, writing as the century came to a close, reminded families of John Locke's declaration, "Children love liberty, and therefore they should be brought to do the things that are fit for them without feeling any restraint laid upon them" (Sully 1896, p. 83). Sully declared that children resented any check on their impulses, and that a child's deep antagonism to the law and adult restraint was grounded on the expectation of liberty, which Sully viewed as natural.

We should not care to see a child give up his inclinations at another's bidding without some little show of resistance. These conflicts are frequent and sharp in proportion to the sanity and vigor of the child. The best children, best from a biological point of view, have, I think, most of the rebel in them. (p. 269)

Three decades later, a textbook in child psychology declared:

The whole process of a child's development has as its goal its emancipation from the parents, so that its own life may be free to develop to the fullest without the hindrances that are inevitable if there continues an attachment to the home ... parents who are wise will grant freedom gradually and increasingly and will welcome rather than resent signs of a desire for independence on the child's part. (Rand, Sweeny, and Vincent 1930, p. 352)

A physician friendly to Freudian theory declared simply, "The greatest of all sins of parenthood is to stand between the child and self-realization—to obstruct his psychological freedom" (Miller 1922, p. 19).

The friendliness to a permissive regimen—which, incidentally, prepared Western society for Freud's ideas—has lasted until the present decade. But there are already signs that America is about to begin a period in which restriction is viewed more benevolently (Stone 1977).

Permissiveness and Freedom The concern with restriction among modern American parents is attributable, in part, to the celebration of individual freedom and private conscience. Many American parents are afraid that restriction will make children fearful of authority. As a consequence, children may be reluctant to exploit opportunities when free choice is necessary, and their veneer of civilized behavior will be based on fear of disapproval rather than on a personal conscience.

Children in American cities, unlike those in small traditional villages, are often in situations where no family member, distant relative, or friend is nearby to supervise their behavior. Hence, it is recognized that each person must develop a private conscience. The child must inhibit stealing from a friend because he believes such action is wrong, not because he will be ashamed if he is discovered or anxious if chastised by his family. If modern society is to work, contemplation of cheating, stealing, or hurting another must generate anticipation of self-condemnation. It is widely assumed that, in order to develop a private conscience and the attendant emotion of guilt, the child must believe he has a choice with respect to conforming to a particular standard. If the only reason a child does not steal is fear of punishment, then when that child is in a situation where he cannot be discovered—for example, on his own in a busy department store where no one will see him steal a toy—he may steal because there is no reason not to do so. Hence, many parents who want to promote a private conscience in their child are gentle in their socialization. They use verbal reasoning, mild reproof, and deprivation of privileges because these practices do not generate extreme fear or anger, but provoke the child to think about why he has misbehaved.

This philosophy of child rearing resembles the advice given to Chinese parents almost sixty years ago by an author who warned of the dangers of frightening the child. He urged parents to avoid any form of punishment that would produce fear, and never to punish the child early in the morning or in the evening: the former would spoil the day's work, and the latter would interfere with a quiet night's sleep (Chen 1925).

The Effects of Restriction: The Evidence   Ambiguity surrounds all conclusions pertaining to the consequences of excessive parental restriction or punitiveness because these consequences are based not only on the degree of parental restraint, but also on the reasons given to the child, on the bond of affection between parent and child, and on the harshness of the punishment. There is no scientific study of the effect of parental restrictiveness alone.

Diana Baumrind (1983) of the University of California, who has conducted some of the most extensive scientific work on this issue, notes that a child's compliance to the parents is not related in any simple way to parental restriction or punitiveness. Baumrind has observed preschool children from middle-class homes in group and individual settings as well as at home with their parents, and invented three types of parents: authoritative, authoritarian, and permissive. Authoritative parents are controlling, but affectionate, and encourage autonomy in their children; authoritarian parents are controlling but less affectionate; while permissive parents are minimally controlling but affectionate. It is difficult to do justice to the wealth of rich detail contained in Baumrind's important monograph (Baumrind 1971). But an important result is that the consequences of these different parental patterns are not the same for boys and girls; and that the combination of restrictive control, warmth, and encouragement of autonomy, not restriction alone, affects a child's aggressiveness and independence. For example, although daughters of authoritarian parents are less independent and daughters of authoritative parents are more independent, these relations are less clear for sons.

A different long-term study of the consequences of early parental restriction on adolescent and adult behavior also revealed inconsistent, and even counterintuitive, results. For example, excessive maternal restriction of sons during the first three years of life predicted minimal dependency on others in adulthood, but excessive restriction had no predictive consequences for girls (Kagan and Moss 1962).

The Mehinaku Indians of central Brazil, who are very indulgent with their infants, treat a consistently disobedient older child in a special way. They "grab a child by the wrists, drag him to a corner, slosh a dipper full of water on his legs, and vigorously scarify his calves and thighs," using a fish-tooth scraper. "Children scream in anger and rage, and for some it is a terrifying experience" (Gregor 1977, p. 276). Yet the adults in this community who were punished this way as children do not appear to be more aggressive or more conforming than the children growing up in groups who do not follow this seemingly harsh practice.

Seventeenth-century Puritan parents beat their children or locked them in a room for a day to socialize unacceptable behavior, apparently persuaded by the Pilgrim pastor, John Robinson, who wrote that the pride children develop "must in the first place be broken and beaten down; that, so the foundation of their education being laid in humility and tractableness, other virtues may, in their time, be built thereon" (Demos 1970, p. 135). These strategies are disapproved of today—we call such parents abusive—because of the belief that children who are physically punished become afraid of and hostile toward their parents.

But fear and hostility are not inevitable if the punishment is perceived by the child as part of a relation that is supportive and respectful in other ways. Japanese children and adults, who are noted for their conformity to family and to social standards, have close attachments and feel strong loyalty to their families. But before the Second World War, and the introduction of Western values favoring gentler socialization, many Japanese fathers were harshly punitive. Yet the reminiscences of successful Japanese adults contain little hostility toward these strict fathers. A Japanese stage director retrieves some memories of his father: "He was very strict in teaching us manners and etiquette. Morning and evening we children bowed to our father in the traditional fashion with both our hands on the tatami" (Wagatsuma 1977, p. 199). A president of a Japanese automotive company recalls, "Once his anger was over he did not nag or complain, but when he was angry I was really afraid of him. His scolding was like thunder.... I learned from my father how to live independently, doing everything on my own. He was the greatest model for my life" (p. 199). A physician novelist recalls his father, a prominent doctor and poet:

My father was, above all, an awesome, frightening being. He was often enraged. When he became angry, it was with all his physical and spiritual strength. Even when I overheard my father reprimand somebody in the next room, a cold shiver used to run down my spine, not to speak of the times when I was chastised.... And yet, he was truly a support as I grew up. (p. 200)

Perhaps an American child treated like these Japanese sons would become far less successful in our society and would harbor strong antipathy toward the parent. But such an outcome is likely only if the child perceives the parental behavior as arbitrary and reflecting hostility. Baumrind notes, "It is not the exercise of firm control per se, however, but the arbitrary, harsh, and nonfunctional exercise of firm control that has negative consequences for child behavior" (1983, p. 139).

Additionally, the significance of severe restriction and harsh punishment, like the consequences of any family experience, is a function of how variable that experience is in the broader culture. Imagine a community where all parents prohibited and punished children harshly for domination of other children. All children would be similarly motivated to inhibit the bullying of peers; and so when they became pre-adolescents, there would not be a large number of children dominating a small group of timid ones. But in our society, where few parents punish a child for dominance, while most parents are permissive, children from the latter families are more likely to dominate those from the former, maintaining an attitude of passivity in them.

Although many Americans see only negative consequences of parental restriction and punishment, there is one potentially desirable outcome. The child who accepts most parental restrictions elicits praise and acceptance and comes to feel valued and even virtuous. Children who consistently refuse to accept parental restriction may acquire a sense of freedom but may also develop a feeling of unworthiness that is not adaptive (Baumrind 1983).

Some of the adult members of the Fels Research Institute longitudinal population told me in an interview that they recalled their parents as restrictive and punitive when they were younger children. The descriptions written twenty years earlier by visitors to the homes of these adults revealed that the parents had, indeed, been excessively punitive and, in a few cases, harsh. But twenty years later, these adults were productive, happily married, and without symptoms and regarded their parents' earlier restrictiveness of them as benevolently motivated. They were happy that their parents had been punitive because those practices inculcated habits they found to be valuable in adult life (Kagan and Moss 1983).

Since the consequences of restriction and punishment are complex and tenuous, why are there strong feelings on this matter? The answer lies, as I indicated earlier, with the popular belief that children need to be free. Excessive restriction—the nineteenth century called it "breaking a child's will"—is supposed to make it difficult for children to assume responsibility and accept the freedom of adulthood. This argument against restriction, which was renewed at the turn of the century, was a reaction to two earlier trends: the excessive punitiveness characteristic of most of the nineteenth century; and the excessively protective attitude of late nineteenth century mothers, who, it was suggested, were producing a degree of dependence on the family that was inconsistent with the characteristics our wisest commentators thought necessary for adjustment in twentieth-century America. As a result, writers in the psychoanalytic tradition urged parents to be less punitive, less prohibitive, and less protective, in order to permit their children to become emotionally free of the family. Today our society contains too much isolation, too little involvement with family, and too much loneliness. We can expect the next generation of essayists writing for American families to urge more restriction rather than less, for, as I noted earlier, the popularity of restriction cycles about every one hundred years. A recent study of young American mothers suggests this trend may have already begun.

Middle- and working-class mothers of three-year-old children listened to a recording of a short essay, approximately four hundred words, comparing the relative wisdom and utility of a restrictive or a permissive mode of socialization, and then tried to remember as much of the essay as they could. More of the middle- than working-class mothers remembered more words from the argument that promoted restrictiveness as a desired regimen. One of the striking differences between the two groups of mothers involved a pair of sentences in the middle of the essay. One sentence noted that excessive permissiveness with a young child could produce an adolescent who would perform poorly in school, take drugs, and become a delinquent. Most of the middle-class mothers remembered this idea in great elaboration, and none distorted it. By contrast, fewer working-class mothers remembered this idea; and for those who did, over one third distorted the meaning of the passage. They stated in their recall that excessive restrictiveness would predispose a child to acquire these undesirable qualities (Kagan et al., in preparation).

Each mother's selective memory for each of the themes in the essay reflects a balance between her concern over having a child who is capable of reasonable conformity to authority and one who is fearless. Middle-class mothers, who are generally more permissive than working-class parents regarding open disobedience, worry that their permissiveness might be inimical to the development of effective study habits and a sense of responsibility—qualities that are necessary for good school performance, college entrance, and a professional vocation. Hence, when this apprehension was articulated in the essay, the middle-class mothers elaborated the relevant information in their recall. By contrast, working-class mothers, who are more punitive, worry that too much restraint and punishment might make their child excessively fearful of authority, passive with peers, and vulnerable to exploitation in the competition for jobs. When information in the essay articulated those worries, it was registered with special salience and recalled in greater detail. Middle-class Japanese mothers living in the city of Sapporo also remember more of the information promoting the permissive argument, because they believe that a child's anger toward a parent obstructs the development of a closely interdependent relationship, and that restrictiveness, by producing anger toward the mother, interferes with a harmonious relation to the parent.

Is there any advice possible in all of this frustrating complexity? Because private conscience, self-confidence, and suppression of anxiety are likely to remain adaptive characteristics in our society, the best advice to parents is to establish an affectionate relation with the child, to decide on the particular behavior to be socialized, and to communicate disapproval of undesirable behavior when it occurs, along with the reasons for punishment. If this strategy does not work, deprivation of privileges the child enjoys can be used to accomplish the socialization goal. Harsh physical punishment and excessive threat of withdrawal of love are probably unwise and, I may add, unnecessary if the first two conditions are met.

THE YEARS FOUR THROUGH SEVEN: THE SENSE OF BEING VALUED

As children enter the fourth year, it is more difficult to list the experiences they must have for optimal development. Four-year-olds can provide variety for themselves, have established an attachment to their parents, and are aware of and practice many of the standards their families promote. The four-year-old is self-consciously in control of much of her behavior, linguistically sophisticated, motorically coordinated, and able to anticipate the wishes and actions of others. The four-year-old is almost self-sufficient enough to survive if left without any caregivers. Hence, in order to prescribe, we must look forward and ask what the child must master in the future in order to adjust to his or her society.

In most contemporary cultures of the world, as in those throughout history, seven- and eight-year-old children are assigned the tasks of gathering wood, planting, sewing, hunting, cooking, and taking care of younger children. Children in modern societies have only one outstanding challenge: they must master the tasks of the school—reading, spelling, writing, and arithmetic. Thus, four-year-olds in modern societies require experiences that will prepare them for coping with this special challenge. The preparation involves preliminary knowledge of letters and numbers, the ability to persist in the face of difficult intellectual problems that generate anxiety, valuing intellectual talent, and a willingness to conform to the arbitrary requests of adults. Because these qualities help the child during the first years of school, interaction with parents that promotes these skills—reading books, solving problems, playing with numbers, and the creation of an accommodating, rather than a disobedient, posture toward unfamiliar adults—should be helpful to the child when he reaches school.

Second, parents are role models with whom the child identifies; hence, parents should display behavior the child classifies as good, for the five-year-old who perceives the parents as nurturant, just, and virtuous, and identifies with them, will come to regard the self as possessing these desirable qualities.

Third, the five-year-old must believe she is valued by her family. This belief is not an obvious derivative of the state of attachment established during infancy. I have noted that Western society attributes considerable power to parental love, and has done so since the seventeenth century (see chapter 2). The psychological power ascribed to parental love, or its absence, has a parallel in the potency attributed in other societies at other times to spirits, loss of soul, sorcery, sin, gossip, God, and witchcraft. "Parental love" has two meanings. One refers to the special emotion parents feel toward a child. A second refers to the child's belief regarding the favor in which he or she is held by the parents. Western society is preoccupied with the significance of the first—a mother's feeling of love for her young child—and assumes that the child's belief will follow automatically. But these two meanings are not always correlated. Experts warn of the potential danger of diluting the mother-child attachment with substitute caregivers. The film *Autumn Sonata* (1978) provokes private assent from hushed audiences who hear a married woman tell her aging mother that the former's psychic anguish is a historical transformation of the mother's failure to love her thirty years earlier. A mother's love for the child is treated as a mysterious force which, if sprinkled plentifully over young children, guarantees salvation. But for the child who is not fortunate enough to have had a loving mother, the future is poisoned. If most human societies held this belief, one might be persuaded of its validity; all people believe that one must eat to survive. But the contemporary Western belief in the long-lasting psychological danger of insufficient maternal love is not shared by many societies, nor was it held by our own society several centuries ago.

The Child's Perception of Rejection   There are many reasons modern American children and adolescents worry about whether they are loved by their parents, and many adults believe that their anxiety and insecurity have been partially caused by their parents' earlier rejection of them as children. These beliefs stem, in part, from the child's failure to meet parental standards. It will be recalled from chapter 4 that, as the child approaches her second birthday, she shows behavioral signs of anxiety if she cannot implement a behavior she feels obliged to display. The recognition that one cannot meet a standard regarded as appropriate provokes distress. Let us apply that conclusion to the contemporary parent-child relationship. The child cannot ignore parental standards because she is in a "closed" situation, dependent upon the care and instrumental help of the parents. The child accepts these standards as reasonable demands to be met. Additionally, the child recognizes that the parents, and many other children, have met these standards, and thus that they are within human capacity. It is not possible for the child to rationalize the standards away.

But if a particular child finds the standards too difficult to attain, she becomes vulnerable to distress. Some people may call this emotion shame; others, guilt; others, a sense of unworthiness. This emotion can generate a feeling of impotence either to cope with problems or to attract the approval and affection of others. The child believes that the self is not worthy of positive regard. The increasing suicide rate among Japanese adolescents who fail to gain university admittance is an extreme reaction to this feeling of unworthiness. This is one reason the child should not be permitted to violate the standards of family and society too frequently or too seriously. Parents should help their children avoid temptations that lead to the violation of standards, should not be so restrictive that the child is forced to disobey, and should reassure the child who is unable to meet parental standards for mastery.

The Role of the Family

A central fact of modern, middle-class Western society is that standards of academic accomplishment are so high that many children fail to meet them. More important, there is no easy way for a child to do penance for this failure. There are no useful instrumental activities that the American child can engage in to prove his effectiveness, utility, or value. The average middle-class child is an object of sentiment with no useful economic role in the household. This situation contrasts sharply with the child in a rural village in a less developed community, who is aware that his work is of value to the family, or with the average Massachusetts adolescent during the late nineteenth century, who provided about one third of the family's income (Kett 1977).

As the one-year-old American child runs to the mother for reassurance when anxious over a discrepant event, the anxious seven-year-old seeks reassurance of his worthiness if he fails to meet a parental standard. The best form of reassurance is a sign of parental acceptance and love. However, some parents find it difficult to award such reassurance honestly, and their children continue to feel distressed and unworthy. The adults in our society who believe that their anxiety and apprehension are due to lack of parental love during childhood may have failed to meet parental standards and, not receiving the needed reassurance, carried this belief into adulthood. This argument implies directly that the child who does not experience distress over failing to meet parental standards, either because the standards are too permissive or because the child is fortunate enough to meet them, is less likely to attribute adult distress to earlier parental rejection, even if the parents were not particularly loving when he or she was young.

Adults who have grown up in families that impose minimal standards on cognitive competence or proper character are also vulnerable to distress, but they should be less likely to attribute their *angst* to lack of earlier parental love. They are more likely to attribute it to other forces—their own incompetence, poor motivation, bad schooling, or an unjust society. On the other hand, those who feel secure as adults may attribute that mood to the fact that they are loved as children. But it is likely that they were fortunate enough to have come close to meeting the standards their parents encouraged. In Third World villages, where the standards set for children are relatively easy to meet (to cook, clean, gather wood, or take care of babies), children less often experience the distress of failure, and adults are less likely to believe that their feelings of anxiety are due to earlier maternal rejection or hostility.

The Signs of Love Parents should communicate to the child whatever local cultural signs indicate that he or she is valued. Some psychologists have assumed that there is a specific set of parental behavior that always signifies acceptance or rejection, for there is remarkable agreement among American parents and psychologists regarding the behavior that defines these attitudes. Harsh physical punishment, lack of social play, and absence of hugging or kissing are supposed to be signs of rejection, and it would be impossible for an American observer to categorize a mother as being both aloof and loving at the same time. But in isolated rural areas of northern Norway, where farms are separated by many miles, mothers behave in ways that an American observer would regard as symptomatic of rejection in an American parent. If a Norwegian mother sees her four-year-old sitting in a doorway and blocking the passage to the next room, she does not ask him to move but bends down, picks him up, and silently sets him aside so she can pass through. Although a middle-class observer might view this apparent indifference as indicative of dislike, most mothers in this Arctic outpost act that way, and the children do not behave the way our theories suggest.

An uneducated young mother slaps her four-year-old across the face when he does not come to the table on time. The intensity of the act tempts an observer to conclude that the mother resents her child. However, during a subsequent conversation, the mother indicates her deep love for the boy. She struck him because she does not want him to grow up to be a bad boy, and she believes that physical punishment is the most effective way to inculcate her standards. Now the mother's behavior seems to serve an affectionate, and not a hostile, attitude. Feeling loved or rejected is a belief held by a child, not a set of parental actions; hence, a parent's behavior is not always a sensitive clue to the child's sense of being valued. When the child is mature enough—about three or four years of age—to recognize that certain resources that parents possess are difficult to obtain, the child regards the receipt of these resources as a sacrifice and as a sign that he or she is valued. The child constructs a "tote board" of the respective values of various parental gifts, whether embraces, privileges, or presents. The value of the gift depends, in part, on its scarcity. Most parents are sufficiently busy, economically constrained, or selfish that they are unable to give the child long periods of uninterrupted companionship or expensive presents; hence, most children place a premium on these prizes. Additionally, children from many cultures learn that physical affection is an essential sign of love, and assign high value to embraces and kisses. After the first World War, child experts emphasized the importance of parental display of physical affection to the child, implying that a lack of such affection might generate anxiety. To the question, "How was your childhood different from the experiences your child is having now?" many older American mothers reply, "I knew my mother loved me, but she didn't show it." Such a statement suggests that a child's belief in his value does not require physical affection but rests on behavior that has come to signify a parent's interest in his happiness. Therefore, there will be uniformity among children in a culture with respect to the parental behaviors that signify love, but the reference for those signs is in the child.

The display of maternal anger toward a child has, during this century, come to signify a rejecting attitude. The family is one of the few settings where anger can be expressed without the inhibiting anticipation of social rejection, loss of status, or counterattack. One spouse often dominates the other, and both parents are always dominant relative to the child. Society is relatively accepting of the misplaced hostility in a husband's display of anger to a wife, which is, in actuality, a reaction to disappointment at work, to difficulties with friends, or to unfulfilled aspirations. But the child, too, is often a target for misplaced parental hostility. Because the mother is usually home with the young child more continually than is the father, the slightest provocation from the child, usually a violation of one of the mother's standards, can release the parent's anger in yelling, physical punishment, or, less commonly, physical abuse. Such behavior is often interpreted by psychologists as indicating a rejecting attitude, even though they are reluctant to make the same inference in the case of the angry husband. They interpret the husband's anger toward the wife as being due to his personal frustrations outside the home, rather than as a sign of deep resentment toward the spouse. Why, then, do psychologists fail to make a similar inference when the mother is hostile to her child?

One reason for this asymmetry in judgment is that most Americans view the love relation between mother and child as inherently stronger, perhaps more natural, than the bond between husband and wife; hence, the expression of hostility toward a child requires an intensity of anger far greater than the irritation that is generated by a frustrating day at work. Second, we find it more difficult to attribute intense anger to women than to men. Thus, most adults assume that a mother's aggression toward her child has to surmount strong internal opposition.

The stereotypes held for the sexes lead most Americans to interpret aggression in men and women differently. Men are categorized as dominant or nondominant; women as loving or nonloving. When aggression, which reflects anger, hostility, and disappointment, occurs in men, we assume it is due to frustration of their motive for dominance or control of their affairs. When aggression occurs in women, we are more likely to assume it springs from a nonloving attitude.

One of the major sources of frustration in modern life is economic insecurity. Marital quarrels are often sparked by one spouse having spent more money than the other regards as proper. Because mothers from lower-class homes experience the uncertainty of economic stress more continually than affluent mothers, they should be more prone to outbursts of anger. And mothers from economically disadvantaged homes do yell, scream, and strike their children more often than advantaged mothers (Kagan and Reznick, unpublished). That fact is interpreted by some psychologists as reflecting a less loving (or more rejecting) attitude toward the child, rather than as indicative of greater frustration.

Of course, it is not possible for the young child to know the real cause of the parent's hostility. The child reacts to the parent's behavior and, if mature enough, to a private interpretation of the parent's intentions. Because mothers typically rationalize their punishment to the child as having been provoked by the violation of a standard, and, therefore, as being in the service of the child's development, the child with an excessively punitive mother is likely to believe that he is bad. The perpetuation of this belief about the self lowers his expectations of accomplishment in school and increases the probability that, when the child becomes an adult, he will be frustrated and prone to anger, thus repeating the cycle.

The Role of the Family

But the fundamental cause of the cycle may be due not, as some psychoanalysts claim, to the continuity of the emotional consequences of maternal rejection, but rather to the re-creation in adulthood of the conditions that made the previous generation prone to anger and hostility. The child may be the immediate provocateur of parental hostility, but not necessarily its real target.

Does Love Matter? I now ask whether lack both of parental affection and a loving attitude seriously contribute to the likelihood of future psychological symptoms in the child. There is no easy answer for reasons that are not strictly empirical. When we ask whether the outside temperature contributes to the probability of snowfall, we need only gather objective data to find out. But when we inquire about the contribution of parental rejection to future psychic illness, we are asking whether a certain set of parental actions usually produces a special mental state in the child—the belief that he or she is not favored—and a future mental state in the same person as an adult—excessive anxiety, depression, or anger. The answers to this question take two different forms.

The first answer is in the subjective frame (see chapter 1) and is concerned only with a person's private belief. The adult who believes that earlier parental rejection determined his present dysphoric state will act as if that hypothesis were true. The second answer, in the objective frame, depends upon whether there is a lawful relation among particular parental behaviors toward the child, the child's perception of favor or disfavor, and a specific adult profile twenty years later. This question has not been answered satisfactorily. Kipsigis mothers in Kenya have older siblings care for young children, Israeli mothers living on kibbutzim use *metaplot,* and many Fijian mothers give their recently weaned two-year-old child to a cousin for adoption. There is no evidence indicating that one group of adolescents feels more in parental favor than another.

The belief that the quality of love between the mother and the young child has a major influence on the latter's future psychological health—a relatively new idea in Western society—may be part of a more general theme: namely, the ascendance of women in Western society over the last three centuries.

It is natural to award sacred qualities to those who represent the ideals of the society. As European middle-class women began to assume primary responsibility for the child's character and to adopt the Enlightenment virtues of charity, kindness, humaneness, and unselfishness in the service of husband and children, they became candidates for sanctification. Men did the evil work of the world; women, by loving, did God's work.

Further, as close loyalties between men became weaker during the nineteenth and twentieth centuries (due, in part, to increased mobility, lack of opportunity to establish long-lasting bonds, and the competitive mood that permeated male relationships), and as moral relativism became attractive to twentieth-century minds, adults searched for some unsullied ideal state that was worthy of commitment. A love relationship—combining mutual psychological enhancement, unquestioned, reciprocal loyalty, and pleasure— was a good candidate. Today many Western adults sanctify love as the primary healing experience. We satirize power and status, politicize and, therefore, corrupt professional competence, belittle the impractical "ivory tower" scholar, and are forced to subordinate natural beauty to the pragmatic need for energy and industrial productivity. The erosion of these ideals leaves the average citizen eager to protect one of the few ideas that remains untainted, and ready to award to women the power to administer one of the last sacraments.

THE YEARS SEVEN THROUGH THIRTEEN

The half-dozen years that precede puberty are preparation for adult life. Young adults in every society must learn an economic skill, accept the responsibility of being parent and spouse, and the duties that come from being a participating member of the society. Children in Third World villages help with cooking, washing, and cleaning; those in modern society learn the necessary intellectual and technical skills. During the years before the Civil War, both middle- and lower-class ten-year-olds left their homes to apprentice with a craftsman in order to learn an adult vocational skill. Ezra Gannett, grandson of a Yale president, left home at eight years of age to live and study with a minister. The sons of the poor had to be unusually enterprising. One seven-year-old boy, Asa Sheldon, began to hire himself out to wealthy farmers and, at age ten, left home to live with a family. But Sheldon's autobiography contains no anger or bitterness over the fact that he had to leave home. He treated this experience as a portentous event in his youth (Kett 1977).

During the years before puberty, the American child needs experiences that promote academic talents, a sense of responsibility, and, most important, a belief that he or she can attain the goals that self and community value. An expectation of success is central to these goals. The priority of a particular motive in consciousness is a function of the person's expectancy of gratifying that motive. The motives of an American ten-year-old include: mastery of academic tasks, peer acceptance, and acquisition of behavior that defines the sex roles. The child needs reassurance that these goals are attainable. If one's daily experience does not contain that information, one is likely to stop investing effort, and the motive will become less pressing. The dangers inherent in this sequence are obvious. Failure to gain desired goals produces distress and can provoke antisocial behavior. Hence, the seminal experiences of this era are those that persuade youth that they can successfully gain the prizes they want. A father in a cornfield teaching his eight-year-old son how to plant maize finds it easy to create a situation that will accomplish this goal. It is more difficult when the child is with one teacher in a class of thirty children. From the child's perspective, the private evaluation of progress is based primarily on a comparison of one's performance with that of one's peers. The larger the number of peers used for comparison, the less likely will a particular child conclude that he or she can master a particular talent (Festinger 1954). A child with an average I.Q. and a particular ability profile attending a class of thirty-five children, in a school of one thousand pupils, in a city of one hundred thousand people, will meet or know about more children who are more talented than he or she than will a comparable child in a class of fifteen in a school of three hundred located in a town of twenty thousand people. That is one reason American children growing up in small towns are disproportionately represented among eminent adults. The majority of the original group of astronauts spent their childhoods in towns and small cities, not in our largest municipalities with their many cultural resources.

Each person remains continually sensitive to the presence of individuals who are more potent than self, whether the source of the potency is size, intellectual talent, strength, beauty, wealth, status, or endurance. When there are a large number of these more potent individuals, the child or adult may inhibit initiations that might be implemented if the more powerful persons were absent. A phenomenon observed in certain tropical fish provides a persuasive analogy. Among a species of wrasse found in the coral reefs off the Hawaiian islands (*Thalassoma duperrey*), females who swim in the presence of smaller, but no larger, fish—whether male or female—undergo a morphological change. These females stop producing eggs and begin to produce sperm—a change they do not undergo when they are in the presence of larger fish (Ross and Losey 1983).

Although families cannot easily change their place of residence so that their child can be with children of equal talent, parents can try to arrange the lives of their children so that successes are more likely than failures. Schools, too, can create classrooms that do not contain children of seriously different ability in order to prevent the less able children from concluding that they are hopelessly incompetent.

The family's role during this period of development is different from what it was during the first seven years of life. The family now functions less as sculptor and more as monitor, detecting signs of conflict, despair, and anxiety and alleviating or correcting them. In our society, the family should permit the adolescent autonomy of choice in order that he or she may grow up with the confidence of being able to make correct decisions independently and to act with responsibility. I suspect that excessive suppression of an American child's independence is harmful, even though I cannot cite firm data to support that feeling. Finally, parents have to behave in ways that are in accord with the child's standard of virtue, because the identification with family members is still influential. A parent who bursts into tears at the slightest provocation, throws plates, gets drunk, or is disliked by the neighbors threatens a ten-year-old's evaluation of self, insofar as the child is identified with that parent. By contrast, parents who meet the child's ideal provide a base of reassurance when the ten-year-old experiences failure, guilt, or peer rejection.

Conclusion

In this discussion of the family, I have not only failed to state many firm principles that summarize the influence of the mother on the child, but I have not said enough about the role of fathers or siblings. The reason is that scientists have been unable to discover many profound principles that relate the actions of mothers, fathers, or siblings to psychological characteristics in the child (see Clarke-Stewart and Hevey 1981, as well as Dunn 1983, for a similar view). After a thorough examination of the evidence on family socialization, two respected psychologists concluded that the relations between parental behavior and the child's qualities are generally ambiguous: "In most cases, the relationships that have appeared are not large. . . . The implications are either that parental behaviors have no effect, or that the only effective aspects of parenting must vary greatly from one child to another within the same family" (Maccoby and Martin 1983, p. 82).

The mood of this chapter is captured by a verse invented to describe the current state of the foundations of mathematics:

> Little by little we subtract
> Faith and fallacy from fact.
> The illusory from the true
> And then starve upon the residue.
> (Hoffenstein, cited in Kline 1980, p. 241)

How can we explain such a pessimistic conclusion?

One possibility is that most of the research has not been sufficiently sophisticated. Some evidence is weak because it is based on asking a mother what she does with her child, while other evidence comes from less than an hour of observation in a laboratory waiting room. Neither of these methods is powerful enough to yield sound inferences. Furthermore, psychologists, in expecting to find a relation between what parents do and a particular outcome in the child, have generally failed to appreciate that the child is always interpreting the actions of parents.

The child lives in a network of relationships with siblings, peers, and adults and is continually evaluating his or her qualities in relation to these people, while identifying selectively with some of them. Thus, the effect of an emotionally significant experience—like a father's prolonged absence or a bitter divorce—will depend on how the child interprets these events. Such interpretations are based on the child's knowledge, moral evaluations, and inferences about the causes of his or her current mood. Rarely will there be a fixed consequence of any single event—no matter how traumatic—or special set of family conditions.

This timid conclusion does not mean that families are of little influence, but that parents affect their children in subtle and complex ways. During the first half-year, the infant born to parents who have not attended college is not very different from the one born to parents who graduated from college. Yet, by age six, the differences between the two youngsters are dramatic. Something has happened in the intervening years to produce the divergent psychological profiles; it is likely that the reasons for the differences at age six lie with family experiences. Older brothers growing up in middle-class homes are generally more obedient, more conforming to parental requests, and better pupils than are younger brothers, despite the fact that first- and later-born boys do not differ much during the opening months of life. Once again, the reasons for the variation must lie with parental treatment, as well as with each boy's perception of the other. The power of the family is also evident in the psychological profiles of children from different ethnic groups, all of whom watch the same television programs, attend the same movies, and read the same primers. Children from Mexican-American families growing up in the Southwest are more cooperative and less competitive than black or Anglo children living in the same towns and cities. Children of Japanese parents growing up in California work harder in school and obtain higher grades than do Mexican-American children. Perhaps during the next twenty years we will gain some understanding of how a family's mood, actions, and philosophy mediate these robust differences among older children.

Epilogue

It is FITTING at the end of our journey to see how the five themes I discussed in chapter 1 have been elaborated.

First, I have tried to right the bias that, during the last half-century, has awarded too little influence to biological maturation. The fear of separation from the mother, the awareness of the self's intentions, the emergence of guilt and pride, the ability to compare self with others, and the detection of inconsistency in one's beliefs—together with many other universal qualities—rest on cognitive abilities that depend upon maturation of the central nervous system. Of course, to be actualized, both maturation and its psychological products require encounters with people and objects, but their appearance must wait upon biological changes.

I have also tried to correct the preoccupation with the preservation of a child's distinctive characteristics and the faith in connectedness across the life course by noting why change and discontinuity are also inherent in development. Indeed, because the cognitive competences continually maturing over the first dozen years are producing important changes in thought, it is unreasonable to expect a great deal of stability in any entity from infancy through adolescence. The evidence fails to support the popular view that the infant provides a good preview of the young adult.

I have argued that some psychological attributes are better understood if they are conceptualized as distinct qualities, rather than as a set of graded instances. The temperamentally inhibited child with a high and stable heart rate is not just a little more frightened than the average child, but is a qualitatively different type of youngster. A principled standard on loyalty to the family is not just a little more pressing than a conventional standard on mode of dress, but, because the former rests on emotion, is qualitatively different. Although psychologists use a continuous set of numbers to gather and to analyze their observations and rely on statistical techniques that assume continuous qualities, these practices may not rest on the best working assumptions. Ptolemy made many correct predictions about planetary phenomena by assuming the sun moved around the earth.

The utility of conceptualizing human qualities as tied to separate contexts was amply illustrated in chapter 6. The evidence is overwhelmingly persuasive. Most of the time, cognitive abilities do not exist apart from a specific class of problem. There are no general memory, perceptual, or reasoning abilities. If there were, students who did their homework correctly would rarely fail an examination, and job training would be superfluous, because, for most vocations, one would need only to master a small set of principles. Human qualities are not colors that are easily applied to any surface, but more like sentences whose meaning is completely dependent on a particular context.

The final theme returns us to the origins of modern academic psychology in the nineteenth century. The discipline began by taking the contents of consciousness as its primary domain of study; hence, the subjective frame of the individual was the focus of interest. But in less than a quarter-century, investigators came to realize that a subjective frame is severely limiting because it does not provide access to deeper phenomena. Moreover, the surface that is available to the investigator is often composed of a set of language forms that may not be well suited to the nonlinguistic processes that are the real targets of curiosity. Hence, the subjective frame was exiled for fifty years. But it has returned in disguised form—in interviews, questionnaires, and subjective reports of symptoms, feelings, and problem-solving sequences. As I noted in the chapters on emotion and the family, the subjective frame can provide useful information for an objective description; and, of course, it is always valid for the subject. When a mother, who has just struck her three-year-old daughter with the heavy, blunt end of a chopping block, explains with sincerity to an observer that she loves her child and is only trying to make sure that the daughter learns to control her strong will, we must reflect on that subjective interpretation—but we do not have to accept it in our objectively framed explanation.

278

Epilogue

These reflections are to be treated not simply as a list of complaints against contemporary social science, but rather as a constructive request to think about human development in a richer way. Do not automatically assume, the next time that you brood about a three-year-old's fear of spiders, a six-year-old's malicious teasing of a sibling, or an adolescent's sudden depression, that these reactions can be understood best as the final culmination of a long history of encounters with family members and friends, and that each is the tip of an iceberg that prophesies a dark future. Of course, past experience can make a significant contribution to the present. But if, in addition, one acknowledges the role of the maturation of novel cognitive functions, temperamental qualities, and the possibility of discontinuity, one will attain a deeper understanding.

As I noted in the preface, the central theme hidden in and between the chapters of this book is that the person's interpretation of experience is simultaneously the most significant product of an encounter and the spur to the next. How else could we understand the affection a Japanese fifty-year-old feels for a father who frightened him throughout his boyhood, or the shame a fourth-century Athenian youth felt if he enjoyed a period of intimate physical contact with his teacher, but the sense of generosity if he did not. The problem psychologists have been unable to solve is how to diagnose these interpretations from the actions, statements, and undetected physiological reactions of children. But if Ernest Rutherford was able to infer the nuclei of gold atoms from the scattering of flashes of light striking a sheet of zinc sulfide, then surely psychologists need not be overly pessimistic about the future.

Although maturation guarantees certain fundamental similarities among all children who grow up with others, it is the differences among youngsters that are harder to understand. They derive from special temperamental qualities, profiles of identification, opportunities to resolve uncertainties generated during earlier stages, and unique historical and sociological conditions. All of these factors finally funnel down to each person's reasons for deciding which action should be awarded priority. Some adolescents and young adults base major life decisions primarily on the likelihood of economic gain; others, on the attainment of status, power, or social acceptance. Still others use personal transformations of the stand-

279

ards of the authority figures they respect. And some base many decisions on the hedonic pleasure an action is likely to produce. The criterion each chooses is influenced by factors that are still not understood.

My own image of a life is that of a traveler whose knapsack is slowly filled with doubts, dogma, and desires during the first dozen years. Each traveler spends the adult years trying to empty the heavy load in the knapsack until he or she can confront the opportunities that are present in each fresh day. Some adults approach this state; most carry their collection of uncertainties, prejudices, and frustrated wishes into middle and old age trying to prove what must remain uncertain while raging wildly at ghosts.

Bibliography

Abramov, I.; et al. 1982. "The Retina of the Newborn Human Infant," *Science,* 217: 265–67.

Ainsworth, M. D. S. 1967. *Infancy in Uganda.* Baltimore: Johns Hopkins University Press.

Ainsworth, M. D. S.; et al. 1978. *Patterns of Attachment.* Hillsdale, N.J.: Lawrence Erlbaum.

Almond, G. A.; Chodorow, M.; and Pearce, R. H., eds. 1982. *Progress and Its Discontents.* Berkeley: University of California Press.

Anderson, J. R. 1983. *The Architecture of Cognition.* Cambridge: Harvard University Press.

Arend, R.; Gove, F. L.; and Sroufe, L. A. 1979. "Continuity of Individual Adaptation from Infancy to Kindergarten: A Predictive Study of Ego Resiliency and Curiosity in Preschoolers," *Child Development* 50: 950–59.

Arlitt, A. H. 1928. *Psychology of Infancy and Early Childhood.* New York: McGraw-Hill.

Arsenian, J. M. 1943. "Young Children in an Insecure Situation," *Journal of Abnormal and Social Psychology* 38: 225–49.

Averill, J. R. 1980. "On the Paucity of Positive Emotions." In K. R. Blankstein, P. Pliner, and J. Pulivy, eds., *Assessment and Modification of Emotional Behavior,* pp. 7–45. New York: Plenum.

Averill, J. R. 1982. *Anger and Aggression.* New York: Springer-Verlag.

Azuma, H. 1982. "Current Trends in Study of Behavioral Development in Japan." *International Journal of Human Development* 5: 153–69.

Baldwin, J. D.; and Baldwin, J. I. 1973. "The Role of Play in Social Organization," *Primates* 14: 369–81.

Baumrind, D. 1971. "Current Patterns of Parental Authority," *Developmental Psychology Monographs* 4 (1, part 2).

Baumrind, D. 1983. "Rejoinder to Lewis's Reinterpretation of Parental Firm Control Effects: Are Authoritative Families Really Harmonious?" *Psychological Bulletin* 94: 132–42.

Bem, S. L. 1981. "Gender Schema Theory: A Cognitive Account of Sex Typing," *Psychological Review* 88: 354–64.

Bentham, J. 1789. *An Introduction to the Principles of Morals and Legislation.* London: T. Payne and Son.

Berlin, B.; Breedlove, D. E.; and Raven, P. H. 1973. "General Principles of Classification and Nomenclature in Folk Biology," *American Anthropologist* 75: 214–42.

Bernard, H. R.; Killworth, P. D.; and Sailer L. 1982. "Informant Accuracy in Social Network Data. V. An Experimental Attempt to Predict Actual Communication from Recall Data," *Social Science Research* 11: 30–66.

Bernfeld, S. 1929. *The Psychology of the Infant.* New York: Brentano's.

Bloom, A. H. 1981. *The Linguistic Shaping of Thought.* Hillsdale, N.J.: Lawrence Erlbaum.

Boag, P. T.; and Grant, P. R. 1981. "Intense Natural Selection in a Population of Darwin's Finches (Geospizinae) in the Galapagos," *Science* 214: 82–85.

Bowerman, M. 1978. "Systematizing Semantic Knowledge," *Child Development* 49: 977–87.

Bowlby, J. 1969. *Attachment* (Vol. I of *Attachment and Loss*). New York: Basic Books.

Bowlby, J. 1973. *Separation—Anxiety and Anger* (Vol. II of *Attachment and Loss*). New York: Basic Books.

Bowlby, J. 1980. *Loss: Sadness and Depression* (Vol. III of *Attachment and Loss*). New York: Basic Books.

Boyd, J. P. 1955. *The Papers of Thomas Jefferson,* vol. XII. Princeton, N.J.: Princeton University Press.

Bradley, R. H.; Caldwell, B. M.; and Elardo, R. 1979. "Home Environment and Cognitive Development in the First Two Years: A Cross Lag Panel Analysis," *Developmental Psychology* 15: 246–50.

Bridgman, P. W. 1958. "Determinism in Modern Science." In S. Hook, ed., *Determinism and Freedom in the Age of Modern Science.* New York: New York University Press.

Briggs, J. L. 1970. *Never in Anger.* Cambridge: Harvard University Press.

Brim, O. G.; and Kagan, J. 1980. "Constancy and Change: A View of the Issues." In O. G. Brim and J. Kagan, eds., *Constancy and Change in Human Development,* pp. 1–25. Cambridge: Harvard University Press.

Bronson, G. W. 1970. "Fear of Visual Novelty," *Developmental Psychology* 2: 33–40.

Bronson, W. C. 1981. *Toddlers' Behaviors with Age Mates: Issues of Interaction, Cognition, and Affect.* Norwood, N.J.: Ablex.

Brown, A. L.; et al. 1983. "Learning, Remembering and Understanding." In J. H. Flavell and E. M. Markman, eds., *Cognitive Development,* vol. 3. In P. H. Mussen, ed., *Handbook of Child Psychology,* pp. 77–166. New York: John Wiley.

Brown, R. W. 1973. *A First Language: The Early Stages.* Cambridge: Harvard University Press.

Bruner, J. 1983. *Child's Talk.* New York: W. W. Norton.

Bullock, M.; Gelman, R.; and Baillargeon, R. 1982. "The Development of Causal Reasoning." In W. J. Friedman, ed., *The Development of the Psychology of Time,* pp. 209–54. New York: Academic Press.

Bushnell, E. W. 1982. "Visual-Tactual Knowledge in 8-, 9½-, and 11-Month-Old Infants," *Infant Behavior and Development,* 5: 63–75.

Cairns, R. B.; and Hood, K. E. 1983. "Continuity in Social Development: A Comparative Perspective on Individual Difference Prediction." In P. Baltes and O. G. Brim, eds., *Life Span Development,* vol V., pp. 301–58. New York: Academic Press.

Campos, J. J.; and Stenberg, C. R. 1981. "Perception, Appraisal, and Emotion." In M. Lamb and L. Sherrod, eds., *Infant Social Cognition,* pp. 273–314. Hillsdale, N. J.: Lawrence Erlbaum.

Campos, J. J.; et al. 1983. "Socio-emotional Development." In M. M. Haith and J. J. Campos, eds., *Infant Development,* vol. II. In P. H. Mussen, ed., *Handbook of Child Psychology,* 4th ed., pp. 783–915. New York: John Wiley.

Carey, S. 1982. "Semantic Development." In E. Wanner; and L. R. Gleitman, eds., *Language Acquisition: The State of the Art,* pp. 347–89. New York: Cambridge University Press.

Carmichael, L. 1927. "A Further Study of the Development of Behavior in Vertebrates Experimentally Removed from the Influence of External Stimulation," *Psychological Review,* 34: 34–47.

Bibliography

Carstairs, G. M. 1967. *The Twice-Born.* Bloomington, Indiana: Indiana University Press.

Cass, L. K.; and Thomas, C. B. 1979. *Childhood Pathology and Later Adjustment.* New York: John Wiley.

Chave, E. J. 1937. *Personality Development in Children.* Chicago: University of Chicago Press.

Chen, H. 1925. *Home Education.* Shanghai, China: China Commercial Press.

Chen, H. 1929. *Family Education.* Southeast University, China.

Clark, E. V. 1983. "Meanings and Concepts." In J. H. Flavell and E. M. Markman, eds., *Cognitive Development,* vol. III. In P. H. Mussen, ed., *Handbook of Child Psychology,* 4th ed., pp. 787–840. New York: John Wiley.

Clarke-Stewart, K. A.; and Hevey, C. M. 1981. "Longitudinal Relations in Repeated Observations of Mother-Child Interaction from 1 to 2½ Years," *Developmental Psychology,* 17: 127–45.

Clarke-Stewart, K. A.; VanderStoep, L. P.; and Killian, G. A. 1979. "Analysis and Replication of Mother-Child Relations at Two Years of Age, *Child Development* 50: 777–93.

Colby, A.; et al. 1983. "A Longitudinal Study of Moral Judgement," *Monographs of the Society for Research and Child Development* 48 (1–2): 1–123.

Compayré, G. 1914. *The Development of the Child in Later Infancy.* Part 2. New York: D. Appleton.

Crockenberg, S. B.; and Smith, P. 1981. "Antecendents of Mother-Infant Interaction and Infant Irritability in the First Three Months of Life." Unpublished manuscript.

Curtiss, S.; et al. 1975. "An Update on the Linguistic Development of Genie." In D. P. Data, ed., *Georgetown University Roundtable on Language and Linguistics,* pp. 145–57. Washington, D.C.: Georgetown University Press.

Daly, E. M.; Lancee, W. J.; and Polivy, J. 1983. "A Conical Model for the Taxonomy of Emotional Experience," *Journal of Personality and Social Psychology* 45: 443–57.

Darwin, C. 1965. *The Expression of Emotions in Man and Animals.* Chicago: University of Chicago Press (Phoenix book).

Davis, N. Z. 1977. "Ghosts, Kin, and Progeny," *Daedalus* 106: 87–114.

Degler, C. 1980. *At Odds: Women and the Family in America from the Revolution to the Present.* New York: Oxford University Press.

Demos, E. V. 1974. "Children's Understanding and Use of Affect Terms." Unpublished doctoral dissertation, Harvard University.

Demos, J. 1970. *A Little Commonwealth.* New York: Oxford University Press.

Dewey, John. 1922. *Human Nature and Conduct.* New York: Henry Holt.

Diamond, A. 1983. "Behavioral Changes Between 6 and 12 Months." Unpublished doctoral dissertation, Harvard University.

Doi, T. 1973. *The Anatomy of Dependence.* Tokyo: Kodansha International.

Dollard, J.; and Miller, N. E. 1950. *Personality and Psychotherapy,* New York: McGraw-Hill.

Donaldson, M. 1978. *Children's Minds.* New York: W. W. Norton.

Donaldson, M. 1982. "Conservation: What is the Question?" *British Journal of Psychology* 73: 199–207.

Dunn, J. 1983. "Sibling Relationships in Early Childhood," *Child Development* 54: 787–811.

Dusek, J. B.; and Flaherty, J. F. 1981. "The Development of the Self Concept during the Adolescent Years," *Monographs of the Society for Research in Child Development* 46(4): 191.

Dyson, F. 1979. *Disturbing the Universe.* New York: Harper & Row.

Eisenberg-Berg, N.; and Hand, M. 1979. "The Relationship of Preschoolers' Reasoning about Prosocial Moral Conflicts and Prosocial Behavior," *Child Development* 50: 356–63.

Ekman, P. 1980. "Biological and Cultural Contributions to Body and Facial Movement in the Expressions of Emotions." In A. O. Rorty ed., *Explaining Emotions*, pp. 73–102. Berkeley: University of California Press.

Ellis, H. 1900. "The Analysis of the Sexual Impulse," *The Alienist and the Neurologist* 21: 247–62.

Emde, R. N.; et al. 1978. "Infant Smiling at Five and Nine Months: Analysis of Heart Rate and Movement," *Infant Behavior and Development* 1: 26–35.

Erasmus. 1530. *De Civilitate Marum Puerilium.* Basel.

Erikson, E. H. 1963. *Childhood and Society.* New York: W. W. Norton.

Erikson, E. H. 1969. *Gandhi's Truth.* New York: W. W. Norton.

Erikson, E. H. 1974. *Dimensions of a New Identity.* New York: W. W. Norton.

Evans, E. E. 1975 [1875]. *The Abuse of Maternity.* New York: Arno.

Ewer, R. F. 1968. *Ethology of Mammals.* London: Logos.

Farley, J. 1974. *The Spontaneous Generation Controversy.* Baltimore: Johns Hopkins University Press.

Fenton, J. C. 1925. *A Practical Psychology of Babyhood.* Boston: Houghton Mifflin.

Festinger, L. 1954. "A Theory of Social Comparison Processes," *Human Relations* 7: 117–140

Festinger, L. 1957. *A Theory of Cognitive Dissonance.* Stanford: Stanford University Press.

Fiske, J. 1909. *The Meaning of Infancy.* Boston: Houghton Mifflin.

Flavell, J. H.; Flavell E. R.; and Green, F. C. 1983. "Development of the Appearance-Reality Distinction," *Cognitive Psychology* 15: 95–120.

Flavell, J. H.; and Wellman, H. M. 1977. "Metamemory." In R. Kail and J. Hagen, eds., *Perspectives on the Development of Memory and Cognition*, pp. 3–34. Hillsdale, N.J.: Lawrence Erlbaum.

Forbush, W. B. 1915. *Child Study and Child Training.* New York: Scribners.

Franklin, B. 1868. *Autobiography.* Philadelphia: J. B. Lippincott.

Freud, S. 1964 [1938]. *An Outline of Psychoanalysis.* Standard Edition of the Works of Sigmund Freud. Vol. XIII, pp. 131–208. London: Hogarth Press.

Freud, S. 1965 [1933]. *New Introductory Lectures on Psychoanalysis.* New York: W. W. Norton.

Friberg, J. 1984. "Numbers and Measures in the Earliest Written Records." *Scientific American* 250: 110–18.

Fried, C. 1978. *Right and Wrong.* Cambridge: Harvard University Press.

Fuller, J. L.; and Clark, L. D. 1968. "Genotype and Behavioral Vulnerability to Isolation in Dogs, *Journal of Comparative and Physiological Psychology* 66: 151–56.

Fung, Y. 1973. *A History of Chinese Philosophy.* Trans. D. Bodde, Princeton, N.J.: Princeton University Press.

Gaensbauer, T. J.; Connell, J. P.; and Schultz, L. A. 1983. "Emotion and Attachment," *Developmental Psychology* 19: 815–31.

Garcia-Coll, C. 1981. "Psychophysiological Correlates of a Tendency toward Inhibition in Infants." Unpublished doctoral dissertation, Harvard University.

Garcia-Coll, C.; Kagan, J.; and Reznick, J. S. "Behavioral Inhibition to the Unfamiliar," *Child Development*, in press.

Gardner, H. 1983. *Frames of Mind.* New York: Basic Books.

Garner, W. R. 1981. "The Analysis of Unanalyzed Perceptions." In M. Kubovy and J. R. Pomerantz, eds., *Perceptual Organization*, pp. 119–39. Hillsdale, N.J.: Lawrence Erlbaum.

Bibliography

Geach, P. 1977. *The Virtues.* Cambridge, England: Cambridge University Press.
Gelman, R.; and Meck, A. 1983. "Preschoolers' Counting: Principles Before Skill," *Cognition* 13: 343–59.
Gewirth, A. 1978. *Reason and Morality.* Chicago: University of Chicago Press.
Gilligan, C. 1982. *In a Different Voice.* Cambridge: Harvard University Press.
Goldmann, L. 1973. *The Philosophy of the Enlightenment.* Cambridge: M.I.T. Press.
Goodnow, J. J.; and Cashmore, J. 1982. "Culture and Competence Performance." Paper presented at the Jean Piaget Society, Philadelphia, Pennsylvania, June 1982.
Gould, S. J. 1980. *The Panda's Thumb.* New York: W. W. Norton.
Gouze, K.; Gordon, L.; and Rayias, M. "Information Processing Correlates of Aggression." Paper presented at a meeting of the Society for Research and Child Development, Detroit, April 1983.
Gregor, T. 1977. *Mehinaku.* Chicago: University of Chicago Press.
Gresham, F. M. 1981. "Validity of Social Skills Measures for Assessing Social Competence in Low Status Children," *Developmental Psychology* 17: 390–98.
Grossmann, K.; et al. 1981. "German Children's Behavior toward Their Mothers at 12 Months and Their Fathers at 18 Months in Ainsworth Strange Situation," *International Journal of Behavioral Development* 4: 157–81.
Gunnar, M. R.; Leighton, K.; and Peleaux, R. 1983. "The Effects of Temporal Predictability on Year-Old Infants' Reactions to Potentially Frightening Toys." Paper presented at the meeting of the Society for Research in Child Development, Detroit, April 1983.

Haith, M. M. 1971. "Developmental Changes in Visual Information Processing and Short-Term Memory," *Human Development* 14: 249–61.
Haith, M. M. 1980. *Rules that Babies Look By.* Hillsdale, N.J.: Lawrence Erlbaum.
Hall, G. S. 1906. *Youth, Its Education, Regime and Hygiene.* New York: Appleton.
Hall, W. G. 1975. "Weaning and Growth of Artificially Reared Rats," *Science,* 190: 1313–15.
Hampshire, S. 1983. *Morality and Conflict.* Cambridge: Harvard University Press.
Hanson, N. R. 1961. *Patterns of Discovery.* Cambridge, England: Cambridge University Press.
Harkness, S.; Edwards, C. P.; and Super, C. M. 1981. "Social Roles and Moral Reasoning," *Developmental Psychology* 17: 595–603.
Harlow, H. F.; and Harlow, M. K. 1966. "Learning to Love," *American Scientist* 54: 244–72.
Harris, I. 1964. *The Promised Seed: A Comparative Study of Eminant First and Later Sons.* New York: Free Press of Glencoe.
Hartshorne, H.; and May, M. 1928. *Studies in Deceit.* New York: Macmillan.
Herdt, G. H. 1981. *Guardians of the Flutes.* New York: McGraw-Hill.
Herrick, C. J. 1956. *The Evolution of Human Nature.* Austin: University of Texas Press.
Herrnstein, R. J. 1970. "On the Law of Effect," *Journal of Experimental Analysis of Behavior,* 13: 243–66.
Herrnstein, R. J. 1979. "Acquisition, Generalization, and Discrimination Reversal of a Natural Concept," *Journal of Experimental Psychology: Animal Behavior Processes* 5: 116–29.
Herrnstein, R. J.; and de Villiers, P. A. 1980. "Fish as a Natural Category for People and Pigeons." In G. H. Bower, ed., *The Psychology of Learning and Motivation,* vol. XIV, pp. 59–95. New York: Academic Press.
Hetherington, E. M.; and Parke, R. D. 1979. *Child Psychology,* 2nd ed. New York: McGraw-Hill.

Hock, E.; and Clinger, J. B. 1981. "Infant Coping Behaviors," *Journal of Genetic Psychology* 138: 231–43.

Hoffman, M. L. 1981. "Perspectives on the Difference Between Understanding People and Understanding Things." In J. H. Flavell and L. Ross, eds., *Social Cognitive Development*, pp. 67–81. Cambridge, England: Cambridge University Press.

Holton, G. 1973. *Thematic Origins of Scientific Thought: Keppler to Einstein.* Cambridge: Harvard University Press.

Hood, L.; and Bloom, L. 1979. "What, When and How About Why," *Monographs of the Society for Research in Child Development*, 44(6).

Hubel, D. H.; and Weisel, T. M. 1970. "The Period of Susceptibility to the Physiological Effects of Unilateral Eye Closure in Kittens," *Journal of Physiology* 206: 419–36.

Huesman, L. R.; et al. 1983. "The Stability of Aggression over Time and Generations." Paper presented at the meeting of the Society for Research in Child Development, Detroit, Michigan, April 1983.

Hume, D. 1969 [1739–40]. *A Treatise of Human Nature.* E. C. Mossner, ed. Hammondsworth, England: Penguin.

Iggers, G. G. 1982. "The Idea of Progress in Historiography and Social Thought since the Enlightenment." In G. A. Almond, M. Chodorow, and R. H. Pearce, eds., *Progress and Its Discontents*, pp. 41–66. Berkeley: University of California Press.

Izard, C. E. 1977. *Human Emotions.* New York: Plenum Press.

James, W. 1981*a* [1890]. *Principles of Psychology*, vol. I. F. Burkhardt, ed. Cambridge: Harvard University Press.

James, W. 1981*b* [1890]. *Principles of Psychology*, vol. II. Cambridge: Harvard University Press.

James, W. 1983 [1904]. "What Is an Emotion?" In F. Burkhardt, ed., *Essays in Psychology*, pp. 168–87. Cambridge: Harvard University Press.

Janik, A.; and Toulmin, S. 1973. *Wittgenstein's Vienna.* New York: Simon and Schuster.

Johnson, W. F.; et al. 1982. "Maternal Perception of Infant Emotion from Birth through 18 Months," *Infant Behavior and Development* 5: 313–22.

Jordan, J. V. 1973. "The Relationship of Sex-Role Orientation to Competitive and Noncompetitive Achievement Behaviors." Unpublished doctoral dissertation, Harvard University.

Kaffman, M.; and Elizur, E. 1977. "Infants Who Become Enuretics," *Monographs of the Society for Research in Child Development* 42(2).

Kagan, J. 1964. "The Child's Sex Role Classification of School Objects," *Child Development*, 35: 1051–56.

Kagan, J. 1967. "On the Need for Relativism," *American Psychologist* 22: 131–42.

Kagan, J. 1971. *Change and Continuity in Infancy.* New York: John Wiley.

Kagan, J. 1978. "On Emotion and Its Development: A Working Paper." In M. Lewis and L. A. Rosenblum, eds., *The Development of Affect*, pp. 11–42. New York: Plenum Press.

Kagan, J. 1981. *The Second Year.* Cambridge: Harvard University Press.

Kagan, J.; and Hamburg, M. 1981. "The Enhancement of Memory in the First Year," *Journal of Genetic Psychology* 138: 3–14.

Kagan, J.; Kearsley, R. B.; and Zelazo, P. R. 1978. *Infancy: Its Place in Human Development.* Cambridge: Harvard University Press.

Kagan, J.; Lapidus, D.; and Moore, M. 1978. "Infant Antecedents of Cognitive Functioning," *Child Development* 49: 1005–23.

Bibliography

Kagan, J.; and Moss, H. A. 1962. *Birth to Maturity.* New York: John Wiley. (Reissued 1983, New Haven: Yale University Press.)

Kagan, J.; et al. 1964. "Information Processing in the Child: The Significance of Analytic and Reflective Attitudes," *Psychological Monographs* 78: 578.

Kagan, J.; et al. 1973. "Memory and Meaning in Two Cultures," *Child Development* 44: 221–23.

Kagan, J.; et al. 1979. "A Cross-Cultural Study of Cognitive Development," *Monographs of the Society for Research in Child Development* 44(5).

Kagan, J.; et al. 1982. "Validity of Children's Self Reports of Psychological Qualities." In B. A. Maher and W. B. Maher, eds., *Progress in Experimental Personality Research,* vol. XI, pp. 171–212. New York: Academic Press.

Kagan, J.; et al. "Behavioral Inhibition in the Young Child." *Child Development,* in press.

Kagan, J.; et al. "Inhibition to the Unfamiliar." In M. G. H. Coles, J. R. Jennings, and J. Stern, eds., *Lacey Festschrift.* Stroudsburg, Pa.: Hutchinson Ross, in press.

Kagan, J.; et al. "Selective Memory and Maternal Attitudes." In preparation.

Kahneman, D.; and Henik, A. 1981. "Perceptual Organization of Attention." In M. Kubovy and J. R. Pomerantz, eds., *Perceptual Organization,* pp. 181–211. Hillsdale, N.J.: Lawrence Erlbaum.

Kakar, S. 1982. *Shamans, Mystics, and Doctors.* New York: Alfred A. Knopf.

Kant, I. 1959 [1785]. *Foundations of the Metaphysics of Morals.* trans. L. Beck. Indianapolis: Bobbs-Merrill.

Kant, I. 1966 [1781]. *Critique of Pure Reason.* New York: Anchor Books.

Kato, S. 1979. *A History of Japanese Literature.* Tokyo: Kodansha International.

Katz, M. M. W. 1981. "Gaining Sense at Age Two in the Outer Fiji Islands." Unpublished doctoral dissertation, Harvard Graduate School of Education.

Kaye, K. 1982. *The Mental and Social Life of Babies.* Chicago: University of Chicago Press.

Keil, F. C. 1983. "On the Emergence of Semantic and Conceptual Distinctions," *Journal of Experimental Psychology: General* 112: 357–85.

Kenney, M.; Mason, W. A.; and Hill, S. 1979. "Effects of Age, Objects, and Visual Experience on Affective Responses of Rhesus Monkeys to Strangers," *Developmental Psychology* 15: 176–84.

Kett, J. F. 1977. *Rites of Passage.* New York: Basic Books.

Klein, D. F.; Zitrin, C. M.; and Woerner, M. 1978. "Anti-depressants, Anxiety, Panic, and Phobia." In M. A. Lipton; A. DiMascio; and K. F. Killam, eds., *Psychopharmacology,* pp. 1401–7. New York: Raven.

Klein, M.; et al. 1952. *Developments in Psychoanalysis.* London: Hogarth Press.

Kleinman, A. 1980. *Patients and Healers in the Context of Culture.* Berkeley: University of California Press.

Kline, L. W.; and France, C. J. 1907. "The Psychology of Ownership." In T. L. Smith, ed., *Aspects of Child Life and Education,* pp. 250–300. Boston: Ginn.

Kline, M. 1980. *Mathematics.* New York: Oxford University Press.

Klinnert, M. D.; et al. "Social Referencing: Emotional Expressions as Behavior Regulators." In R. Plutchik and H. Kellerman, eds., *Emotions in Early Development.* New York: Academic Press, in press.

Kohlberg, L. 1981. *The Philosophy of Moral Development,* vol. I, *Moral Stages and the Idea of Justice.* New York: Harper & Row.

Kohn, M. L. 1977. *Class and Conformity.* Chicago: University of Chicago Press.

Kosslyn, S. 1980. *Image and Mind.* Cambridge: Harvard University Press.

Kreutzer, M. A.; Leonard, C.; and Flavell, J. H. 1975. "An Interview Study of Children's Knowledge about Memory," *Monographs of the Society for Research in Child Development* 40(159).

Kuhn, D.; Nash, S. C.; and Brucken, L. 1978. "Sex Role Concepts of Two- and Three-year-olds," *Child Development* 49: 445–51.

Lagerqvist, P. 1971. *The Eternal Smile.* New York: Hill and Wang.

Lamb, M. E.; et al. 1982. "Security of Mother- and Father-Infant Attachment and Its Relation to Sociability with Strangers in Traditional and Nontraditional Swedish Families," *Infant Behavior and Development* 5: 355–67.

Lamb, M. E.; et al. "Security of Infantile Attachment as Assessed in the Strange Situation," *Behavioral and Brain Sciences,* in press.

Langer, J. 1980. *The Origins of Logic.* New York: Academic Press.

Langsdorf, P.; Izard, C. E.; and Rayias, M. 1981. "Interest, Expression, Attention, and Heart Rate Changes in Two- to Eight-Month-Old Infants." Unpublished manuscript, University of Delaware.

Laxon, V. J. 1981. "On the Problems of Being More or Less the Same," *Journal of Experimental Child Psychology* 31: 531–43.

Ledingham, J. E., and Schwartzman, A. E. 1983. "A Longitudinal Investigation of Aggressive and Withdrawn Children." Paper presented at the meeting of the Society for Research in Child Development, Detroit, April 1983.

Le Douarin, N. 1982. *The Neural Crest.* Cambridge, England: Cambridge University Press.

Lerner, R. 1984. *The Nature of Human Plasticity.* New York: Cambridge University Press.

Levine, S. 1982. "Comparative and Psychobiological Perspectives on Development." In A. Collins, ed., *The Concept of Development,* pp. 29–53. Minnesota Symposium, vol. XV, Hillsdale, N.J.: Lawrence Erlbaum.

Lewis, C. C. 1981. "The Effects of Parental Firm Control," *Psychological Bulletin* 90: 547–63.

Lewis, M.; and Brooks-Gunn, J. 1979. *Social Cognition and the Acquisition of Self.* New York: Plenum Press.

Linn, S.; et al. 1982. "Salience of Visual Patterns in the Human Infant, *Developmental Psychology* 18: 651–57.

Livingston, K. R. 1977. "The Organization of Children's Concepts." Unpublished doctoral dissertation, Harvard University.

Locke, J. 1892. *Some Thoughts Concerning Education.* Cambridge, England: Cambridge University Press.

Locke, J. 1894 [1690]. *Essay Concerning the Human Understanding,* ed. A. O. Fraser. Oxford, England: Clarendon Press.

Londerville, S.; and Main, M. 1981. "Security of Attachment and Compliance in Maternal Training Methods in the Second Year of Life," *Developmental Psychology* 17: 289–99.

Lovejoy, A. O. 1936. *The Great Chain of Being.* Cambridge: Harvard University Press.

Lusk, D. 1978. "Empathy in Young Children." Unpublished doctoral dissertation, Harvard University.

Lutz, C. 1982. "The Domain of Emotion Words on Ifaluk," *American Ethnologist* 9: 113–28.

Lyons, W. 1980. *Emotion.* Cambridge, England: Cambridge University Press.

McCall, R. B.; Kennedy, C. B.; and Appelbaum, M.I. 1977. "Magnitude of Discrepancy and the Direction of Attention in Infants," *Child Development* 48: 772–85.

Maccoby, E. E. 1980. *Social Development.* New York: Harcourt Brace Jovanovich.

Maccoby, E. E.; and Feldman, S. S. 1972. "Mother-Infant Attachment and Stranger Reactions in the Third Year of Life," *Monographs of the Society for Research in Child Development* 37: 1.

Maccoby, E. E.; and Martin, J. A. 1983. "Socialization and the Context of the Family: Parent-Child Interaction." In E. Mavis Hetherington, ed. *Socialization,*

288

Bibliography

Personality, and Social Development. vol. IV, pp. 1–101. In P. H. Mussen, ed., *Handbook of Child Psychology,* 4th ed. New York: John Wiley.

McDougall, W. 1908. *An Introduction to Social Psychology.* London: Methuen.

McGuire, W. J.; and Padawer-Singer, A. 1976. "Trait Salience in a Spontaneous Self-concept, *Journal of Personality and Social Psychology* 33: 743–54.

MacIntyre, A. 1981. *After Virtue.* Notre Dame, Ind.: Notre Dame University Press.

Mackinnon, D.W. 1965. "Personality and the Realization of Creative Potential," *American Psychologist,* 20: 273–81.

Mackintosh, N. J. 1983. *Conditioning and Associative Learning.* Oxford, England: Clarendon Press.

Mandelbaum, M. 1971. *History, Man, and Reason.* Baltimore: Johns Hopkins University Press.

Mandler, G. 1975. *Mind and Emotion.* New York: John Wiley.

Maratsos, M. 1983. "Some Current Issues in the Study of the Acquisition of Grammar," In J. H. Flavell and E. M. Markman, eds., *Cognitive Development,* pp. 707–86. P. H. Mussen, ed., *Handbook of Child Psychology,* vol. III. New York: John Wiley.

Marcel, A. J. 1983. "Conscious and Unconscious Perception: An Approach to the Relations Between Phenomenal Experience and Perceptual Processes," *Cognitive Psychology,* 15: 238–300.

Margolis, H.; et al. 1980. "The Validity of Forms of the Matching Familiar Figures Test with Kindergarten Children," *Journal of Experimental Child Psychology* 29: 12–22.

Markman, E. M. 1981. "Two Different Principles of Conceptual Organization." In M. Lamb and A. Brown, eds., *Advances in Developmental Psychology,* vol. I, pp. 99–236. Hillsdale, N.J.: Lawrence Erlbaum.

Markman, E. M.; and Siebert, J. 1976. "Classes and Collections," *Cognitive Psychology* 8: 561–77.

Marler, P. A. 1970. "A Comparative Approach to Vocal Learning: Song Development in White Crowned Sparrows," *Journal of Comparative and Physiological Psychology* 6: 1–25.

Marx, K. 1904 [1867, 1894]. *Capital: A Critique of Political Economy,* 3 vols. Chicago: Kerr.

Mason, W. A. 1978. "Social Experience in Primate Cognitive Development." In G. M. Burghardt and M. Bekoff, eds., *The Development of Behavior: Comparative and Evolutionary Aspects,* pp. 233–51. New York: Garland Press.

Mast, V. K.; et al. 1980. "Immediate and Long-term Memory for Reinforcement Context: The Development of Learned Expectancies in Early Infancy," *Child Development* 51: 700–707.

May, H. 1959. *The End of American Innocence.* New York: Alfred A. Knopf.

Mayr, E. 1982. *The Growth of Biological Thought.* Cambridge: Harvard University Press.

Menzel, E. W.; and Juno, C. 1982. "Marmosets (Saguinus Fuscicollis): Are Learning Sets Learned?" *Science* 217: 750–52.

Messer, S. M.; and Brodzinsky, D. M. 1981. "Three-Year Stability of Reflection-Impulsivity in Young Adolescents," *Developmental Psychology* 17: 848–50.

Milewski, A. E. 1979. "Visual Discrimination and Detection of Configurational Invariance in Three-Month-Old Infants, *Developmental Psychology* 15: 357–63.

Milgram, S. 1964. "Group Pressure and Action Against a Person," *Journal of Abnormal and Social Psychology* 69: 137–43.

Mill, J. S. 1879 [1843]. *A System of Logic, Ratiocinative and Induction,* 2 vols., 8th ed. New York: Harper.

Miller, H. C. 1922. *The New Psychology and the Parent.* London: Jarrolds.

Moberg, G. P.; and Wood, V. A. 1981. "Neonatal Stress in Lambs," *Developmental Psychobiology* 14: 155–62.

Moore, G. E. 1903. *Principia Ethica.* Cambridge: Cambridge University Press.

Moore, G. E. 1959 [1922]. *Philosophical Papers.* London: Allen & Unwin.

Moore, M.; Kagan, J.; and Haith, M. 1978. "Memory and Motives," *Developmental Psychology* 14: 563–64.

Morgan, E. S. 1944. *The Puritan Family.* New York: Harper.

Morris, D. P.; Soroker, E.; and Burruss, G. 1954. "Follow-up Studies of Shy, Withdrawn Children," *American Journal of Orthopsychiatry* 24: 743–54.

Moss, H. A.; and Susman, E. J. 1980. "Longitudinal Study of Personality Development." In O. G. Brim and J. Kagan, eds., *Constancy and Change in Human Development.* pp. 530–95. Cambridge: Harvard University Press.

Mussen, P. H.; Conger, J. J.; and Kagan, J. 1969. *Child Development and Personality,* 3rd ed. New York: Harper & Row.

Newcombe, N.; Rogoff, B.; and Kagan, J. 1977. "Developmental Changes in Recognition Memory for Pictures of Objects and Scenes," *Developmental Psychology* 13: 337–41.

Newman, P. L. 1960. "Wildman Behavior in a New Guinea Highlands Community," *American Anthropologist* 66: 1–19.

Newman, S. A.; and Frisch, H. L. 1979. "Dynamics of Skeletal Pattern Formation in Developing Chick Limb," *Science* 205: 662.

Nickerson, R. S. 1968. "A Note on Long-term Recognition Memory for Pictorial Materials," *Psychonomic Science* 11: 58.

Nisbet, R. 1980. *History of the Idea of Progress.* New York: Basic Books.

Nolan, E. 1979. "Emergence of Self-awareness in Three- to Four-year-old Children." Unpublished doctoral dissertation, Harvard University.

Nolan, E.; and Kagan, J. 1978. "Psychological Factors in the Face-Hands Test," *Archives of Neurology* 35: 41–42.

Nolan, E.; and Kagan, J. 1980. "Recognition of Self and Self's Products in Preschool Children," *Journal of Genetic Psychology* 137: 285–94.

Novey, M. S. 1975. "The Development of Knowledge of Others' Ability to See." Unpublished doctoral dissertation, Harvard University.

Obrist, P. A.; Light, K. C.; and Hastrup, J. L. 1982. "Emotion and the Cardiovascular System: A Critical Perspective." In C. E. Izard, ed., *Measuring Emotions in Infants and Children,* pp. 199–316. New York: Cambridge University Press.

Olson, S. L.; Bates, J. E.; and Bayles, K. 1982. "Maternal Perceptions of Infant and Toddler Behavior," *Infant Behavior and Development* 5: 397–410.

Olweus, D. 1981. "Stability in Aggressive, Inhibited, and Withdrawn Behavior Patterns." Presented at the meeting of the Society for Research in Child Development, Boston, April 1981.

Oppenheim, R. W. 1981. "Ontogenetic Adaptations and Retrogressive Processes in the Development of the Nervous System and Behavior: A Neuroembryological Perspective." In K. J. Connolly and H. F. R. Prechtel, eds., *Maturation and Development: Biological and Psychological Perspectives,* pp. 73–109. Philadelphia: J. B. Lippincott.

Ozment, S. 1983. *When Fathers Ruled.* Cambridge: Harvard University Press.

Paine, T. 1973 [1776]. *Common Sense.* New York: Anchor Books.

Parikh, B. 1980. "Development of Moral Judgment and Its Relation to Family Environmental Factors in Indian and American Families," *Child Development.* 51: 1030–39.

Patterson, P. H.; Potter, D. D.; and Furshpan, E. J. 1978. "The Chemical Differentiation of Nerve Cells," *Scientific American* 239: 50–59.

Bibliography

Pearlin, L. I. 1971. *Class Context and Family Relations.* Boston: Little, Brown.

Petitto, L. A. 1983. "From Gesture to Symbol," Unpublished dissertation, Harvard Graduate School of Education.

Piaget, J. 1913. "Premieres Recherches sur les Mollusques profonds du lac de Neuchâtel, *Bulletin de la Société Neuchâtel des Sciences naturelles* 40: 148–71.

Piaget, J. 1950. *The Psychology of Intelligence.* Trans. M. Piercy and D. E. Berlyne. London: Routledge & Kegan Paul.

Piaget, J. 1951. *Play, Dreams, and Imitation in Childhood.* Trans. C. Gattegno and F. M. Hodgson. London: Routledge & Kegan Paul.

Piaget, J. 1952 [1936]. *The Origins of Intelligence in Children.* New York: International Universities Press.

Piaget, J. 1965 [1932]. *The Moral Judgment of the Child.* New York: Free Press.

Piaget, J. 1970. *Structuralism.* New York: Basic Books.

Piaget, J. 1972. *The Principles of Genetic Epistemology.* Trans. W. Mays. New York: Basic Books.

Piaget, J.; and Inhelder, B. 1958. *The Growth of Logical Thinking from Childhood to Adolescence* Trans. A. Parsons and S. Milgram. New York: Basic Books.

Piaget, J.; and Inhelder, B. 1969. *The Psychology of the Child.* New York: Basic Books.

Pinchbeck, I.; and Hewitt, M. 1969, 1973. *Children in English Society,* vols. I and II. London: Routledge & Kegan Paul.

Plomin, R.; and Rowe, D. C. 1979. "Genetic and Environmental Etiology of Social Behavior in Infancy," *Developmental Psychology,* 15: 62–72.

Polanyi, M. 1966. *The Tacit Dimension.* Garden City, N.Y.: Doubleday.

Polivy, J. 1981. "On the Induction of Emotion in the Laboratory," *Journal of Personality and Social Psychology* 41:803–17.

Pollock, J. L. 1982. *Language and Thought.* Princeton: Princeton University Press.

Premack, D.; and Premack, A. J. 1983. *The Mind of an Ape.* New York: W. W. Norton.

Preyer, W. 1888. *The Mind of the Child, Part I: The Senses and the Will.* New York: D. Appleton.

Prothro, E. J. 1966. "Socialization and Social Class in a Transitional Society," *Child Development* 37:219–28.

Queen, S. A.; Haberstein, R. W.; and Adams, J. B. eds. 1961. *The Family in Various Cultures.* New York: J. B. Lippincott.

Quine, W. V. 1981. *Theories and Things.* Cambridge: Harvard University Press.

Ramey, C. T.; Farran, D. C.; and Campbell, F. A. 1979. "Predicting IQ from Mother-Infant Interactions," *Child Development* 50: 804–14.

Rand, W.; Sweeny, M. E.; and Vincent, E. L. 1930. *Growth and Development of the Young Child.* Philadelphia: W. B. Saunders.

Rathbun, C.; DiVirgilio, L.; and Waldfogel, S. 1958. A Restitutive Process in Children Following Radical Separation from Family and Culture," *American Journal of Orthopsychiatry* 28: 408–15.

Rawls, J. 1971. *A Theory of Justice.* Cambridge: Harvard University Press.

Reznick, J. S. 1982. "The Development of Perceptual and Lexical Categories in the Human Infant." Unpublished doctoral dissertation, University of Colorado.

Reznick, J. S.; and Kagan, J. 1982. "Category Detection in Infancy." In L. Lipsitt, ed. *Advances in Infancy Research,* vol. II, pp. 80–111. Norwood, N.J.: Ablex.

Richardson, F. H. 1926. *Parenthood and the Newer Psychology.* New York: G. P. Putnam.

Ritchie, J.; and Ritchie, J. 1979. *Growing Up in Polynesia.* Sydney, Australia: George Allen & Unwin.

Rogoff, B., Newcombe, N., Kagan, J. 1974. "Planfulness and Recognition Memory," *Child Development* 45: 972–77.
Rorty, A. O., ed. 1980. *Explaining Emotions.* Berkeley: University of California Press.
Rorty, R. 1979. *Philosophy and the Mirror of Nature.* Princeton: Princeton University Press.
Rosch, E. 1973. "On the Internal Structure of Perceptual and Semantic Categories." In T. E. Moore, ed., *Cognitive Development and the Acquisition of Language,* pp. 111–44. New York: Academic Press.
Rosch, E. 1978. "Principles of Categorization." In E. Rosch and B. B. Lloyd, eds., *Cognition and Categorization,* pp. 27–48. Hillsdale, N.J.: Lawrence Erlbaum.
Rose, S. A.; Gottfried, A. W.; and Bridger, W. H. 1983. "Infants' Cross-Modal Transfer from Solid Objects to their Graphic Representations," *Child Development* 54: 686–94.
Rosenblum, L. A.; and Harlow, H. F. 1963. "Approach-Avoidance Conflict in the Mother-Surrogate Situation," *Psychological Reports* 12: 83–85.
Ross, G. 1980. "Concept Categorization in 1- to 2-Year-Olds," *Developmental Psychology* 16: 391–96.
Ross, R. M.; and Losey, G. S. 1983. "Sex Change in a Coral Reef Fish," *Science,* 221: 574–75.
Rubin, D. C.; Groth, E.; and Goldsmith, D. J. 1983. "Olfactory Cueing of Autobiographical Memory." Unpublished manuscript, Duke University.
Rousseau, J. J. 1911 [1762]. *Emile.* Trans. B. Foxley. New York: E. P. Dutton.
Russell, B. 1940. *An Inquiry into Meaning and Truth.* London: Allen & Unwin.

Sackett, G. P. 1972. "Isolation Rearing in Monkeys." In R. Ohauvin, ed., *Animal Models of Human Behavior.* Paris: Colloques Internationaux du C.N.R.S.
Sackett, G. P.; et al. 1981. "Social Isolation Rearing Effects in Monkeys Vary with Genotype," *Developmental Psychology* 17: 313–18.
Salkind, N.; Kojima, H.; and Zelniker, T. 1978. "Cognitive Tempo in American, Japanese and Israeli Children," *Child Development* 49: 1025–27.
Sameroff, A. J.; Seifer, R.; and Elias, P. K. 1982. "Socio-cultural Variability in Infant Temperament Ratings," *Child Development* 53: 164–73.
Sartre, J.-P. 1964. *The Words.* Trans. B. Frechtman. New York: George Braziller.
Scarr, S. 1969. "Social Introversion-Extraversion as a Heritable Response," *Child Development* 40: 823–32.
Scherer, K. 1981. "Speech and Emotional States." In J. Darby, ed., *Speech Evaluation in Psychiatry.* New York: Grune & Stratton.
Schiller, F. 1865. *The Philosophical and Aesthetic Letters and Essays of Schiller,* trans. J. Weiss. London: J. Chapman.
Schwartz, G. E. 1982. "Psychophysiological Patterning of Emotion Revisited: A Systems Perspective." In C. E. Izard, ed., *Measuring Emotions in Infants and Children,* pp. 67–93. New York: Cambridge University Press.
Scott, J. P.; and Fuller, J. L. 1965. *Genetics and the Social Behavior of the Dog.* Chicago: University of Chicago Press.
Seligman, M. E. P. 1975. *Helplessness.* San Francisco: W. H. Freeman.
Sellers, M. J. 1979. "The Enhancement of Memory in Costa Rican Children." Unpublished doctoral dissertation, Harvard University.
Shepard, R. 1967, "Recognition Memory for Words, Sentences, and Pictures," *Journal of Verbal Learning and Verbal Behavior* 6: 156–63.
Shields, S. A.; and Stern, R. M. 1979. "Emotion: The Perception of Bodily Change." In P. Pliner, K. R. Blankstein, and I. M. Speigel, *Perception of Emotion in Self and Others,* pp. 85–106. New York: Plenum Press.
Shigaki, J. S. 1983. "Child Care Practices in Japan and the United States," *Young Children.* May, pp. 13–24.

Bibliography

Shweder, R. A. "Menstrual pollution, Soul Loss, and the Comparative Study of Emotions." In A. Kleinman and B. J. Good, eds., *Culture and Depression*. In press.

Shweder, R. A.; Turiel, E.; and Much, N. C. 1981. "The Moral Intuitions of the Child." In J. H. Flavell and L. Ross, eds., *Social Cognitive Development*, pp. 288–305. Cambridge, England: Cambridge University Press.

Siegler, R. S. 1981 "Developmental Sequences within and between Concepts," *Monographs of the Society for Research in Child Development*. 46 (2).

Siegler, R. S. 1983. "Information Processing Approaches to Development." In W. Kessen, ed, *History, Theories, and Methods*. P. H. Mussen, ed., *Handbook of Child Psychology*, vol. 1, pp. 129–212. New York: John Wiley.

Skinner, B. F. 1938. *The Behavior of Organisms*. New York: Appleton Century.

Slobin, D. I. 1982. "Universal and Particular in the Acquisition of Language." In E. Wanner and L. R. Gleitman, ed, *Language Acquisition: The State of the Art*, pp. 128–70. New York: Cambridge University Press.

Smith, S. H. 1965. "Remarks on Education." In F. Rudolph, ed., *Essays on Education in the Early Republic*. pp. 167–224. Cambridge: Harvard University Press.

Sorce, J. F.; and Emde, R. N. 1981. "Mother's Presence is Not Enough: The Effect of Emotional Availability on Infant Exploration," *Developmental Psychology*, 17: 737–41.

Speer, J. R.; and Flavell, J. H. 1979. "Young Children's Knowledge of the Relative Difficulty of Recognition and Recall Memory Tasks," *Developmental Psychology*. 14: 214–17.

Spelke, E. S. 1976 "Infants' Intermodal Perception of Events," *Cognitive Psychology* 8: 553–60.

Sroufe, L. A. 1979 "The Coherence of Individual Development," *American Psychologist* 34: 834–40.

Standing, L.; Conezio, J.; and Haber, R. N. 1970 "Perception and Memory for Pictures: Single Trial Learning of 2500 Visual Stimuli," *Psychonomic Science* 19: 73–74.

Stanley, S.M. 1981. *The New Evolutionary Timetable*. New York: Basic Books.

Starkey, P.; and Cooper, R. G. 1980. "Perception of Numbers by Human Infants." *Science* 210: 1033–35.

Stein, G. G.; Rosen, J. J.; and Butters, N. 1974. *Plasticity and Recovery of Function in the Central Nervous System*. New York: Academic Press.

Stern, W. 1930. *Psychology of Early Childhood*. Trans. A. Barwell. 6th ed. New York: Henry Holt.

Sternbach, R. A. 1968. *Pain: A Psychophysiological Analysis*. New York: Academic Press.

Stevenson-Hinde, J.; Stillwell-Barnes, R.; and Zunz, M. 1980a. "Subjective Assessment of Rhesus Monkeys over Four Successive Years," *Primates*. 21: 66–82.

Stevenson-Hinde, J.; Stillwell-Barnes, R.; and Zunz, M. 1980b. "Individual Differences in Young Rhesus Monkeys: Consistency and Change, *Primates*, 21: 498–509.

Stone, L. 1977. *The Family, Sex, and Marriage in England 1500–1800*. New York: Harper & Row.

Strauss, M. S. 1979. "Abstraction of Prototypical Information by Adults in Ten-Month-Old Infants," *Journal of Experimental Psychology: Human Learning and Memory*. 5: 618–32.

Sulloway, F. 1972. "Family Constellations, Sibling Rivalry, and Scientific Revolutions." Unpublished manuscript.

Sully, J. 1896. *Studies of Childhood*. New York: Appleton.

Suomi, S. J.; et al. 1981. "Inherited and Experiential Factors Associated with Individual Differences in Anxious Behavior Displayed by Rhesus Monkeys." In

D. F. Kline and J. Rabkin, eds., *Anxiety: New Research and Changing Concepts*, pp. 179–99. New York: Raven Press.

Super, C. M. 1972. "Long-term Memory in Early Infancy. "Unpublished doctoral dissertation, Harvard University.

Sutherland, H. E. G. 1930. "The Relationship between IQ and Size of Family in the Case of Fatherless Children," *The Pedagogical Seminary and Journal of Genetic Psychology*. 38: 161–70.

Tanji, J.; and Evarts, E. V. 1976. "Anticipatory Activity of Motor Cortex Neurons in Relation to Direction of an Intended Movement," *Journal of Neurophysiology*, 39: 1062–68.

Tennes, K. 1982. "The Role of Hormones in Mother-Infant Interaction." In R. N. Emde and R. J. Harmon, eds., *The Development of Attachment and Affiliative Systems*, pp. 75–88. New York: Plenum Press.

Tennes, K.; Downey, K.; and Vernadakis, A. 1977. "Urinary Cortisol Excretion Rates and Anxiety in Normal One-Year-Old Infants," *Psychosomatic Medicine* 39 (3): 178–87.

Thomas, A.; and Chess, S. 1977. *Temperament and Development*. New York: Brunner/Mazel.

Thompson, R. A.; and Lamb, M. E. 1983a. "Security of Attachment and Stranger Sociability in Infancy," *Developmental Psychology* 19: 184–91.

Thompson, R. A.: and Lamb, M. E. 1983b. "Assessing Qualitative Dimensions of Emotional Responsiveness in Infants." Paper presented at the meeting of the Society for Research in Child Development, Detroit, April 1983.

Thompson, R. A.; Lamb, M. E.; and Estes, D. 1982. "Stability of Infant-Mother Attachment and Its Relationship to Changing Life Circumstances in an Unselected Middle-Class Sample," *Child Development* 53: 144–48.

Thorndike, E. L. 1905. *The Elements of Psychology*. New York: A. G. Seiler.

Tizard, B.; and Hodges, J. 1978. "The Effect of Early Institutional Rearing on the Development of Eight-Year-Old Children, *Journal of Child Psychology and Psychiatry* 19: 99–118.

Tizard, B.; and Rees, J. 1975. "The Effect of Early Institutional Rearing on the Behavioral Problems of Affectional Relationships of Four-Year-Old Children," *Journal of Child Psychology and Psychiatry* 16: 61–74.

Trehub, S. 1976. "The Discrimination of Foreign Speech Contrasts by Infants and Adults" *Child Development* 47: 466–72.

Trehub, S. 1979. "Reflections on the Development of Speech Perception," *Canadian Journal of Psychology* 39: 368–81.

Tronick, E. Z.; Winn, S.; and Morelli, G. A. "Multiple Caretaking in the Niche of Human Evolution." In T. Field and M. Reite, eds., *The Psychology of Attachment*. New York: Academic Press. In press.

Tversky, A. 1977. "Features of Similarity," *Psychological Review* 84: 327–52.

Tversky, A.; and Gati, I. 1978. "Studies of Similarity." In E. Rosch and B. B. Lloyd, eds., *Cognition and Categorization*, pp. 79–98. Hillsdale, N.J.: Lawrence Erlbaum.

Tversky, A.; and Kahneman, D. 1981. "The Framing of Decisions and the Rationality of Choice," *Science*, 211: 453–58.

Tylor, E. B. 1878. *Researches into the Early History of Mankind*. New York: Henry Holt.

Vidal, F. 1981. "Piaget on Evolution and Morality." Unpublished honors thesis, Harvard University.

Vihman, M.V. 1983. "Language Differentiation by the Bilingual Infant." Unpublished manuscript, Stanford University.

Bibliography

Von Frisch, K. 1974. "Decoding the Language of the Bee," *Science* 185: 663–68.

Waddington, C. H. 1969. "Paradigm for an Evolutionary Process." In *Towards a Theoretic Biology II. Sketches,* pp. 106–28. Edinburgh: Edinburgh University Press.

Wagatsuma, H. 1977. "Some Aspects of the Contemporary Japanese Family: Once Confucian, Now Fatherless," *Daedalus* 106 (Spring): 181–210.

Wagner, S. et al. 1981. "Metaphorical Mapping in Human Infants," *Child Development* 52: 728–31.

Waters, E.; Wippman, J.; and Sroufe, L.A. 1979. "Attachment, Positive Affect, and Competence in the Peer Group," *Child Development* 50: 821–29.

Watson, J. 1928. *Psychological Care of Infant and Child.* New York: W.W. Norton.

Weiner, K.; and Kagan, J. 1976. "Infants' Reactions to Changes in Orientation of Figure and Frame," *Perception* 5: 25–28.

Weiskrantz, L. 1977. "Trying to Bridge Some Neuropsychological Gaps between Monkey and Man," *British Journal of Psychology* 68: 431–45.

Wellman, H. M. 1978. "Knowledge of the Interaction of Memory Variables," *Developmental Psychology* 14: 24–29.

Werner, E. E.; and Smith, R. S. 1982. *Vulnerable but Invincible.* New York: McGraw-Hill.

White, H. 1973. *Metahistory: the Historical Imagination in Nineteenth-Century Europe.* Baltimore: Johns Hopkins University Press.

Whitehead, A. N. 1929. *Process and Reality.* New York: Macmillan.

Williams, B. 1971. "Morality and the Emotions." In J. Casey, ed., *Morality and Moral Reasoning.* London: Methuen.

Wilson, E. O. 1975. *Sociobiology.* Cambridge: Harvard University Press.

Wilson, R. S.; Brown, A. M.; and Matheny, A. P. 1971. "Emergence and Persistence of Behavioral Differences in Twins," *Child Development.* 42: 1381–98.

Winick, M.; Meyer, K. K.; and Harris, R. C. 1975. "Malnutrition and Environmental Enrichment by Early Adoption," *Science* 190: 1173–75.

Winograd, E.; and Killinger, W. A. 1983. "Relating Age at Encoding in Early Childhood to Adult Recall: Development of Flashbulb Memories," *Journal of Experimental Psychology: General* 112: 413–22.

Wittgenstein, L. 1922. *Tractatus Logico-Philosophicus.* London: Routlege & Kegan Paul.

Wittgenstein, L. 1953. *Philosophical Investigations.* New York: Macmillan.

Wohl, R. 1979. *The Generation of 1914.* Cambridge: Harvard University Press.

Wolfson, H. A. 1962. *The Philosophy of Spinoza.* Cambridge: Harvard University Press.

Woodger, J. H. 1952. *Biology and Language.* New York: Cambridge University Press.

Woodley, J. D.; et. al. 1981 "Hurricane Allen's Impact on Jamaican Coral Reefs," *Science* 214: 749–54.

Zahn-Waxler, C.; Radke-Yarrow, M.; and King, R. A. 1979. "Child Rearing and Children's Prosocial Initiations toward Victims of Distress," *Child Development.* 50: 319–30.

Zajonc, R. 1976. "Family Configuration and Intelligence," *Science.* 192: 227–36.

Index

Abramov, I., 31
accommodation, 192
actions: consistency between beliefs and, 134–35; generated by ideas, 152; meanings imposed on, 107–8; preservation of, 95, 99–100
activation of cognitive processes, 231
active memory, 40, 42–43, 49, 50; fear and, 44
actual competences, 198–202; age-related, 229–30
Adams, J. B., 244
adjustment, 30
adolescents: ability to assume hypothetical set of, 215; anxious, quality of attachment in infancy of, 253, 254; attitude toward obedience of, 135; beliefs of, 9; consequences of early parental restrictions for, 260; derivations of perinatal stress in, 109, 110; emotions of, 179–82; failure in adaptation of, 107; impact of historical events on, 92; impact of social class differences on, 27; observations versus self-reports of, 22–23; questioning of propositions by, 220; range of academic competence in, 238–39; sources of standards for, 142–43; suicides of, 266
adopted children, studies of, 100–101
adulthood, stages of, 76
aesthetic sense, 81
affect, see emotions
age standards, 141–43
aggression: in adulthood, origins in infancy of, 82; disapproval of, 128; in inhibited children, 68, 70; inhibition of, 129, 131, 175; Kleinian view of, 29–30; meanings imposed on, 108; morality and, 113, 114, 121–22; preservation of, 100, 103–4; restraint of, 253, 256; sex-role stereotypes about, 141, 270

Ainsworth, Mary, 57–60
alternation, rule of, 231
Anderson, John R., 202n, 210
anger: development of capacity for, 173, 174; display of, in family, 269–71
animal studies: arguments against connectedness implied by, 90–91; of attachment, 51, 56, 57, 62; of central nervous system maturation, 5–6, 186, 189; of discrimination, 200; of dominance, 176; of fear of unusual, 46–47; of internal changes associated with emotion, 158; of memory growth, 43; objective frame in, 20; of separation anxiety, 44; of sources of knowledge, 35; of synaptic change, 87; of temperament, 70
anxiety, 38, 72, 175; ability to cope with, 60–62; anticipation of, 119, 120; attachment and, 51, 52, 56, 57; control of, 232; disappearance of symptoms of, 100; dispelled by action, 46; over failure to meet standards, 266; insecure attachment and, 253; mothers' concern with control of, 161–62; sources of, 156; subjective experience of, 157, 160; to task failure, 173–74; unconscious, 160; over violation of standards, 145, 147; vulnerability to, 58–60, 62, 105
appearance of objects, salience and, 187
Appelbaum, M. I., 38
Arend, R., 58
Aristotle, 5, 13, 118, 145
arousal, 165
Arsenian, Jean M., 60
articulation of problem and solution, 230
assimilation, 192
Athens, ancient, 120, 248
attachment, *xiii,* 30, 31, 50–64, 71; assumption of persistence of, 90; Bowlby on, 54–55; cultural beliefs and, 55–57; differen-

Index

tal milestones and, 74; developmental transitions and, 92; fear of the unusual and, 46–48; impact of experience on, 87; memory growth and, 43

charity, virtue of, 120

Chave, E. J., 133

Chen, H., 245, 258

Chess, Stella, 64

China: child-rearing practices in, 259; filial love in, 244, 245

Chinese language, 215

Chinese philosophy, *xiv;* emphasis on change in, 12; human nature in, 123

Christianity: morality and, 115; science and, 87

"Chuang-tzû Commentary," 12

Cicero, 147

Clark, Eve V., 189, 212

Clark, L. D., 70

Clarke-Stewart, K. A., 251, 275

classes of persons, preservation of, 96, 99–100

cleanliness, standard of, 134–35

Clinger, J. B., 61

cognitive development, *xiii, xv,* 30–31, 185–239; actual vs. potential competence and, 198–202; basic units of cognition, 203–4; and change in frame, 9; CNS maturation and, 5, 6; complementary relation between maturation and experience in, 186–95; computer model of, 202; emotional development and, 77–78, 172–83; and evaluation of ideas, 227–29; and executive processes, 229–36; and family experience, 251–52; in infancy, 31–50; inferences and categories and, 210–23; intelligence and, 195–97; memory and, 223–27; morality and, 134, 150; neurophysiological model of, 202–3; perception and schemata in, 205–10; Piaget's view of, 48–50, 190–95; of premature infants, 10–11; selection of terms to describe, 195–205; separation anxiety and, 90

cognitive dissonance, 179–82

Colby, A., 151

color, perception of, 13

communication: consensual meaning in, 214; hidden understanding essential to, 201; potential of emotions for, 165

Compayré, G., 133

competences, actual vs. potential, 198–202

concepts, 203, 204; validity of notion of, 237; *see also* categories

concrete operational stage, 76, 77, 134, 192

conditioned fear reaction, 45

Conezio, J., 211

confidence, 176, 178

conformity, harsh toilet training and, 81, 83

Conger, J. J., 83

connectedness, *xiv,* 73–111; arguments against, 89–93; arguments for, 86–89; in cognitive development, 191; cultural beliefs about, 73–74; discontinuity and, 11–12; Piaget's assumption of, 50; and preservation of individual qualities, 93–99; and stability of differences, 99–110; and stage of development, 75–93

Connell, J. P., 59

conscience, *xiv;* faith in inevitability of, 131; historical notions of, 30; private, promotion of, 259

consciousness, states of, 95–96

conservation of quantity, 80, 233, 237

constructs, general vs. specific, 14–19

conventional standards, 121–22

Cooper, R. G., 81

Copernicus, 223, 251

coping mechanisms, 159; exhaustion of, 182

courage, 120

creativity, 222–23

Crockenberg, S. B., 105

Cross, A., 255*n*

cultural differences: in anxiety, 156, 173–74; attachment and, 52, 53, 59–63, 252, 254; in behavior selected for socialization, 256; in beliefs about childhood characteristics, 88; in childhood fears, 44, 45; in cognitive development, 197, 199, 215, 225–26, 233; in emotional terminology, 166–68; in family, 242, 244, 245, 248; in influence of experience, 240–41; in middle childhood, 272; in morality, 115–21, 123, 126, 129, 135, 146–48, 150; in parental love, 271; in parental restrictiveness, 260–61, 263–64; in parental standards, 267–68; in primary emotions, 163–64; in signs of parental love, 269; in status of women, 243

Curtiss, S., 102

Dallinger, William, 86

Daly, E. M., 168

Darwin, Charles, *xii,* 28, 82, 144, 222–23

Index

240-41; meanings children impose on, *xvi*; morality and, 132-33; schemata based on, 206; as source of knowledge, 35, 71; subjective, 20-21; temperament and, 64, 69-70; written knowledge and, 88-89

exploitation, ability to resist, 249

face-hands test, 209, 235
facial expression, measurement of changes in, 171
factor analysis, 197, 198
faith, virtue of, 120
family, *xv*, 240-76; behavior selected for socialization in, 255-56; child's perception of rejection in, 266-68; infant in, 251-54; language acquisition and, 255; middle childhood and, 272-74; mode of socialization in, 256-57; parental theories about children and, 245-50; as referent, 177-78; restrictive, 257-64; sense of being valued by, 264-72; signs of love in, 268-70; social class differences in, 249-50
Farley, J., 86
Farran, D. C., 251
fatigue, subjective experience of, 160
fear(s), 38; cognitive bases of, 43-48; control of, 248; differentiating among states relating to, 155-56; inhibition and, 66; of parental punishment, 77; schema for, 209
feeling states: capacity to infer, 235; developmental changes in, 183; features of concepts referring to, 212; internal tone and, 158-60; measurement of, 170-71; naming of, 163-69; schema of, 208-9; self-report data on, 162-63
Festinger, L., 273
Fijians, 44, 56*n*, 129, 271
filial love, 244
First World War, 56
Fiske, J., 53
fixation, 80
Flaherty, J. F., 23
Flavell, E. R., 187
Flavell, John H., 187, 225, 230
flexibility, 231-32
Forbush, W. B., 132
formal operational stage, 142, 179, 182, 192
frames, 9; *see also* objective frame; subjective frame

Franklin, Benjamin, 72
freedom, 114; ethical status of, 115; permissiveness and, 258-59
Freud, Sigmund, *xii*, 15, 27-29, 53, 75-77, 82, 223, 258
Friberg, J., 168
Fried, Charles, 115, 116
frustration, anger to, 173
Fuller, J. L., 51, 70
functional qualities, 212
Fung, Y., 12

Gaensbauer, T. J., 59
Galileo, 13
Gannett, Ezra, 272
Garcia-Coll, C., 66
Gardner, Howard, 201, 203*n*
Garner, Wendell R., 20
Gati, I., 218
Gauss, Karl, 213
Geach, Peter, 120
Gelman, R., 188, 198
genetic factors in temperament, 69, 70
geographical mobility, 56
Gewirth, A., 115
Gilligan, Carol, 140, 249
Goldman, L., 116
Goldsmith, D. J., 226
good, meaning of, 113-18
Gordon, L., 226
Gouze, K., 226
Gove, F. L., 58
Grant, P. R., 79
gratification: fatigue following, 119; relaxation to, 172
Green, F. C., 187
Gregor, T., 260
Grossman, K., 60, 62
Grossman, K. E., 60, 62*n*
Groth, E., 226
guilt, 145, 147, 152, 175, 259; appearance of, 77; over failure to meet standards, 266
Gunnar, M. R., 39, 46
Gururumba, 168

Haber, R. N., 211
Haberstein, R. W., 244

Index

internal changes associated with emotions, 157–63, 165

internal tone, 158; measurement of, 170–71

Inuit Eskimos, 143

intuition, logic vs., 190

irritability: derivatives of, 105–6; inhibition and, 67; security of attachment and, 59–60

Israeli kibbutzim, 75, 271; changes in standards in, 135

Izard, C. E., 171

James, William, 27, 71, 117, 150, 155

Janik, A., 123

Japan: adolescent suicide in, 266; cognitive dissonance of adolescents in, 182; concepts of intelligence in, 88; morality in, 117, 146–47; primary emotional categories in, 163–64; reflection-impulsivity in, 228–29; socialization practices in, 260–61, 264; sources of fear in, 156; view of infancy in, 29; vulnerability to anxiety of infants in, 59

Jefferson, Thomas, 151

Jensen, Arthur, 87

Johnson, W. F., 172

Juno, C., 200

justice, 120; ideal of, 116; sense of, 122

Kaffman, M., 69

Kahneman, D., 220

Kant, Immanuel, 114, 123, 193

Katz, M. M. W., 44, 56n

Kauai, 109

Kaufmann, I. C., 44n

Kaye, K., 249

Kearsley, R. B., 41, 52, 229

Keil, F. C., 189

Kennedy, C. B., 38

Kenney, M., 6, 35, 47, 189

Kepler, Johann, xii

Kett, J. F., 267, 273

Killian, G. A., 251

Killinger, W. A., 224

Killworth, P. D., 23

kin groups, 242

kindness, standard of, 142

King, R. A., 127

Kipsigis tribe, 119, 146, 271

Klein, D. R., 156

Klein, Melanie, 29–30

Kleinman, A., 20

Kline, M., 124, 275

Klinnert, M. D., 183

knowledge: alteration of emotions by, 183–84; dynamic and changing nature of, 217–18; forms of, 35–40; initial, of infant, 31; multiple functions of, 48–49; nonsymbolic, 202; permanence of, 209–10; Piaget on, 190–92, 194; sources of, 35, 71; written, 88–89

Kohlberg, Lawrence, 115, 117, 150, 151

Kohn, Melvin L., 249–50

Kojima, H., 228

Kosslyn, S., 206

Kreutzer, M. A., 225, 230

Kuhn, D., 177

Lagerqvist, Pär, 152

Lamb, M. E., 58, 59, 63

Lancee, W. J., 168

Langer, Jonas, 82

language: capacity for symbolism and memory prior to, 80; categories and, 212–15, 217, 219–20; complementarity of maturation and experience in acquisition of, 186; and conceptualization of self, 137; connection between infants' babbling and, 81; cultural beliefs reflected in, 88; evaluative, 112; family experiences and, 255; influence of contexts on interpretation of, 235; intelligence and, 197, 198; memory and, 224; percepetual contrasts and, 37; and Piagetian theory, 193

Lapidus, D., 106, 210

"law of effect," 80

"law of practice," 80

Ledingham, J. E., 103

Le Douarin, N., 111

Leonard, C., 225, 230

Lerner, R., 90

Levine, S., 62

Lewis, M., 137

libertarians, 114

libidinal energy, 28; reallocation of, 80

linguistics, 14

Linn, S., 33

303

Index

naturalism, 113
neural crest cells, embryology of, 111
neurotransmitters, 5
New Guinea, *xvi,* 108, 240
Newcombe, N., 197, 231
Newman, P. L., 108, 168
Newton, Isaac, *xii,* 164
Nickerson, R. S., 211
nightmares, 66
Nolan, E., 130, 207, 209
normative events, 92
novelty, surprise to, 172
Novey, M. S., 127
nuclear family, 242
nuclear weapons, 56
number, discovery of, 194

obedience, 135; measurement of tendency for, 97–98; motivation for, 143
objective frame, 19–25; emotions and, 157, 160–63; meanings in, 204; parental love and, 271
object permanence, 49
Odyssey (Homer), 118
oedipal stage, 77
Ogden, Charles K., 154
olfactory schemata, 206
Olweus, D., 99, 100
operant, definition of, 95
operation, cognitive process of, 191
operationalism, 19
Oppenheim, R. W., 90
opposites, appreciation of, 189
oral stage, 28, 29

Padawer-Singer, A., 177
"paradoxial sleep," 19
parasympathetic nervous system, 68–69
parents: adolescents' beliefs about, 180–81; identification with, 139; *see also* family
Parikh, B., 151
particle physics, 16
Pascal, Blaise, 123
Pavlovian theory, 133
Peabody Picture Vocabulary Test, 228

peer group: acceptance by, 249, 273; as referent, 178
perception: of color, 13; in infancy, 31–32; qualities available to, 212; of rejection, 266–68; schemata and, 205–10; subjective vs. objective, 20
perinatal stress, 109–10
permissiveness, 257–59
Petitto, L. A., 43, 137
philosophical assumptions, *xi, xii*
phobias, 80
physical privation, distress to, 172
physics: primary theoretical entities in, 94; quantitative approach of, 13
Piaget, Jean, 27, 29, 41, 48–50, 75–77, 81–82, 117, 134, 150, 167, 169, 179, 189–95, 233–35, 237
Pinchbeck, I., 241
Plato, 13, 36
pleasure, 7; attachment and, 51; as criteria for good and bad, 113–14; subjective feelings of displeasure and, 165
Plomin, R., 69
Polanyi, M., 21
Polivy, J., 163, 168
Pollock, John L., 116
Polynesian societies, 52, 243
possession, sense of, 137–38
potential competences, 198–202
pragmatism, 114
Premack, A. J., 188
Premack, D., 188
premature infants: cognitive development of, 10–11; psychological profile of, 109
preservation of structure, 80–82
Preyer, William, 132
pride, 176
principled standards, 121–22
procedures, relation of conclusions to, 15–19
prohibitions, parental, 255–57
propositions, 203, 204, 211, 219–23; computers and, 202; counterfactual conditional, 215; memory of, 226; preservation of, 94–95; validity of notion of, 237
prototypes, schematic, 206–9
proto-Elamites, 168*n*
prudence, virtue of, 120
psychopaths, 131
puberty, 78–79; role changes at, 179
Puritans, *xvi,* 147–48; socialization practices of, 260

Index

23; evaluation of, 124, 128–29, 138, 176–77; evaluation of actions of, 112; family group and conception of, 242; love objects and, 55; primary loyalty to, 245; verbal reports of, 24

self-blame, 145–46

self-control, 30

self-interest, 114; freedom to act in service of, 115–16; honesty and, 116

self-report data, problems in use of, 162–63

Seligman, M. E. P., 182

Sellers, M. J., 227

sensory-motor scheme, 48

sensory-motor stage, 192, 251

separation anxiety, 44–48, 71; attachment and, 55, 57; cognitive basis of, 90

sex roles, 77; acquisition of behavior defining, 273; standards for, 140–41, 143

sexual excitement, 179

sexuality: adolescents' beliefs about, 181; cultural views on importance of, 244; motivation and, 144; similarity postulated between nursing infant and, 84–85; standards and, 121

shame, 145–48, 152, 175, 176; over failure to meet standards, 266

Sheldon, Asa, 272

Shepard, R., 211

Shweder, R. A., 121

Siebert, J., 235

Siegler, R. S., 219

single-parent families, 243

Skinner, B. F., 6, 95

Slobin, Dan I., 214

smiling, emergence of, 78

Smith, Adam, 240

Smith, P., 105

Smith, R. S., 11, 109, 110

sociability, parental encouragement of, 248, 249

social class: cognitive development and, 10–11; developmental influence of, 107; and display of anger in family, 270; early school achievement and, 22; impact in adolescence of, 27; and parental theories about children, 249–50; reflection-impulsivity and, 229

socialization: behavior selected for, 255–56; modes of, 256–64

societal change, sudden, 79

Sorce, J. F., 51

sorting behavior, 211

spatial ability, 195

Speer, J. R., 230

Spinoza, Baruch, 147

Sroufe, L. Alan, 58, 98

stability of differences, 99–110

stages, developmental, 75–93; connections between, 80–86; gradual vs. abrupt transitions between, 78–80

standards, 112, 152; abstract, 117; adolescents' rejection of, 181–82; age and role, 141–43; attachment and acceptance of, 233; for best solutions, 232; and conceptualization of self, 136–38; and consistency of belief and action, 134–36; emergence of, 124–43; family prohibitions and, 255–57; identification and acquisition of, 139–41; rejection for failure to meet, 266–69; sex-role, 140–41; sexual, 179; as source of motives, 143–44; universal, 118–24; violation of, 145–49, 175, 176, 220

Standing, L., 211

Stanley, S. M., 107

Starkey, D., 187n

Starkey, P., 81

states of consciousness, preservation of, 95–96

Stein, G. G., 87

stepping reflex of fetus, 90

Stern, William, 53, 81

Stevenson-Hinde, J., 104

Stillwell-Barnes, R., 104

Stone, L., 258

Strange Situation (est), 57–63, 98

stranger anxiety, 44, 47, 71

Strauss, M. S., 36

stress, arousal and, 66–67

subjective frame, 19–25; emotions and, 157, 160–63; meanings in, 204; parental love and, 271; of understanding, 235, 236

success, expectation of, 273

suicide, adolescent, 266

Sulloway, Frank, 222

Sully, James, 131, 257–58

Super, C. M., 119, 146, 223

superego, xiv, 15; motives of, 144

Susman, E. J., 100, 106

Sutherland, H. E. G., 241

Sweeney, M. E., 81, 258

symbolic attitude, 188

symbolism, 80

sympathetic nervous system, 68–69

sympathy, 123

synapses, 202–3; change in, psychological experience and, 87; elimination of, 5, 210

Index